DIGS AND DIGGERS

A Book of World Archaeology

Digs
AND
Diggers

A BOOK OF WORLD ARCHAEOLOGY

by LEONARD COTTRELL

Illustrated with photographs

THE WORLD PUBLISHING COMPANY

Cleveland and New York

J
913
C

Published by The World Publishing Company
2231 West 110th Street, Cleveland 2, Ohio
Published simultaneously in Canada by
Nelson, Foster & Scott Ltd.
Library of Congress Catalog Card Number: 64-19997
FIRST EDITION
WP 964

Designed by Jack Jaget.

To my niece KATHERINE ANN

Contents

THE NEW WORLD

FROM THE PACIFIC TO THE MEDITERRANEAN

GUIDE TO FURTHER READING AND INDEX

Illustrations are on pages 49-56, 89-96, 161-168 and 233-240.

THE
BEGINNINGS

What Is Archaeology?

Archaeology is about human beings like ourselves—people who lived hundreds, thousands, perhaps tens of thousands of years ago—most of them before writing was invented. We know about our own age through such things as newspapers, books, magazines, movies, TV, and radio. We know about our immediate ancestors mainly through the books they wrote and the pictures they painted and the buildings they bequeathed to us. We know them, too, through their music and other arts.

Now archaeology can be applied to the study of these people, too, because it is simply, according to the dictionary definition, "the scientific study of the life and culture of ancient people," or to expand that a little, the study of the past through the tangible objects which people left behind. For instance if you find and study objects dating from the American Colonial period, say wine bottles or old weapons, you could apply archaeological techniques to learn something about the period from the *things* the people made and used. But, generally speaking, most archaeologists are concerned either with people who lived before writing was invented—before 3000 B.C.—or people who, though they lived at the same time as or even after the peoples of Egypt and Mesopotamia had invented writing, were still illiterate.

For example the people who built the huge, mysterious stone circles such as Stonehenge and Avebury in England, and also in France and Spain, lived more than fifteen hundred years after the Egyptians and the Sumerians of the Middle East had invented writing systems, but they themeslves could not write. Archaeologists who specialize in this period are called prehistorians; they have to rely entirely on buried remains of buildings, pottery, tools discarded objects left in rubbish dumps, weapons, jewelry, and more valuable objects sometimes buried with the dead. These in themselves do not sound very promising, but the modern archaeologist, unlike his predecessors, can call in the aid of many scientific disciplines—physics, chemistry, zoology, botany, besides mechanical aids such as photography, especially aerial photography, to help him interpret his finds.

Let us briefly consider the side of archaeology with which most people are familiar. The great museums, such as the Metropolitan Museum of Art in New York, the British Museum in London, the Louvre in Paris, the Egyptian Museum in Cairo, are full of lovely and valuable things discovered by archaeologists past and present in many parts of the world. In the Metropolitan Museum, for example, you can see the gold and jeweled crowns and ornaments worn by Egyptian kings, queens, and princesses more than four thousand years ago. There is even a jewel box of an Egyptian princess, complete with her golden girdle, anklets, mirror, mascara pot, rouge dish, and toilet jars. This jewelry was discovered near an Egyptian pyramid by the British archaeologist Sir Flinders Petrie. In the same museum you can see a set of Egyptian models dating from about the same period—2000 B.C. These, found by the American archaeologist Herbert Winlock in 1920, enable you to enter into that vanished world of long ago. There are beautifully rigged ships, with model men at the oars. There is a model brewery, a model granary, statues of women servants carrying baskets of food and wine. All these models, which had lain undisturbed in a small rock-cut burial chamber for forty centuries, were intended to provide the dead man, by a process of magic, with all the good things which he had enjoyed during his life on earth.

In Chicago there is another wonderful Egyptian collection including objects found by the American archaeologist Dr. George Reisner; and in the Egyptian Museum in Cairo is Reisner's greatest find—the bed, throne, carrying chair, and jewelry of Queen Hetepheres, mother of the Pharaoh Cheops who built the Great Pyramid five thousand years ago; in fact it is more than likely that Cheops was born on that bed. In the same museum in Cairo is the greatest Egyptian treasure of all, the complete funeral regalia of the Pharaoh Tutankhamen, filling several galleries. This glorious treasure house is like an Aladdin's cave, full of glittering wonders. There is the king's inner coffin of solid gold set with semi-precious stones, the four huge gold-encased shrines which surrounded it, a solid gold portrait mask of the young king, and literally thousands of other objects ranging from a large number of walking sticks—Tutankhamen collected them, apparently—to his hunting bows, his golden chariots, and even the toys he played with as a boy.

Then, in the British Museum in London, there are some of the astounding finds made by Sir Leonard Woolley at Ur of the Chaldees in Mesopotamia. Ur, according to the Bible, was the home of Abraham, but the objects Woolley found date from long before Abraham's time. In a series of deep-cut tombs he came upon the bodies of large numbers of people who appear to have gone to their deaths voluntarily to accompany their royal or priestly masters to the grave. In ramps or slopes leading to the tombs, Woolley found rows of men and women who, having probably taken poison, died as the earth was thrown back on top of them.

There were soldiers still carrying their spears; there were court ladies in fine regalia, including silver headbands; there were court musicians, and Woolley was able to recover the beautiful harp of gold inlaid with tortoise shell which one of them had carried. And in the tombs themselves the archaeologist found the corpse of a Queen Shub-ad, on whose head was an intricate head-dress made of petals of gold, with gold leaves hanging over her brow, a piece of feminine finery such as the most sophisticated modern woman would have been delighted to wear. These and other things can be seen at the museum, where also stand the proud, grim-looking winged bulls which once guarded the portals of the palaces of the kings of Assyria. They were discovered by Sir Austen Henry Layard in Mesopotamia over a century ago. Similar magnificent sculptures, dug out of ruins of buried Nineveh, were found by the Frenchman Paul Emile Botta and can be seen in the Paris Louvre.

Perhaps even more impressive than the objects exhibited in museums are the remains of long-buried cities. In America there are the mysterious buildings erected by the Mayas in the jungles of southern Mexico and Guatemala: pyramids and temples and tombs, constructed of huge stone blocks by people who did not even have the wheel or a pack animal. In Italy, of course, there are the well-known sites of Pompeii and Herculaneum, overwhelmed nineteen centuries ago by the eruption of the volcano Vesuvius. With barely time to escape the rain of lava dust—indeed many did not escape—the inhabitants had to leave everything behind: the baker left his loaves in the oven; the lady of a great house left her tea service on the table; an unfortunate dog was left chained at the door and suffocated to death, as did many of the human inhabitants, the impressions of whose bodies were found in the solidified lava dust.

These are just a few examples of the glories of the past revealed first by treasure hunters and curio seekers, and later by scientific archaeologists. For archaeology began simply as treasure hunting, and even today many people imagine that the archaeologist is only a man looking for buried treasure. Sometimes, it is true, he does come upon magnificent things buried under the ground, or something which appeals to everyone's imagination, such as the imprint in the earth of a complete Viking ship, the timbers of which rotted away many centuries ago. But that is not his main task. More often than not the things he finds and studies are no more exciting than fragments of pottery, or the scanty foundations of a primitive hut, holes in the ground left by timber roof supports long-since perished, or even the side of an earthen trench, meaningless to the average onlooker but containing stratified deposits in which the archaeologist can recognize many centuries of human occupation. Yet, properly understood, these things can be as exciting in their own way as the buried treasure of kings.

For the archaeologist of today is a kind of super-detective, looking for clues and facts. That muddy fragment of pottery stuck in the side of a trench may provide the clue to the date of a building which some other archaeologist found hundreds or thousands of miles away. A tiny bead of blue faience, found in a British burial mound of 1500 B.C., proves that those primitive hut-dwelling inhabitants of early Britain were in trading contact, at least, with the rich, sophisticated civilization of Ancient Egypt; because faience, a kind of glazed clay, was made in Egypt at that time.

Again, through studying carefully the changing styles of pottery, and establishing a sequence of development (for fashions in pottery design changed as do women's clothes today) scholars may be able to establish at least the comparative dates of various buildings, even when there are no written records which give precise dates. This comparative method, called "sequence dating," was the contribution of an archaeologist of genius, Sir Flinders Petrie, of whom we shall be hearing more later.

Have you ever thought why archaeologists pay so much attention to pottery, and why there is so much of it in museums? Well, consider what happens on the site of a city or settlement which has been continuously occupied for hundreds, perhaps thousands, of years. From generation to generation the occupants build and rebuild, usually on the foundations of their predecessors' dwellings. Little of value is left in these foundations, except rubbish which people have discarded. Valuable objects were sometimes buried in important tombs, but these, all too frequently, have been plundered. Perhaps in the end the last generation leaves the city, or it is sacked and burned by invaders. Practically everything of value gets carried away, but the pottery remains, since who wants to keep a broken pot?

But as the archaeologist digs down through the successive strata or layers representing phases of occupation, he finds these ceramic fragments, and skilled "pot menders" piece them together. Some of the vessels may be beautiful in themselves—they often are—but their main value is for dating purposes. Because obviously, if the mound covering the buried city has not been disturbed, the pottery mound at the lowest level will be the oldest, and that at the highest level the latest, with gradations in between. And since the shapes and style of decoration changed and developed over the centuries, an archaeologist finding a fragment of pottery of a certain known design can give the approximate date to the layer in which that fragment was found.

The astute reader will ask, How are these dates arrived at in the absence of written records giving dates? The answer, in the case of Crete and prehistoric Greece, is that these people were in contact with Ancient Egypt which produced objects which can be dated with reasonable precision, because the Egyptians had a calendar and dated the reigns of their kings. And occasionally, very occasionally, some Egyptian object has turned up in Crete bearing the name of an Egyptian king. Perhaps it is only a little statuette or a signet ring. But when such objects are found in association with—that is, the same layer as—a certain type of Cretan pottery, archaeologists have secured a datum line. If, say, the Egyptian object bears the name of a Pharaoh who reigned between 1500 and 1450 B.C., it is highly probable that the Cretan pottery surrounding it and the building in which it was found are of about the same date; therefore the layers below it must be earlier and those above later, always assuming that the layers have not been disturbed by subsequent digging.

Of course this is not invariably the case. For instance, if some future archaeologist found a Roman coin in the foundations of modern New York, he would be wrong in assuming that New York was built in the second century A.D.! But modern archaeologists are usually scrupulously cautious, like good detectives examining clues. And when other Egyptian objects of the same date turned up alongside similar Cretan remains, then they knew they had a firm date.

Now you see how important were those tiny Egyptian faience beads found under a British burial mound; those beads could be dated to approximately 1500 B.C., giving a date for the mounds and also, perhaps, for the huge stone circles associated with them.

Dating is one of the cornerstones of scientific archaeology. For archaeology is essentially about people, and it is necessary to know, at least approximately, when those people lived, who came before them, and who came after them. It also shows the archaeologist in his role of detective, and just as police forces have international contacts to help them in their work, so is archaeology also international. Archaeologists communicate with each other, not necessarily by personal contact, though many do, but by publishing the results of their finds in learned publications which are read throughout the world.

But, it may be asked, if the archaeologist is not searching mainly for precious and beautiful things, what is the point of all this laborious research? What is its purpose and value? There are several possible answers, all incomplete. One could say that archaeology is a kind of exploration, and just as many human beings long to ascend hitherto unclimbable mountains, travel to the arctic, or explore jungles inhabited by primitive tribes, so other men and women are impelled to penetrate the unknown or little-known past, to study the successive stages through which man has passed to become what he is. One might answer that archaeology is a study of history, but extending deep into regions to which the historian, relying mainly on written records, has no access. As to its having any practical value, surely any study which helps to illuminate man's progress through the ages, which reveals his successive attempts to establish civilizations, and the possible reason for the fall of those civilizations—Sumerian, Babylonian, Egyptian, Greek, Roman, Aztec, Maya, Inca—is of value to us in our own exciting but dangerous world.

The Romantic
Approach

Archaeology has changed, in less than two centuries, from a mere search for old, valuable, or beautiful things to a more scientific discipline. This does not mean it has lost its romance and become dull. Nowadays, when the earth yields ancient treasure of "gold, silver, ivory, and precious woods," it is far more likely to be preserved from destruction or decay than in the old days of indiscriminate plunder and treasure hunting.

Nevertheless there were true archaeologists two or even three hundred years ago—men who studied sites with care and intelligence, made accurate surveys and drawings, and tried to understand their meaning. In England William Camden was recording Roman monuments as far back as the reign of Queen Elizabeth I; John Aubrey and William Stukely made records of British antiquities not much later which are still of value today. And in the seventeenth century Sir Thomas Browne, a Norwich physician, expressed the true archaeologist's curiosity about the past in some of the most beautiful prose ever written in the English language. Of some funerary urns found in a Norfolk field he wrote:

What song the Syrens sang, or what name Achilles assumed when he hid himself among women, though puzzling Questions, are not beyond all conjecture. What time the Persons of these Ossuaries entered the famous Nations of the Dead, and slept with Princes and Counsellors, might admit of a wide solution. But who were the proprietaries of these bones, or what bodies these ashes made up, were a question above Antiquarism. . . . Had they made as good provision for their names, as they have done for their Relics, they had not so grossly erred in the art of perpetuation. But to subsist in bones, and be but pyramidally extant, is a fallacy in duration.

A modern archaeologist finding those urns would be able to date them, to say who made them, and relate the find to a mass of other material. But he would not, of course, write his report in prose-poetry. And this illustrates another difference between archaeologists past and present. As archaeology becomes more and more specialized and scientific in its approach, so do archaeological publications tend to become more like scientific textbooks. There are, of course, brilliant exceptions. For instance Sir Mortimer Wheeler who, after excavating Maiden Castle, an Iron Age hill-fortress in Dorset, England, thus describes the attack upon it by a Roman legion under Vespasian.

Approaching from the direction of the Isle of Wight, Vespasian's legion may be supposed to have crossed the river Frome at the Dorchester crossing and found itself confronted, some two miles away, by the sevenfold ramparts of the fortress-town, towering above the cornfields which then, as now, flowed up to the defences. . . . Vespasian moved his main attack to the somewhat less formidable eastern end. What happened there has been revealed by excavation. First the regiment of artillery put down a barrage of ballista arrows [fired from powerful spring-guns]. The arrows have been found about the site, and buried among the outworks was a man with an arrowhead still buried in his backbone.

Following the barrage, the Roman infantry advanced up the slope, cutting its way from rampart to rampart until it reached the innermost bay, where some circular huts . . . were set alight, and under the rising clouds of smoke the gates were stormed and the position carried. But resistance had been obstinate and the fury of the legionaries was roused. For a space, confusion and massacre dominated the scene. Men and women, young and old, were savagely cut down before the troops could be called to heel. A systematic slighting of the defences followed, where-after the legion was withdrawn, doubtless taking hostages with it, and the dazed inhabitants were left to bury their dead among the ashes of the huts beside the gates. . . . With their food vessels and trinkets, the bones, often two or more skeletons huddled into a single grave and many of the skulls deeply scored with sword-cuts, made a sad and dramatic showing—the earliest British war-cemetery known to us.

That description might have come from a historical novel, yet no fiction enters into it. Apart from the fact, mentioned by Tacitus, that Vespasian's Second Augustan Legion attacked certain *oppida* (strong points) in the west of England, no contemporary written record of that event exists. It was built up entirely by Wheeler from his excavations at Maiden Castle—and from his personal experience as an ex-Brigadier, which helped him to put himself in the shoes of the attacking Roman general.

You can see, therefore, that the drama of archaeology, when it exists, need not arise only from the discovery of buried treasure.

Another factor which should be noticed is the disciplined imagination which Wheeler brings to his discovery; all truly great archaeologists have had it. They did not indulge in random fancies and far-fetched speculation. They were looking for facts, facts, facts all the time. But to the interpretation of those facts they brought imagination, in the same way as great scientists such as Isaac Newton and Michael Faraday, and great inventors such as Thomas Edison.

But though some of the early archaeologists used a scientific approach, they brought something else to their explorations and discoveries, a sense of romance and adventure. In their reports they were not ashamed to show emotion and reveal excitement, which is what makes their books so enthralling. In the remainder of this chapter we shall examine, very briefly, the lives and personalities of some of these pioneers of the past.

First, the voice of John Lloyd Stephens, an American explorer and writer, who with his English-born colleague Frederick Catherwood, hacked his way into the jungles of Central America over 120 years ago. Since the departure of the Spanish four hundred years ago they were probably the first white men ever to see the mysterious Maya cities, and Stephens' description captures all their enchantment:

> America, say historians, was peopled by savages; but savages never reared these structures, savages never carved these stones. . . . Architecture, sculpture and painting, all the arts which embellish life, had flourished in this overgrown forest; orators, warriors, and statesmen, beauty, ambition and glory had lived and passed away, and none knew that such things had been, or could tell of their past existence. . . . The beauty of the sculpture, the solemn stillness of the woods disturbed only by the screaming of monkeys and the chattering of parrots, the desolation of the city, and the mystery that hung over it, all created an interest higher, if possible, than I had ever felt among the ruins of the Old World.

Neither Stephens nor Catherwood was an archaeologist in the modern sense; rather they were explorers, though Catherwood, who was a talented artist, made many drawings of Maya buildings which were of value to future generations of scholars.

At about the same period, some of the most romantic and historically important discoveries were being made in the Middle East, and especially in Mesopotamia. There was a reason for the special interest in this region.

Until Darwin and Huxley proved that man's past extended over hundreds of thousands of years, most Christian Europeans and Americans accepted the chronology laboriously worked out by Archbishop James Ussher in the seventeenth century. Working from the Hebrew date of the Flood, 2348 B.C., and back through the Book of Genesis, Ussher calculated that the world had come into existence in the year 4004 B.C.; in fact on a Sunday evening.

Early editions of the Authorized Version of the Bible contain this date.

This acceptance of Ussher's chronology, and of the literal truth of the Old Testament, tended to focus men's minds on the Bible lands, and especially on Mesopotamia, where the great civilizations mentioned in the Hebrew records—Babylon and Assyria—had flourished. The site of the Assyrian cities such as Ashur and Nineveh had long been forgotten. Even in Roman times the poet Lucian could write: "As for Nineveh . . . it is already gone, and there is no trace of it left; you couldn't even say where it was. . . . But there is Babylon, the well-towered city with its enormous walls; before long it will be as hard to find as Nineveh."

However, Lucian was wrong; the site of Babylon continued to be known, and during the Middle Ages the few venturesome Europeans who penetrated to Mesopotamia saw it and brought back reports of it. And if Babylon was a reality, why not other cities mentioned in the Bible?

But for six hundred years, since the end of the Crusades, the Middle East had been virtually cut off from Europe. Then, early in the nineteenth century, communications were reopened and interest in the Middle East began to stir among European and American explorers.

Now it was possible, though with great difficulty, for European explorers to obtain a *firman* (permit) from the Turkish Government and explore lands hitherto closed to them. Not that their task was easy; they had to contend with hostile tribesmen who attacked and robbed them, with corrupt Turkish officials who put obstacles in their way, not to mention the hardships of travel over those harsh desert wastes on horseback (there were no railways) and the constant threat of diseases bred in the foul, insanitary conditions prevailing in cities and villages.

Men willing to risk these dangers, *and* carry out archaeological research, had to be people of extraordinary quality, and so they were. It is with them, and with the earliest Egyptologists, that modern archaeology begins.

Here is the discoverer of Nineveh, Austen Henry Layard, age twenty-four, describing his first sight of the huge mounds of crumbling mud brick which rise between the Tigris and Euphrates:

Desolation meets desolation; a feeling of awe succeeds to wonder; for there is nothing to relieve the mind, to lead to hope or to tell of what has gone by. These huge mounds of Assyria made a deeper impression on me, gave rise to more serious thoughts and earnest reflection, than the [Roman] temple of Balbec, and the [Greek] theatres of Ionia.

Layard, with a young fellow countryman, Edward Mitford, had traveled on horseback or by post chaise across Europe, from the Low Countries to Germany, from Germany via Switzerland to Italy and Dalmatia, thence into Turkey, and then, on horse or muleback, across the Armenian mountains and down into the Syrian plain. When Mitford left for India, Layard stayed behind, took part in the tribal wars between the Bakhtiari tribes of Persia and their Persian oppressors (on the side of the Bakhtiari of course), then introduced himself to the British Ambassador to Constantinople, Sir Stratford Canning.

When, in 1843, the Frenchman Paul Botta unearthed Assyrian sculptures in a mound near Khorsabad, in Mesopotamia, Layard hurried across the mountains to Constantinople and persuaded Canning to make him a small financial grant so that he too could dig. As soon as he received sanction, he got astride his horse again, and in his own words: "I crossed the mountains of Pontus and the great steppes of the Usun Yilak as fast as post-horses could carry me, descended the high lands into the valley of the Tigris, galloped over the vast plains of Assyria, and reached Mosul in twelve days." Then, pretending to be going on a hunting expedition (to deceive the suspicious Turkish authorities in Mosul), he rode to the great mound called Nimrud, named after the mighty hunter who is mentioned in the Book of Genesis.

"I had slept little during the night," he wrote. "Hopes, long cherished, were now to be realised, or were to end in disappointment. Visions of palaces under-ground, of gigantic monsters, of sculptured figures and endless inscriptions floated before me." In the morning, when he left his tent, "the lofty cone and broad mound of Nimrud broke like a distant mountain against the morning sky."

Layard suspected that the mound, like that at Khorsabad, would conceal the palace of an Assyrian king. He possessed none of the elaborate technical equipment which would accompany a modern archaeologist about to excavate such a site. He stood alone, in a desolate country, with no one to help him except a few locally recruited Arab workmen; also he possessed no professional training as an archaeologist.

Yet within a few days his workmen had revealed wonders; as they tunneled into the mound, chanting their monotonous songs to the swing of their picks, great stone-lined chambers and galleries were revealed. On the walls of these chambers strode sculptured figures of kings and gods; there were scenes depicting the siege of cities, as described in the Bible, and battle scenes of terrifying power.

> Two chariots, drawn by horses richly caparisoned [wrote Layard] were each occupied by three warriors, the principal was clothed in a complete suit of mail. . . . The left hand, the arm being fully extended, grasped a bow at full stretch. . . . A second warrior urged, with reins and whip . . . three horses, which were galloping across the plains. . . . Under the horses' feet, and scattered about the relief, were the conquered, wounded by the arrows of the conquerors.

And Layard was reminded of the words of the prophet Nahum, in the Old Testament: "Woe to the bloody city! it is all full of lies and robbery; the prey departeth not. The noise of the whip, and the noise of the rattling wheels, and the prancing horses, and of the jumping chariots."

The "bloody city" was Nineveh, capital of Assyria. Later, when he excavated an even larger mound at Kuyunjik, near Mosul, Layard found himself in a still bigger palace, of which he wrote:

> I opened no less than seventy-one halls, chambers and passages whose walls, almost without exception, had been panelled with slabs of sculptured alabaster recording the wars, the triumphs and great deeds of the Assyrian king. By a rough calculation about 9,880 feet, or nearly two miles, of bas-reliefs, with

twenty-seven portals formed by colossal winged bulls and lion-sphinxes, were uncovered in that part of the building explored during my researches.

The sculptured reliefs which Layard describes were accompanied by written inscriptions in wedge-shaped characters called *cuneiform*. When Layard first uncovered them they could not be read, but soon afterward another Englishman, Henry Rawlinson, succeeded in deciphering the writing. Then Layard knew that at Kuyunjik he had discovered Nineveh itself, the palace of Sennacherib, the terrible king who laid siege to Jerusalem, and of whom Byron had written:

> The Assyrian came down like a wolf on the fold,
> And his cohorts were gleaming in purple and gold,
> And the sheen of their spears was like stars on the sea,
> When the blue wave rolls nightly on deep Galilee.

The Roman Lucian who, seventeen hundred years earlier, had written, "Nineveh is already gone . . . there is no trace of it," would have been astonished by Layard's discoveries. For the first time in some twenty-six hundred years men saw the terrible Assyrians in action, "a people delighting in war." No longer merely a name, they had stepped out of the pages of the Bible and become real again.

To have revealed these Assyrian cities would have been marvelous enough, but Layard went much further. With only a pitifully small financial grant from the British Museum, he succeeded in lifting and transporting hundreds of tons of these magnificent sculptures to London. Every piece of sculpture capable of being moved, even the winged bulls weighing more than twenty tons, were prized from their foundations with crowbars, hoisted onto specially built carts, hauled across miles of desert under the burning sun, winched aboard ship, and brought, via Bombay and the Cape of Good Hope, to England.

It may be asked, Why take them away? Why not leave them where they were found? If they had been found today undoubtedly they would not have been removed, as the modern Iraqui Government has a staff of archaeologists who would know how to preserve and protect the monuments. But in Layard's time, no such safeguards existed. To the fanatical Moslems of the district the sculptures were mere idols, fit only for destruction.

And in case Layard be labeled a mere antiquity hunter, searching only for spectacular pieces of sculpture to adorn the British Museum, something else should be mentioned. In the Assyrian palace at Nineveh he came upon the royal library, consisting of over twenty-six hundred cuneiform tablets. These, which range in subject from official chronicles to legal documents, diplomatic correspondence, poetry, proverbs, and "wisdom-books," include an ancient epic poem, "The Saga of Gilgamesh," which contains a description of Noah's Flood closely resembling that in the Old Testament.

Once the cuneiform writing had been deciphered, a hunt began for more tablets. It was soon recognized that those found by Layard in the Assyrian palace at Nineveh were mainly copies of much earlier documents—poems, chronicles, medical and religious literature produced by a people who had flourished in Meso-potamia more than a thousand years before the Assyrians rose to power. These ancient people, who had invented writing before 3000 B.C. and who were building fine cities in 2700 B.C., were known as the Sumerians, and the country—southern Mesopotamia —was called Sumer. In the Old Testament it is described as "the land of Shinar."

In 1887 the University of Pennsylvania sent an expedition to explore one of these cities, Nippur. It was led by a Dr. Peters, who, unfortunately had not lived in the East and was ignorant of Arab customs. Instead of recruiting local Arab workmen through the local Sheikh, he put his workmen under a Turkish commissar, whom they hated. The result is vividly described by H. Y. Hil-precht, another American scholar, who was a member of the expedition.

On Thursday, 18 April, long before the sun rose, the whole expedition was in readiness to vacate the mounds and force their way to Hilla, when, upon the treacherous order of Mukota, an Arab secretly set fire to our huts of reeds and mats and laid the whole camp in ashes in the short space of five minutes. For a while the utmost confusion prevailed; the *zabtiye* got demoralized and occupied a neighboring hill; and while we were trying to save our effects, many of the Arabs commenced plundering. Half the horses perished in the flames, firearms and saddlebags and $1,000 in gold fell into the hands of the marauders, but all the antiquities were saved. Under the war-dance and yells of the frantic Arabs the expedition finally withdrew.

But a few years later, when the American expedition returned to Nippur, this time under Hilprecht's direction, it succeeded in finding over thirty thousand inscribed tablets, including over two thousand literary texts of considerable importance. Of all the Sumerian literature known to exist, most was discovered at Nippur by the American excavators. Some of these fascinating documents will be described later; here it is only necessary to illustrate the difficulties under which those early excavators worked, and the things which most interested them. It is very important to remember this in assessing the work of these pioneer archaeologists.

The modern archaeologist, as we shall see, tries to obtain an over-all picture of the site he is excavating. He uses every technique available to him to find out *a*) the period of the culture he is investigating, *b*) evidences of its economic life—what crops did the people grow, what domestic animals did they have, what animals did they hunt? Was there trade and if so what were the trade goods? *c*) What was the form of its society. *d*) What kinds of religious beliefs did the people hold and what were their funerary customs, as evidenced in their cemeteries. *e*) What sort of buildings did they erect and how were they furnished and equipped. *f*) What were their relations with other peoples living at the same period. *g*) What was their standard of artistic achievement, as seen in the manufacture of weapons, pottery, jewelry, furniture, etc. *h*) Did they have a writing system; did they keep records.

Men such as Layard were concerned only with the buildings and sculptured ornamentation of the Assyrians, and the evidence of a writing system. The same was true of Hilprecht and many others. During their time the decipherment of the cuneiform writing-system caused an interest in the discovery of inscribed tablets. So they hunted for these, and for tangible objects connected with the period. Because of their lack of knowledge, and their obsession with the excavation of buried cities in search of works of art for museums, they ignored every other consideration, and in fact they must have destroyed, unwittingly, much valuable evidence of which a modern archaeologist would have made use.

I stated earlier that the archaeologist is generally concerned with acquiring knowledge of ancient peoples through the things they made and used, rather than through written records, and this is true. But it so happens that because of their association with the Old Testament, or because they had been described by Greek and Roman historians, the areas which first attracted archaeologists of the early nineteenth century happened to be Mesopotamia and Egypt, the two lands in which writing first appeared. And as both these writing systems could be read, however imperfectly, our knowledge of these civilizations owes as much to the work of the philologist—a scholar versed in the science of language—as to the pure archaeologist. The philologist or linguist was one of the archaeologist's earliest allies, and remains so to this day, though the two do not invariably agree with each other.

The hunt for early writing systems was carried to other parts of the world. Another example occurred in far-off China. It was known that Chinese civilization and writing stretched back to a very remote era, but how far back was uncertain. The earliest known Chinese historian, Ssu-ma Ch'ien, who flourished sometime between 145–80 B.C., refers to dynasties going back to an ascertainable date of 850 B.C. But did Chinese civilization stretch back even earlier than this? And how old was their writing system?

In the year 1079 A.D., thirteen years after the Battle of Hastings in England, a heavy storm occurred near the town of Anyang, in North China. Chinese historians of the period recorded the fact that a large mound near the village caved in, revealing a splendid tomb of ancient date, containing not only human remains but horses and chariots, and magnificent bronze vessels. These the practical people of Anyang promptly collected and sold, and that was that. Eight centuries passed and then these mounds near Anyang, called "the Mounds of Yin," began to attract the attention of curio hunters. In particular, nineteenth-century collectors sought for fragments of animal bones and turtle shells which had peculiar scratchings on them.

These bones, called later "oracle bones," were inscribed with symbols which turned out to be an early form of the Chinese writing system. They were used for divination or prophecy. You went to the priest or magician and put to him a question: Should I marry this girl? or, Is tonight a good night for hunting? The magician then took a piece of bone, perhaps the shoulder blade of an ox or deer, or a piece of turtle shell, and weakened it by making incisions at certain places. Then he applied a red-hot needle point to the shell, which cracked, leaving a pattern of fissures which the priest-magician claimed to interpret. He would then scratch on the bone the result of his divination. One of these has been translated as follows: "Tonight it will rain, and an elephant will be caught." The signs were primitive, but undoubtedly the ancestors of the modern Chinese script. Like all early forms of writing they were pictographic, that is, a sign usually stood for a thing: the word *yu* ("fish" or "to fish") represents a rod and line; *li*, the word for "harvest," shows the act of threshing; *chiu*— "wine"—shows an overflowing jar, and so on.

Led by these inscriptions, the Chinese authorities began to excavate the area in 1927, and not a moment too soon. For the bronze vessels which the villagers of 1079 A.D. had so carelessly sold proved to have been the funerary equipment of an early Chinese king, a member of the Shang Dynasty. Other tombs were found, magnificently equipped with the dead man's horses, chariots, weapons, and ornaments, and nearby, the archaeologists dug up remains of buildings—the ruler's palace, surrounded by the homes of his dependents, many of them skilled craftsmen in bronze. The date was approximately between 1700 and 1500 B.C., roughly contemporary with the peak period of Ancient Egyptian civilization, the Eighteenth Dynasty of the Pharaohs. Like the

Ancient Egyptians, these early Chinese had the horse and chariot, and worked skillfully in bronze. And like the Egyptians and the peoples of Mesopotamia they had a writing system, though not, at this period, so well developed.

Yet there seems no possibility of any cultural connection between peoples living so far apart. Even as relatively recently as the third century B.C. when Hannibal was fighting the Romans, the Chinese were quite unaware of the existence of European civilization. Where did they get the horse, which also appears in Egypt for the first time round about 1700 B.C.? And where did they learn the art of bronze making? Did it penetrate to both China and western Asia from some common source? Or did the Chinese discover it independently? These and similar questions illustrate yet another fascinating aspect of archaeological research—the interrelationship of peoples as revealed by their artifacts, the things they made.

One may compare the work of pioneer archaeologists with stones dropped in a pool. At first there is only a local splash, but gradually, as the circles of ripples expand they touch the ripples formed by the other stones. At first archaeologists, or "antiquarians" as they used to be called, worked independently on the antiquities of their own or other lands.

The progress of archaeology has been not only in working technique, from romantic exploration to scientific excavation, but in the gradual revelation, over the past hundred years, of the complex history of the human race as a whole, of how by trade, war, invasion, or merely by the transmission of ideas and techniques— for example, farming and metalworking—the whole human race has developed.

EGYPT AND
THE EARLIEST
CIVILIZATIONS

"A Unique
National Park
of Ancient Life"

O F ALL THE COUNTRIES which have attracted archaeologists
none have yielded so many rich and wonderful discoveries as
Egypt. Professor Stephen Glanville, a distinguished Egyptologist,
happily called it "a unique National Park of ancient life." A number of circumstances combined to produce this harvest of antiquities. First, Egypt is, with southern Mesopotamia, the home of
the oldest civilization on earth. Second, from earliest times Egyptian religion laid emphasis on the importance of preparing for
the afterlife, so that Ancient Egyptian kings and nobles lavished
their wealth during their lifetime on building pyramids, mausoleums, or rock-cut tombs designed to last for eternity; in fact the
Ancient Egyptian name for tomb means "House of Eternity."

They were not unique in this, of course; many other peoples
have buried their dead in elaborate tombs, but no one carried
this custom as far as did the Egyptians. The earliest Pharaohs,
from 2800 B.C. onward, were buried under man-made mountains
of stone called pyramids, and their noblemen were laid to rest
in ranks of rectangular tombs called mastabas (an Arabic word
meaning "bench") surrounding the pyramid of the monarch.

33

Later Pharaohs were buried in enormous rock-cut tombs tunneled out of the Theban hills and penetrating many hundreds of feet.

For several thousand years every Egyptian who could afford to build a "House of Eternity" did so, and when he died, his mummified body, sometimes enclosed in coffins encased in gold and semiprecious stones, was laid to rest accompanied by all manner of precious and beautiful objects; the Pharaohs were buried in coffins of solid gold surrounded by a succession of wooden shrines plated with gold. In subsidiary chambers of the sepulcher were placed their chariots and weapons, models of the ships in which they had voyaged along the Nile, gold-encased statues of the gods and goddesses they had worshiped, vases of alabaster, golden jewelry inlaid with carnelian and lapis lazuli, caskets of ivory and ebony containing their clothing and other articles—all the wealth and sumptuousness which had surrounded them in life, and which they fervently hoped would accompany them to the life beyond the grave.

Except in very early times, however, the Egyptians did not kill and bury the household retinues with their monarchs. The great officials and their wives also built themselves handsome sepulchers in which they, too, were accompanied by considerable wealth and on the walls of their tombs they had sculpted or painted scenes depicting the life they had enjoyed on earth, and which they hoped would continue in the life to come. Even the lower middle class who could not afford private tombs had their bodies mummified and buried in corporate mausoleums accompanied by a few trinkets attached to their bodies under the mummy wrappings.

At one period, which Egyptologists call the Middle Kingdom (between 2100 and 1700 B.C.), it was customary to bury with the noble dead elaborate and beautiful models, such as were found in the tomb described in the first chapter. These models, which often represent quite mundane activities such as brewing and baking and stock rearing, give us a picture of ordinary Egyptian life—the life of the common people—which one rarely if ever finds in the tombs of contemporary or later civilizations. It is almost as if the Ancient Egyptians, whose civilization lasted some three thousand years, had deliberately set out to show posterity how they lived.

They kept written records; their tombs are inscribed with descriptions of the scenes depicted on the walls; they covered their temples with inscriptions; and they wrote documents on papyri— a writing material made from the papyrus reed which used to grow beside the river Nile—ranging from school notebooks to poetry, stories, official chronicles, and religious texts. Incidentally our word "paper" comes from "papyrus."

Egypt is a dry, virtually rainless country; its only water supply comes from the mighty Nile, which is the source of Egypt's life, then and now. Pyramids and tombs were built on the rocky fringes of the enclosing desert, where there is hardly any moisture; therefore objects and paintings which would undoubtedly have perished in a more temperate climate have survived down to our own age almost intact. The wall paintings and hieroglyphic inscriptions look as fresh as on the day they were painted; wooden objects such as caskets, statues, and models have been preserved by the dry climate, as have many of the mummies. Even the un-mummified bodies of the so-called predynastic inhabitants—the ancestors of the civilized, tomb-building Egyptians—often preserve their skin and hair, although they were buried in mere shallow pit-graves in the sand, accompanied by a few primitive pots and slate palettes.

At first, as in Mesopotamia, Europeans were attracted to Egypt by its Biblical associations. Who was the Pharaoh Moses served and from whom he fled with the Israelites to the Red Sea, where the king and his pursuing army were drowned? Who was the Pharaoh who "came up against Jerusalem" and took away the treasures of Solomon's temple? In the early nineteenth century, to those who accepted Archbishop Ussher's chronology, these were pertinent questions. They had no idea that the primitive history of Egypt goes back four to five thousand years B.C., and that behind the civilized Egyptians lay an even earlier people.

It is this formative period which attracts many modern Egyptologists, whereas in the early nineteenth century the motive was, all too often, to ransack the country of portable objects which could be sent to American and European museums, who paid their agents well for this work. Men who had no claim to the title "archaeologist" went to Egypt, completely unequipped for serious archaeological research, simply with the intention of digging for antiquities. Among them they committed archaeological outrages which would not be permitted today. Museums and private collections throughout the world are full of Egyptian objects of considerable beauty, the provenance of which is unknown. Sites which today would have been scrupulously excavated, layer by layer, were indiscriminately dug and left wrecked in a frantic search for portable antiquities which were, in Wheeler's apt phrase, "dug up like potatoes."

One of the early adventurers was Giovanni Belzoni, who had been, among other things, the strong man in a circus, and who went to Egypt in 1816. He thus describes how he explored a communal tomb full of mummies:

> After getting through these passages, some of them two or three hundred yards long, you generally find a more commodious place, perhaps high enough to sit. But what a place of rest! surrounded by bodies, by heaps of mummies in all directions, which, previous to my becoming accustomed to the sight, filled me with horror. The blackness of the wall, the faint light given by candles and torches for want of air, the different objects that surrounded me seeming to converse with each other, and the Arabs with the candles and torches in their hands, naked and covered with dust, themselves resembling living mummies, absolutely formed a scene that cannot be described.
>
> After the exertion of entering such a place . . . and nearly overcome, I sought a resting-place, found one and contrived to sit; but when my weight bore down on the body of an Egyptian, it crushed like a band-box; I had naturally no course but to my hands to sustain my weight, but they found no better support; so that I sank altogether among the broken mummies, with a crash of bones, rags and wooden cases. . . .

But Belzoni, for all the crudity of his methods, did make his contribution to Egyptology, if only by bringing the attention of the Western world to the treasures which could be found in Egypt. He was the first man to enter the Second Pyramid in modern times, and discovered its concealed entrance. However his greatest achievement was his excavation of the most splendid tomb in the Valley of the Kings at Luxor, that of Seti I, the mightiest monarch of the Nineteenth Dynasty (1350–1200 B.C.). Of course he was not the first to explore it—it was a popular "show place" in Greek and Roman times—but some of its splendidly sculptured and painted galleries had become choked with fallen rock. These galleries Belzoni penetrated with the aid of battering rams, until he found himself in the burial chamber of Seti himself.

It had been robbed in ancient times, like nearly all the tombs in the Royal Valley, but the king's beautiful alabaster sarcophagus, its surface incised with hundreds of miniature figures and religious texts, had survived. Belzoni brought it triumphantly to London and exhibited it to thousands in a building specially decorated as the Egyptian Hall. The empty stone chest, which once contained the body of one of Egypt's greatest kings, now stands in a small, little-known museum in central London, the Soane Museum in Lincoln's Inn Fields. But when it was first exhibited Belzoni surrounded it with reproductions of the beautifully colored bas-reliefs which he copied from the walls of the tomb, and the total effect must have been striking.

Belzoni's exhibition, was to most visitors their first introduction to the marvels of Ancient Egypt. It was an astonishing revelation to a generation brought up in the traditions of Graeco-Roman art; vulgar and "popular" though it may have been, it helped to create a climate of opinion which encouraged others to go to Egypt and study its antiquities.

But the greatest stimulus to Egyptological research was undoubtedly the decipherment of the Egyptian hieroglyphic writing system which enabled the long-forgotten Ancient Egyptians to speak directly to us. The story of how this was done, though well known, is worth repeating.

When Napoleon invaded Egypt, he took with him a band of savants who carefully surveyed the monuments. At a place called Rosetta, near the mouth of the Nile, some French soldiers came upon a slab of stone inscribed in Greek, which could be read, and in two forms of the Egyptian writing system, the "hieroglyphic" and "hieratic" scripts, which could not be read. Hieroglyph is an Ancient Greek word meaning "Sacred Sign." Very few Greeks could read this ancient "picture writing" of the Egyptians which remained a mystery for two thousand years. Napoleon's scholars made copies of the inscription on the Rosetta Stone and circulated it to their fellow scholars. Among these was a young man named Jean François Champollion. He guessed that the inscriptions were bilingual, that is, they said the same thing in two different languages, Greek and Ancient Egyptian. The Greek inscription turned out to be a copy of a decree passed by the General Council of Egyptian priests to celebrate the first commemoration of Ptolemy V, Epiphanes, king of Egypt. (The Ptolemies, a Greek-speaking dynasty of kings descended from Ptolemy I, one of Alexander's generals, ruled Egypt from 332 to 30 B.C.)

An Englishman, Dr. Thomas Young, shared with Champollion the glory of deciphering a language which had been extinct for more than fifteen centuries, and of unlocking the door to a forgotten world. Both he and Champollion demonstrated that the hieroglyphs were alphabetic and that wherever a royal or proper name occurred in the Ancient Egyptian script it was surrounded by a flattened oval which they called a "cartouche." This is characteristic of all Egyptian writing in which the names of royal persons appear.

One of the names mentioned in the Greek inscription was, of course, Ptolemy, the pronunciation of which was known. So, they reasoned, the name must include the sounds *p, t, l,* and *m.* Another part of the Greek inscription includes the name Cleopatra, which contains the sounds *k, l, p, t,* and *r.* One can imagine the decipherers' excitement when they discovered that within the cartouche enclosing the name Ptolemy the *p* and *t* sounds came first and second, followed by the *l* and *m* sounds, whereas in the cartouche which they suspected enclosed Cleopatra's name, the *l* sound came second, followed by the *p* and *t* and a fifth symbol which could represent the consonant *r.* (Vowel sounds were not represented in the Egyptian writing system, which is one reason why the pronunciation of the language is so difficult to determine.)

In this way Champollion and Young gradually worked out the

phonetic equivalents of other hieroglyphs and so eventually an alphabet began to form. This was only the beginning; it enabled scholars to read the names but not yet to translate the language. Its grammatical structure was still unknown. Probably it might have remained so save for a vital fact. During the Roman period the Egyptians became Christianized and conducted their religious services in their own ancient tongue. When, in the seventh century A.D., the Arabs conquered the country and imposed their Moslem religion and Arab language on most of the inhabitants, a minority of the population, called Copts or Kopts, still adhered to Christianity; they became a persecuted minority which, although it spoke Arabic, the language of the conquerors, retained, in its religious ritual, elements of the ancient language which its ancestors had spoken and written for some three thousand years. By studying this Coptic language scholars such as Champollion and his successors were able to grasp the structure of the Ancient Egyptian writing system and eventually to translate it.

This almost miraculous decipherment, like that of the cuneiform writing of ancient Mesopotamia, gave archaeologists working in these two countries an advantage over their colleagues working in areas where no writing system existed. It explains why, at this period, the attention of some of the foremost archaeologists was concentrated on these two favored regions of the world, and especially on Egypt where there was an abundance of well-preserved stone monuments and tombs. These, even if they had been rifled thousands of years ago (as most were), still contained important inscriptions which could be read. The Egyptologist of the nineteenth century did not have to interpret the Ancient Egyptian civilization entirely through ruins of buildings, pottery and other artifacts, and cemeteries. The Ancient Egyptians, prolific record keepers, had obligingly provided him with written clues.

They kept records of the reign dates of their kings, divided into dynasties from the First Dynasty (about 3200 B.C.) down to the Thirtieth Dynasty (378–332 B.C.) followed by the period of Graeco-Roman occupation, from 332 B.C. to 395 A.D. They had the convenient habit of inscribing, not only on tombs and temples, but even on small objects such as scarabs and miniature statuettes, the name of the reigning king, so that the object could be roughly dated. The same applies to the furniture and other objects found in their tombs. On the walls of their temples the Pharaohs inscribed records of their wars and conquests; the great officials not only left vividly executed wall paintings and bas-reliefs in their tombs, but inscribed these with descriptions of each scene, even down to the dialogue spoken by the participants in the scenes.

Then there were writings on papyrus scrolls, from school note-books to volumes of poetry, folk tales, medical literature, and legal documents. Among the latter the most fascinating are the records of the trial of certain tomb robbers accused of plundering royal and princely sepulchers some three thousand years ago. So Glanville's description of Egypt as "a unique National Park of ancient life" is not an exaggeration. Not only does the park exist but visitors are supplied with a guide book written by the Ancient Egyptians themselves. It is not entirely accurate, and contains many serious gaps; but compared with archaeologists working in prehistoric Europe, Africa, or the Americas, Egyptologists are singularly fortunate.

Pioneers
of Egyptology

Although the army of Napoleon was soon forced to retire from Egypt, French influence remained strong throughout the nineteenth century. It was the Frenchman, Auguste Mariette, who was responsible for founding the Antiquities Service, the Egyptian Government Department responsible for guarding and preserving the antiquities, and which grants or withholds permission to excavate. Its foundation was very necessary in order to control indiscriminate plundering, not only by European antiquity hunters, but by Egyptian peasants who dug (and still dig) illicitly at Luxor and other places to supply dealers.

Some of these illicit diggers are very engaging rascals, particularly those living at el-Gournah, near the Theban Necropolis at Luxor. Their ancestors have been plundering tombs for thousands of years and they see no reason why the government should stop them. They are also adept at faking antiquities if they cannot find genuine articles; the best examples are traded through dealers to collectors; the smaller varieties are exhibited on trays as genuine antiquities to gullible tourists emerging from the

Royal Valley. Recently the government has passed strict laws forbidding the sale of faked antiquities. But the last time I visited Luxor the gay crowd of hawkers was still there, each with his tray of objects. Only this time, above each tray was stuck a sign which read "Genuine Imitations."

Today, thanks to the Antiquities Department, all the principal tombs are guarded by iron gates and protected by formidable-looking Arabs called *ghaffirs,* carrying rifles and bandoliers. Illicit digging still goes on, of course, owing to the inexorable laws of supply and demand. This is the price Egyptology has had to pay for its popularity. As more and more tourists visit Egypt, more and more want to take a bit of it home with them, although this is forbidden by law. So the villagers of el-Gournah and other places neighboring the Theban Necropolis dig shafts in the floors of their homes and then drive tunnels into adjoining tombs in order to chip from the walls fragments of painting or bas-relief which have a high market value. Over the years thousands of square feet of tomb inscriptions have been ruined in this way, and archaeological evidence destroyed forever.

In considering the work of Mariette and his successors in Egypt, it is important to remember that ready-made guidebook which the Ancient Egyptians had provided in the form of king lists, regnal years, monuments and objects inscribed with the names of the reigning Pharaoh. They also had an accurate calendar; they studied and recorded the movement of the sun, moon, and planets and kept records of them. This gives us an additional check on their dating. Therefore, from about 1840 onward, any archaeologist investigating an Egyptian site could roughly ascertain its date if it came within the period when kings' names were inscribed on monuments or objects. They did not have to bother much about changes in pottery styles.

What few of the nineteenth-century archaeologists realized, or bothered to consider, was that a civilization which in 2800 B.C. was sufficiently mature to build pyramids hundreds of feet high, which had a developed writing system and a sophisticated art, could not have come into existence suddenly. It must have had antecedents, whose unspectacular relics were probably buried under the desert sand—objects left by the primitive ancestors of the Ancient Egyptians thousands of years before writing was invented or the first pyramid built. We owe the discovery of these so-called predynastic cultures—before the First Dynasty (circa 3200 B.C.)—to the genius of Flinders Petrie and to those who have followed up the clues he discovered.

Meanwhile Egyptologists were well content to investigate the visible and impressive monuments of the Dynastic Period, from 2800 B.C., the beginning of the Third Dynasty, down to the time of the Macedonian conquerors, the Ptolemies, who annexed Egypt in 332 B.C. At first the monuments of the First to the Fourth Dynasties (roughly from 3200 to 2700 B.C.) were not recognized, although the names of these early kings had been recorded. It was believed that the oldest monument in Egypt was the famous Great Pyramid at Giza, built by the Pharaoh Cheops (or Khufu) about 2700 B.C.

When he investigated the pyramid of Cheops, Belzoni found only a rifled burial chamber within the pyramid, in which all that remained was the king's sarcophagus. Then he penetrated the pyramid of Cheops's successor, Chephren, and found a sarcophagus containing a few bones. Colonel Richard Howard-Vyse and his assistant John Perring penetrated the Third Pyramid (with the assistance of gunpowder) and discovered, within the sarcophagus, fragmentary bones which may have been those of its owner, Menkaure (Mycerinus). They are now in the British Museum, London.

But all three pyramids had been despoiled in remote antiquity, as had the rectangular mastaba tombs of the Pharaohs' officials which were laid out in orderly streets surrounding their masters' pyramid. Then Vyse and Perring investigated the mysterious Step Pyramid at Sakkara, some twelve miles south of Cairo, which eventually turned out to be the sepulcher of King Joser (Neter-khet), first king of the Third Dynasty, circa 2800 B.C., the oldest stone building in the world. Further south, at Dashur and at Medûm, Egyptologists were able to identify two enormous pyramids as belonging to the Pharaoh Snofru, who may have been the last

Pharaoh of the Third Dynasty or perhaps the first Pharaoh of the Fourth. In this they were guided entirely by painted inscriptions on some of the stones bearing the name Snofru. Except for these rough scrawls, probably painted by workmen, these pyramids of the Third and Fourth Dynasties were uninscribed. Nevertheless it was possible, after a time, to trace the evolution of the pyramid form from the simple rectangular mastaba through the Step Pyramid, which was a series of mastabas piled one on top of the other to form a "stepped" structure, to the true straight-sided pyramid.

All these monumental structures (the Great Pyramid was over 450 feet high) were essentially royal tombs and nothing else. In Joser's tomb members of the royal family were buried in galleries adjoining the king's burial chamber beneath the building. Later the king alone rested under or within the pyramid, surmounted by hundreds of thousands of accurately masoned stone blocks, each weighing between two and three tons. Members of his family were buried in miniature pyramids near the main building, and it was in one of these that Petrie discovered the fabulous jewelry of Sit-Hathor-Unet and other Egyptian queens and princesses.

The purpose underlying all this work, which must have occupied great gangs of laborers for upward of twenty years, was quite simple—the preservation of the royal body. And in this, as we have seen, the Egyptians failed. Despite the mass of masonry and the cunningly concealed entrances, portcullis blocks sealing the inner galleries, the Ancient Egyptian tomb robbers always got through in the end. To be "pyramidally extant," as Thomas Browne had written, "is a fallacy in duration."

However, the Egyptians, the most conservative of people, continued to build pyramids for their kings down to the Middle Kingdom (2100–1700 B.C.), though the royal architects kept altering their plans in a vain effort to defeat the robbers. At first they relied on a huge mass of superincumbent masonry and a concealed entrance. Once this was penetrated and the blocking stones removed or by-passed, the plunderers could go straight to the burial chamber. In the Twelfth Dynasty (1900–1790 B.C.) they tended to build smaller pyramids, of which only the outside was of

hewn stone; the core was of rubble. But instead of a simple entrance gallery, they devised ingenious "puzzle passages" and blind
alleys, hoping thus to delay and perhaps exhaust the robbers in
their efforts to find the true burial chamber. In this too they were
unsuccessful.

Finally, at the beginning of the Eighteenth Dynasty (1555 B.C.)
they gave up building pyramids altogether. By this time the capital of Egypt had been moved to Thebes (modern Luxor) in the
southern part of the land, where there were imposing cliffs of
limestone enclosing a secret valley. Here over thirty of the greatest Pharaohs of the New Kingdom (1555–712 B.C.) were buried in
deep rock-cut tombs tunneled out of the mountainside; these
also had their blind alleys and puzzle passages of surpassing inge-
nuity, and some were of colossal size. That of Queen Hatshepsut,
high up in the cliffs, was 700 feet long; that of Seti I, which Belzoni excavated, measured 470 feet in length. But these too (all
except one) were penetrated and plundered by the Ancient Egyptian robbers.

A number of distinguished Greek and Roman writers had
visited Egypt in classical times, and described its monuments. They
could not read the ancient writing, but had enjoyed the enviable
advantage of seeing Egyptian civilization still in being. Nineteenth-century scholars pored over the works of Strabo, Pliny,
Diodorus Siculus, and others, searching for clues. Among them
was the young Auguste Ferdinand François Mariette, later to become founder and first Director of the Antiquities Service. In
1850, when he was twenty-nine, he visited Egypt, nominally to
acquire Coptic manuscripts, but the mighty monuments of the
country so fascinated him that he spent most of his time (and
money) surveying and digging. It was Mariette who discovered the
superb diorite statue of the Pharaoh Chephren, so often reproduced.

He also discovered the sepulcher of the Apis bulls. "One day,"
he writes, "attracted to Sakkarah by my Egyptological studies, I
perceived the head of . . . [a sphinx] obtruding itself from the
sand." A passage in Strabo in which he referred to "a temple of
Serapis in a spot so sandy that the wind causes the sand to accu-

mulate in heaps, under which we could see many sphinxes," suddenly occurred to Mariette's mind. He realized with a thrill of excitement that here, under the sand, might lie the avenue of sphinxes leading to the rock-cut tombs of the Apis bulls, so often sought for but never found.

Engaging a few workmen, and without referring to anybody, the young Frenchman started to dig along the avenue until he disclosed the entrance to one of the most remarkable monuments in all Egypt, and one which most visitors to Sakkara still visit. Deep underground, hollowed out of the rock, are great galleries, off which lead chambers, each containing a huge sarcophagus. These were the burial places of the sacred Apis bulls, which were mummified like kings and buried with rich regalia. All the sarcophagi were empty when Mariette discovered them but this labyrinth of passages is awesome enough in its own right.

Among Mariette's contemporaries were the great German Egyptologist Karl Lepsius who collected an enormous mass of inscriptions and published them in his famous *Denkmäler,* and another German, Adolf Erman, one of the most distinguished philologists and an expert on the interpretation of the Ancient Egyptian language. He and Mariette were rivals, but neither was a treasure hunter. What interested them most was the Egyptian language. When did it first come into use? The pyramids of the Fourth Dynasty, as we have noted, were uninscribed save for quarry marks, and Mariette had formed the fixed opinion that all the pyramids were *muettes* ("dumb"); he saw no point in digging into others in the hope of finding hieroglyphs.

Gaston Maspero, who came out to Egypt in 1880, was less certain. He had heard rumors that in the year before he arrived in Egypt an inscribed pyramid had been found at Sakkara. It turned out to be true, and the discoverer was a fox. The animal had managed to penetrate into a cavity in the rubble of a ruined pyramid. An Arab head-workman *(reis),* following the fox, found himself in a pyramid chamber covered with inscribed texts. It turned out to be that of Pepi I, third Pharaoh of the Sixth Dynasty (2420–2270 B.C.)

Maspero, who shortly afterward succeeded Mariette as Director

of the Antiquities Service, opened up the neighboring pyramids
of Unas, Teti, and Merenre. All were inscribed with fascinating
funerary texts which he published. Altogether four thousand lines
of hymns and formulas were found, of which Maspero wrote,
*"the greater part were written originally during the prehistoric
period of Egyptian history"* (my italics).

Some of the texts made sense in the light of what was already
known about Egyptian religion. The Pharaoh, as son of Ra (Re),
the sun god, serves the god in the after life. "King Pepi receives
to himself his oar; he takes his seat; he sits in the bow of the ship;
he rows Ra to the west," says one text. In another the king
appears to act as scribe or secretary to Ra. "King Unas sits before
him [Ra]; King Unas opens his chest [of papers]; King Unas
breaks open his edicts; King Unas signs his decrees . . . "

But many of the texts were obscure, and appeared to be not
a continuous, meaningful narrative but a haphazard collection of
spells and hymns. There is a reference to a ferryman, "he who
looks behind," who takes the dead Pharaoh across the "Lily Lake"
to "the fields where the gods were begotten"—reminiscent of the
Greek Elysian Fields and Charon the ferryman who carried the
dead across the river Styx. Yet these texts were inscribed at least
fourteen hundred years before the first classical Greeks visited
Egypt, and at least seven hundred years before even the pre-Hel-
lenic Greeks, Homer's Achaeans, could have seen the Nile Valley.

Even more fascinating were certain texts which bore no relationship whatever to the life of the Egyptians of the pyramid-
building period. In one of these the king "devours the gods" and
indulges in a cannibal feast. In another we find the strange words,
"the bricks are removed from thee from the great tomb"; the pyramids were of stone, not brick. And another reads, "cast the sand
from thy face"; why "sand" when the Pharaoh was sealed in
mummy wrappings and in a coffin within a stone sarcophagus
inside a pyramid?

Mariette and his colleagues were right in conjecturing that some
of these texts dated from a period long before the Egyptians
became civilized; but theirs was still merely a conjecture. It was
the archaeologist Petrie, working in regions to which the linguist

could not penetrate, who eventually proved, by excavation, that these texts once had a literal meaning. But his revelation of predynastic Egypt came later. Meanwhile let us return to the historical period and watch Emile Brugsch, Maspero's assistant, make the most remarkable discovery in the history of Egyptian archaeology.

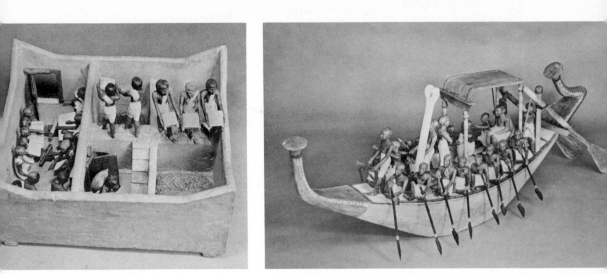

Funerary models of a ship and a granary from the tomb of Meket-Re

Articles from the dressing table of Princess Sit-Hathor-Unet.
A part of the Lahun treasure.

The three great pyramids at Giza and (below) The Temple of
Queen Hatshepsut near the Valley of Kings

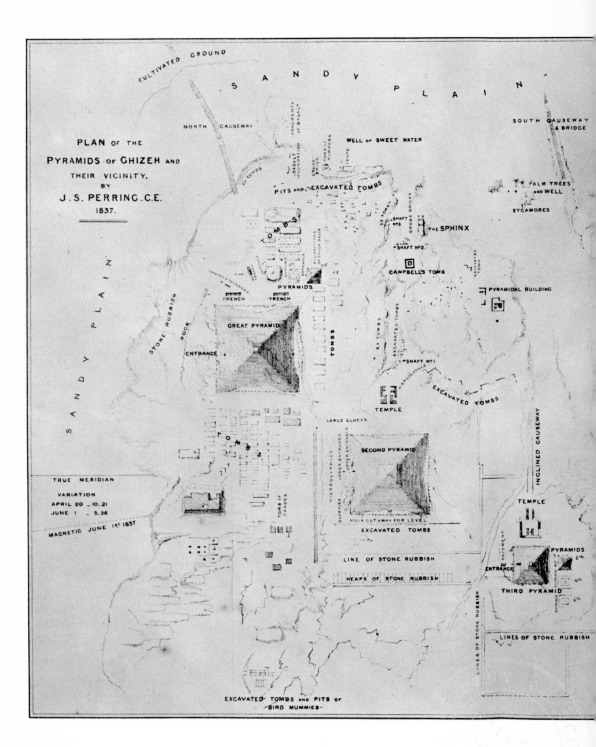

CULTIVATED GROUND

S A N D Y   P L A I N

NORTH CAUSEWAY

SOUTH CAUSEWAY
& BRIDGE

WELL of SWEET WATER

PLAN of the
PYRAMIDS of GHIZEH AND
THEIR VICINITY,
BY
J.S. PERRING.C.E.
1837.

PALM TREES
AND WELL

PITS and EXCAVATED TOMBS

SYCAMORES

SHAFT No 3

THE SPHINX

SHAFT No 2

CAMPBELL'S TOMB

S
A
N
D
Y

P
L
A
I
N

PYRAMIDS

TRENCH   TRENCH

PYRAMIDAL BUILDING

GREAT PYRAMID

ENTRANCE

TOMBS

SHAFT No 1

EXCAVATED TOMBS

TEMPLE

LARGE BLOCKS

LINE OF STONE RUBBISH

SECOND PYRAMID

INCLINED CAUSEWAY

TRUE MERIDIAN

VARIATION
APRIL 20 - 10.21
JUNE 1 - 8.36

MAGNETIC JUNE 1ST 1837

TOMBS OF THADES

ROCK CUT AWAY FOR LEVEL

EXCAVATED TOMBS

TEMPLE

PYRAMIDS

ENTRANCE

THIRD PYRAMID

LINE OF STONE RUBBISH

HEAPS OF STONE RUBBISH

LINES OF STONE RUBBISH

LINES OF STONE RUBBISH

EXCAVATED TOMBS AND PITS OF
BIRD MUMMIES

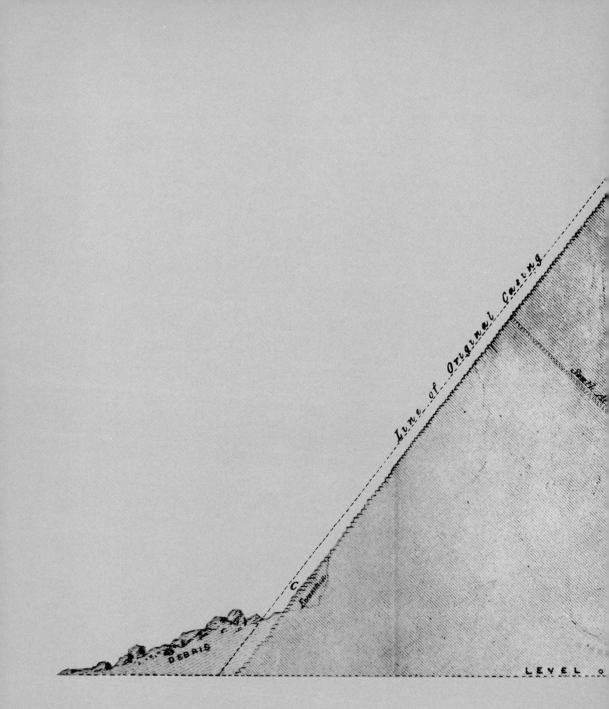

Line of Original Casing
C
DEBRIS
LEVEL O
GREAT
VERTICAL SECTION
THROUGH PASSAGE

Vyse's diagram of the Great Pyramid

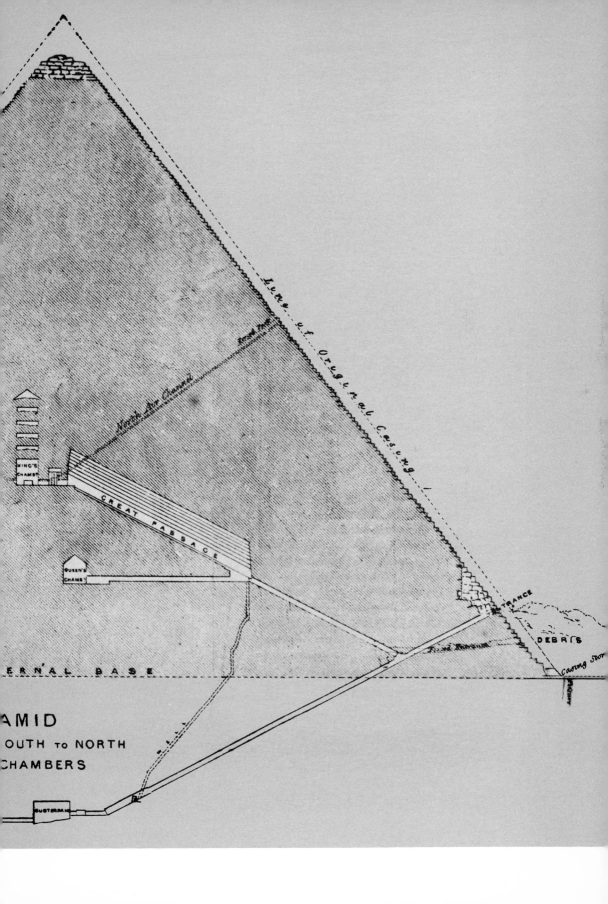

Line of Original Casing

North Air Channel

KING'S CHAMBER

GREAT PASSAGE

QUEEN'S CHAMBER

ENTRANCE

DEBRIS

Casing Stones

INTERNAL BASE

...AMID

...OUTH TO NORTH

...CHAMBERS

SUBTERRAN...

*The burial chamber of Menkaure (Mycerinus) as seen by Colonel
Howard-Vyse and J. S. Perring*

Reconstructed entrance to the outer enclosure of the Step Pyramid of King Joser

*King Joser. The statue on the left is from his mastaba; the stela was found
in one of the underground galleries beneath his pyramid.*

Sir Flinders Petrie in his library at Jerusalem in 1932

Digging Deeper

ONE DAY, in the 1870's, when Mariette was still Director of
the Antiquities Service, a gentleman named Abderassul was conducting an illicit "dig" at Luxor, six hundred miles to the south
of Sakkara. Abderassul was an Egyptian peasant from the village
of El-Gournah and if Mariette had known what he and his companions were up to they would probably have been clapped in jail.
Despite the efforts of the Egyptian authorities, these illicit "diggers" continued their nefarious work. The district surrounding
their homes, in which their ancestors had lived since Pharaonic
times, was honeycombed with tombs, and family traditions stretching back over centuries had given them a shrewd professional
knowledge of where to dig. Their work was secret, clandestine,
and involved them in a constant battle of wits with the authorities.

Westward of the Nile a broad cultivated plain suddenly ends in
an abrupt rocky escarpment occasionally broken by deep clefts in
the cliff. It was in one of these rarely visited clefts—a place called
Deir el-Bahari—that Abderassul and a fellow robber came upon a
deep, vertical, rock-cut shaft. Calling for rope and candles, Abderassul had himself lowered into the shaft, which was very deep.

57

His friend kept on paying out the rope until at last Abderassul called up the shaft that he had struck bottom, and had found a horizontal gallery which he was going to explore.

For a long, long time there was silence. The explorer's companion, waiting anxiously on the surface, watched continually for any sign of intruders. Suddenly he heard Abderassul's voice raised in terror, booming up the echoing shaft. "Pull me up! Pull me up, quickly! There's an *afrit* down here!"

To the superstitious peasants of el-Gournah an *afrit* is an evil spirit, a devil who is believed to live underground. As rapidly as possible Abderassul was hauled up into the daylight, sweating with terror and gibbering about the terrible sight he had seen. Without another word the two mounted their donkeys and hurried back to the river bank as fast as they could go. And that was the end of that. The explorer refused to talk about the incident, and when, some weeks later, his friend ventured back to the top of the shaft, such an obnoxious smell emerged from it that it was obvious that there *was* an *afrit* at the bottom of that dark hole, for these spirits were known to give out a foul odor.

Then, in 1874 there appeared on the antiquities markets of Europe certain objects which puzzled and intrigued Egyptologists. Maspero noted "several figurines, of rough workmanship but coated with charming blue enamel which were being sold in Paris. . . . Though they did not carry a royal name they bore the title Kheperkhare, which was attributed to at least two of the Pharaohs, Senusret II of the Twelfth Dynasty and Pinedjem of the Twenty-First Dynasty."

In 1877 Maspero received, from a British collector, General Campbell, "a hieratic ritual of the High Priest of Amun [or Amen, the chief god of Egypt during the New Kingdom] whose name was Pinedjem. He had bought the papyrus from a Luxor dealer for £400." In the following year a French collector named de Saulcy sent Maspero a photograph of a long papyrus scroll bearing the name Queen Nedjamet. De Saulcy had bought it from a Syrian dragoman (guide) who said he had acquired it in Luxor. Meanwhile Mariette, in Cairo, had obtained a papyrus of the same type in Suez.

"In short," wrote Maspero, "by the year 1878 I felt sure that the Arabs had somewhere discovered one or more vaults of a hitherto unknown group of royal tombs of the Twenty-First Dynasty. . . . To hunt for this site was one of the principal objects of my journey to Upper Egypt in the months of March and April, 1881."

Maspero, who in this year had succeeded Mariette as Director of the Antiquities Service, set about his inquiries with determination, backed by the power invested in him by the Egyptian Government. After a visit to Luxor he established that the principal sellers of royal antiquities were a certain Abderassul Ahmed, his brother Mohammed Abderassul, and Mustapha Agha Ayat, who was Consular Agent in Luxor for the British, Belgian, and Russian governments. Mustapha Agha Ayat could not be touched, since he was protected by diplomatic immunity, so Maspero issued orders for the arrest of Abderassul Ahmed.

Abderassul vigorously denied any knowledge of royal antiquities, despite the unanimous testimony of tourists who had bought such objects from him. His house was searched, but without result. When coaxing and threats had failed, Maspero sent the suspect under guard to the Turkish Governor of the district, Daoud Pasha, who was conducting his own investigations. These lasted two months, during the whole of which time Abderassul Ahmed was kept in prison, except when he appeared in court. Maspero writes smoothly that "the business was gone into with great thoroughness" and commends "the vigour with which the inquiry was conducted." Just how vigorous you may judge from a story told me many years ago by the late Professor Percy Newberry, who, as a young man, had met the aged Abderassul. The old Arab had pointed to the marks on the soles of his feet made by the *bastinado*, a favorite Turkish form of punishment. Daoud Pasha was known for his severity.

Despite all this, Abderassul continued to deny any knowledge of any illicit excavations, and witnesses from el-Gournah all testified to his honesty and integrity. He was, they said, "the loyalest and most disinterested man in Egypt, who never had excavated and never would excavate anything." After two months he was dismissed and went back to his village. Maspero seemed to have failed.

Then, a short while afterward, a bitter quarrel broke out within the Abderassul family. Some believed that the museum authorities had finally been foiled, and would trouble them no longer. Others thought it better to own up and avoid enduring in the future what Abderassul Ahmed had suffered. He, poor man, angrily demanded that in the future he should receive a half share of the loot, whereas till then he had been content with one fifth. Eventually his brother, Mohammed Abderassul, realizing that the secret would soon be out, went privately to Daoud Pasha and told him the truth.

Next day a dispatch from Daoud Pasha arrived in Cairo. Maspero, to his annoyance, had planned to sail immediately to Europe, so he sent his assistant, Emile Brugsch, to Luxor. There he was met by Abderassul Ahmed, who led him, accompanied by Turkish officials and guards, across the plain to the shaft at the foot of the Theban cliffs which Abderassul had found over ten years earlier. What Brugsch discovered when he was lowered into the shaft is best described in his own words. There were two long horizontal galleries, one of them ending in a small chamber. These galleries were crammed with royal mummies,

> every inch . . . was covered with coffins and antiquities of all kinds. My astonishment was so overpowering that I scarcely knew whether I was awake or whether it was only a dream. Resting on a coffin, I mechanically cast my eyes over the lid, and distinctly saw the name of King Sethi Ist, father of Ramesses the Second . . . a few steps further on, with his hands crossed on his breast, lay Ramesses II, the great Sesostris himself. The further I advanced, the greater was the wealth displayed—here Amenophis I, there Ahmes, the three Tuthmoses, Queen Ahmes Nefertari—all the mummies well-preserved, thirty-six coffins, all belonging to Kings or Queens or Princes or Princesses . . .

It was as if, three thousand years from now, most of the greatest kings of France, from Charlemagne to Louis XIV, had been found in one spot, their original tombs having been plundered. For most of these Pharaohs belonged to the period of Egypt's imperial greatness, when she was for a time the most powerful state in the world.

How did they get there? And by what miracle had the tomb escaped detection for thirty centuries?

You will remember that originally each king was buried in his own separate and magnificent tomb hollowed out of the cliffs in the Royal Valley. Each was surrounded by immense wealth in gold, silver, and semiprecious stones. For a brief time following the death of each Pharaoh his treasures were reasonably safe. But sooner or later, during periods of weak government, and doubtless with the connivance of corrupt guards and priestly custodians, tomb robbers got in and removed the treasure. Sometimes, as we know from contemporary records, they even set fire to the mummy, but usually they were content to strip it of its jewelry and leave the body unwrapped. Perhaps, too, a few of the king's possessions, those with little monetary value, would be left by the robbers.

This must have happened again and again from the Eighteenth Dynasty onward, but especially during the Twenty-First Dynasty (1090–945 B.C.) when the authorities were too weak, or too corrupt and indifferent, to guard the tombs adequately. It must have been at this time that the priests of the Necropolis, nominally responsible for protecting the royal tombs, hit on a desperate plan. At night (it must have been at night) they secretly gathered together thirty-six of the royal mummies, hauled them over the bridle path (which can still be followed) leading from the Royal Valley to the eastern edge of the mountain, and then lowered them, one by one, into this single tomb, which, being at the foot of a narrow cliff, could easily be guarded. The secret died with the priests, and the Pharaohs slept undisturbed for three thousand years, until Abderassul stumbled on them by accident.

Abderassul and his associates knew enough about Egyptology to recognize that the *ureus*, or serpent, on the brow of each mummy signified royalty. That was why they had kept quiet about their find for ten years. It would have been impossible for them to remove the mummies without being observed, and in any case, where would they sell them without its becoming known to the Antiquities Service?

So during ten years they visited the tomb only three times, always, of course, at night and were content to remove a few small portable objects which could easily be disposed of. It was these minor antiquities, some of which bore royal names, which first attracted the notice of Maspero and others.

Brugsch discovered dockets with hieroglyphic inscriptions on the mummies, giving the name of the king or queen and in some cases the number of times it had been rewrapped. Ramses II, for example, had been reburied three times, indicating that at first the Pharaohs had been reinterred in their own tombs only to be robbed yet again. Then, checking against their king lists, the archaeologists noticed that there were some notable absentees from the cache. Queen Hatshepsut was missing. So were Amenophis II and his great descendant Amenophis III, father of Akhenaten. Meneptah, the Nineteenth Dynasty Pharaoh whom some Bible students believed to have been the Pharaoh drowned in the Red Sea was absent—significantly, they thought.

But a few years later a French archaeologist opened the tomb of Amenophis II in the Royal Valley and found not only its royal owner but twelve other Pharaohs, including the missing Meneptah. Amenophis II still lay in his original coffin, and beside him lay the great bow which, he boasts in his inscriptions, only he could draw. Clearly the Necropolis priests had selected this tomb as a second hiding place for their royal dead.

For a time the experiment was tried of leaving Amenophis II in his original tomb, but within a few years, in 1901, the modern descendants of the tomb robbers got in, after overpowering the night guards (or so the guards said). When Howard Carter, who was then Chief Inspector of the area, entered the ravaged tomb he found the mummy of the king tossed onto the floor. Its bandages had been slit in the hope of finding jewelry, but alas for the robbers of el-Gournah! Their predecessors of three thousand years ago had done their job only too well. The mummy had been rewrapped after its original ornaments had been stripped from it.

Today privileged visitors to the Egyptian Museum in Cairo can see the actual features of such monarchs as Seti I and Ramses II, preserved even down to their skin and hair. One can easily recognize the chubby features of Tuthmosis III, the "Napoleon of Ancient Egypt," reproduced so often in his statues, proof that the

Egyptian sculptors did make portraits of their kings and noblemen even though they idealized them somewhat at times. But to me there are two aspects of this well-known story which grip the imagination.

One is that, when the royal mummies were safely stowed in the museum steamer and it began to move down the Nile to Cairo, women followed its course along the banks, pouring dust on their disheveled hair and sending up the old, wailing cry for the dead which probably comes directly from Pharaonic times. The other is the story of Abderassul's cunning subterfuge when, having discovered the mummies, he pretended to be terror-stricken by an *afrit*. He did this in order to frighten his companion, and insure that he would not revisit and explore the tomb in Abderassul's absence. To make doubly sure he went back to the shaft a few days later, killed his donkey, and flung it down the hole. It was the stench from the decaying corpse of the animal which convinced any suspicious Arab visitors that the tomb was the home of an *afrit*. I first heard this story from Professor Newberry, who had met Abderassul around 1890 and had heard his version of the story from his own lips.

In such an atmosphere of high romance it is hardly surprising that many Egyptologists of the nineteenth century were less interested in discovering new facts about Egyptian civilization (including its mysterious origins) than in searching for more royal tombs and treasure. But there were distinguished exceptions. One of them was the American scholar Professor James Breasted, whose *Ancient Records* (a painstaking collection of all available Egyptian inscriptions) and *History of Egypt* are of enduring value to students of Egyptology. Another was the American Dr. George Reisner.

Then there was Sir Alan Gardiner, who devoted most of his life to the study of ancient Egyptian writings; Gardiner's *Egyptian Grammar* is a standard textbook throughout the world, though he never conducted a single excavation himself. There was the German scholar Adolf Erman, whose translations of Ancient Egyptian texts, official chronicles, poetry, history, and folk tales have brought us into intimate contact with the thoughts and emotions of these long-dead people. Here, for example, is Erman's translation of an ironical account by an old soldier who had campaigned in the mountains of Syria against the "sand-dwellers." The irony occurs because he is addressing a young subordinate who fancies himself as a soldier.

> You gain the name of a *mahir* [hero] among the officers of Egypt. Your name becomes like that of Kazardi, the chief of Eser. . . . Behold there is a narrow defile, made perilous by Bedouins, who are hidden behind the bushes; some of them are of four cubits and five cubits from the nose to the sole of the foot, fierce of face, their hearts not mild, and they listen not to your coaxing.
>
> You are alone, no helper is with you, and no army is behind you. You cannot find a guide to show you a way of crossing. You are determined to go forward, even without knowing the way. Shuddering seizes you, your hair stands on end. . . . The path is full of boulders and shingle, and there is no passable track. The ravine is one side of you, the mountain on the other. On you go, guiding your chariot beside you . . . *Now* you know what pain tastes like.

That was written in the time of Tuthmosis III, about thirty-four hundred years ago, but apart from the archaic chariot, it might be the experience of any modern young army officer out on a dangerous patrol in hostile country. As a complete contrast, take the following beautiful love poem of the same period, translated by Sir Alan Gardiner.

> Seven days from yesterday I have not seen my
>   beloved,
> And sickness has crept over me,
> And I am become heavy in my limbs,
> And am unmindful of mine own body.
> If the master-physicians come to me,
> My heart has no comfort of their remedies,
> And the magicians, no resource is in them,
> My malady is not diagnosed.

Better for me is my beloved than any remedies,
More important is she for me than the entire
    compendium of medicine.

My salvation is when she enters from without
When I see her, then I am well;
Opens she her eye, my limbs are young again;
Speaks she, and I am strong.
And when I embrace her, she banishes evil,
And it passes from me for seven days.

This situation too is not unfamiliar to us. In fact what we recognize in the writings, the sculptures, and paintings of such people
as the Egyptians, the Sumerians, Babylonians, Hittites, and other
ancient peoples are men and women who, despite their cultural
and religious differences from us, were basically like ourselves.
They were civilized; that is, they had learned to live together in
large, organized communities; they had doctors and lawyers and
soldiers; they had literature and art; and the more fortunate
classes had time to think and reflect upon what life was about.
They enjoyed many of the luxuries which some of us enjoy—good
food and fine wines, elegant clothes and jewelry, splendid, richly
furnished buildings; for entertainment they had music, dancing,
and many forms of sport, especially hunting and fishing. They
knew the elation and horror of battle, the joy and sorrow of love,
and the intellectual pleasures of reading and conversation.

All this has been revealed to us by the archaeologist and his
ally the linguist (or philologist). But as, throughout the nineteenth
century, man's vision of his past expanded, as geologists and prehistorians (mainly in Europe) found relics of man's ancestors
which could be dated to 20,000, 50,000 or even 250,000 years ago,
it became clear that these "ancient civilizations" were relatively
modern. Ancient Egypt, with its Pharaohs and hieroglyphs and
pyramids, may seem incredibly remote from us. With Sumer it is
the oldest civilization on earth, yet both came into existence little
more than five thousand years ago. When one realizes that recognizable human beings like ourselves have been walking the earth

for at least *one hundred times* that span of years, is it really surprising that these first civilizations should appear to have so much in common with our own? Let us imagine that the entire history of the human race was charted within a book of one hundred pages. In that case the Ancient Egyptians would appear at the top of page 100 and we should be at the bottom of the same page.

Researches into remote prehistory were going on, mainly in Europe, at the same time as archaeologists such as Hilprecht, Professor A. H. Sayce, Maspero, Reisner, and Petrie were revealing the buried civilizations of Mesopotamia and Egypt. Inevitably these men were influenced, consciously or unconsciously, by the broader view of man's past revealed by the prehistorians. Petrie in particular moved from a study of Egyptian civilization to an almost obsessional curiosity about its origins.

Petrie Pushes Back
the Time Frontier

Young flinders petrie owed his introduction to Egyptology
to the religious "crankiness" of his father, William Petrie, an
electrical engineer. In the 1870's Petrie senior became almost
obsessed by the theories of a certain Piazzi Smyth, a brilliant
mathematician and one-time Astronomer-Royal for Scotland.
Smyth had formed a theory that the Great Pyramid at Giza, the
tomb of Cheops, was no mere sepulcher but a divinely inspired
compendium of weights and measures, and that its dimensions,
both within and without, had prophetic significance. He believed
that, correctly interpreted, the measurements of the building with
its complex arrangement of inner galleries and chambers would
reveal not only the past history of the world but its future. The
elder Petrie, himself a mathematician, was intrigued by this, but
was not convinced of the accuracy of Smyth's measurements.
Young Petrie, who had already published a book called *Inductive
Metrology,* was sent out to Egypt by his father, equipped with
a set of the most up-to-date measuring and surveying instruments,
and instructed to make a detailed and accurate survey of the Great
Pyramid.

In appearance Petrie was strikingly handsome, with fine eyes, regular features, and a thick black beard. Also, like most geniuses, he tended to be strong-willed, obstinate, and egocentric. Other people's discoveries rarely interested him, unless they bore directly on his own. In the winter of 1880, just before Maspero became Director of the Antiquities Service, this young black-bearded giant arrived on the Giza plateau with a box full of measuring instruments. He was twenty-six, and had never been to Egypt before. He set about making precise measurements of a monument measuring over 750 feet along each base line and 450 feet high. Colonel Howard-Vyse and his colleague Perring had done the same thing in 1836; indeed they had published the first scientific survey not only of the Giza group, of which the Great Pyramid is one, but also those at Sakkara, Dashur, Lisht, Medûm, and Hawara. Petrie must have been aware of their valuable work, but his methods of measurement, involving the most up-to-date instruments available at the time, were much more thorough and accurate.

Petrie spent three full seasons at Giza working mainly on the Great Pyramid. His book *The Pyramids and Temples of Gizeh* is still a standard work, though published first in 1883. It makes absorbing reading, because whereas previous generations of explorers were impressed by the sheer bulk of this enormous pyramid, and the purpose of its complex system of inner galleries, Petrie's survey revealed for the first time the incredible precision with which it was built. He established that its orientation—north, south, east, and west—was so accurate that the errors of a modern compass could be checked against it. He found that the maximum error was little over one-twelfth of a degree, which is extraordinary in a structure of such stupendous size, built five thousand years ago. Who, one wonders, was the master engineer who planned and laid it out?

Even more remarkable was the cutting and finishing of the "casing stones" which Petrie examined at the base of the pyramid. The profile of the Great Pyramid today is like a saw-edge, and on closer approach it resembles a flight of steps. But originally it was sheathed from top to bottom in polished white limestone which shone like a mirror. Most of these stones were removed by the

Arabs as building material, but near the base Petrie found a few still in position. And when he came to measure them he found that

> the mean variation of the cutting of the stone from a straight line is but .01 [one-hundredth part of an inch] of 75 inches up the face . . . these joints, with an area of 35 square feet each, were not only worked as finely as this, but cemented throughout. Though the stones were brought as close as 1/500th of an inch, or, in fact, into contact, the mean opening of the joint was 1/50th of an inch, yet the builders managed to fill the joint with cement, despite the great area of it, and the weight of the stones, each of about 16 tons.

Herodotus, twenty-four hundred years ago, had examined the pyramid and left a description of how it was built, as told to him, with some exaggerations, by the Egyptian priests of his time. The seventeenth-century traveler, John Greaves, exploring the Grand Gallery had marveled at "the coagmentation, or knitting of the joints . . . so close that they are scarcely discernible by a curious eye." Napoleon had calculated that there was enough stone within the building to build a ten-foot wall around the whole of France (which is true). But it was Petrie, with his practical eye and severely technological approach, who first demonstrated what sophisticated craftsmen, engineers, and builders were these Ancient Egyptians of five thousand years ago. Piazzi Smyth and his "Pyramid Theories" were soon discreetly forgotten; in any case Petrie rapidly proved that Smyth's measurements were wrong. Nevertheless, although he seems to have derived some quiet amusement from discussing this theory with local enthusiasts, loyalty to his father prevented him at first from blowing the theory sky-high in the press.

Petrie, who had made his home in a tomb near the Great Pyramid, reserved his anger for those who, before his very eyes, were destroying the monuments out of greed, ignorance, and cupidity. In a letter shown to me by the late Lady Petrie, the young archaeologist writes:

I hear that some Pasha most rascally blasted to pieces all the fallen parts of the granite temple by a large gang of soldiers to clear it out, instead of lifting the stones up and replacing them with tackle. I should like to put a hundredth of the powder in his inside with a fuse.

His youthful impatience (and arrogance) were at white heat, almost burning the paper on which these private letters were written; they are in amusing contrast to the grave, measured style of his later published writings, when he was an established Egyptologist and professor.

Nothing seems to be done with any uniform or regular plan. Work is begun and left unfinished, no regard is paid to future requirements of exploration; and no civilised or labour-saving appliances are used, nothing but what the natives have; all the sand being carried in small baskets on the heads of children. . . . It is sickening to see the rate at which everything is being destroyed. . . . Anything would be better than leaving things to be destroyed wholesale; better spoil half in preserving the other half, than leave the whole to be smashed. After supper, writing and looking over measures, 20.70 is about the granite temple cubit. Then wrote this up and to bed. . . .

And fifty years later, when, knighted and honored by the universities of the world, he recalled this period of his life, Petrie wrote:

The science of observation, of registration, of recording, was as yet unthought of; nothing had a meaning unless it were an inscription or a sculpture. A year's work in Egypt made me feel it was like a house on fire, so rapid was the destruction going on. My duty was that of a salvage man, to get all I could, quickly gathered in, and then when I was sixty I would sit down and write it up. That was a true forecast.

If I may be forgiven a personal note, I remember Lady Petrie saying to me that "Flinders, in his books and reports, adopted a cool, objective, scientific style of writing. He did not approve of the 'jaunty' style of some writers on archaeology." This is perfectly true of Petrie's later writing, when he was a mature man and an internationally respected scholar. However, it is amusing to discover, in his youthful accounts of pyramid exploration, passages like this one:

> I pitched my tent at the edge of the cultivated land [near Dashur] some half mile from the village, beneath a small grove of palms on a sandy rise. . . . The only trouble was the need of having guards, owing to the distance from the village. . . . Those guards slept in an enviable manner; one night I was awoke by a whine, and leaning forward to my man Muhammed, who was also awake, he said that a hyena had been smelling the guards' feet, but thought they were alive, so hesitated to begin on them. On Muhammed's moving, the hyena had slipped into the shadow of a palm and stood whining at a distance from the prospect of supper. The guards were snoring quite steadily, when I just sent a shot towards the beast to scare it off; as the crack of my revolver died away, I heard the same snore continuing without the least break or change.

This adventurous atmosphere has, of course, vanished from Egyptology today, which is probably just as well. Still, it did add excitement to Petrie's pyramid explorations, which were carried out with zest and panache. Petrie had not reached the age when he was ashamed to show enthusiasm. Having completed and published his work on the well-known, much-visited Giza group, he began to explore the little-known pyramids to the south, situated on the fringe of wild desert country where he was untroubled by tourists and overzealous officials, and could work unhindered in his own characteristic way. He tunneled, one by one, into the pyramids of Dashur, Medûm, Illahun, and Hawara, and reported his finds in vivid prose.

Here he is attacking the mud-brick pyramid of Amenemhat III, the great Twelfth Dynasty Pharaoh, at Hawara.

> The opening of the pyramid of Hawara proved a far longer and more troublesome affair than seemed probable at first sight. When we knew that every pyramid yet examined opened from

the north side, and not far from the base, nothing seemed simpler than just to clear the north side . . .

But he could find no entrance in the pyramid structure, so Petrie had to begin, reluctantly, to drive a tunnel under the north face in the hope of finding the subterranean burial chamber and adjacent galleries.

At this period (around 2000 B.C.) pyramids were built of mud brick, only the outer casings and galleries being of stone. Tunneling through this soft substance might appear to have presented little difficulty, but it raised special problems which Petrie describes:

> The sand between the bricks was in very thick layers, usually half to one inch; and being quite dry and clean, it ran out interminably in some parts, coming down as in an hour glass from the joints. It was needful therefore to board up the roof of the tunnel all along, and as no native would treat the place with sufficient tenderness to avoid loosening the bricks overhead, I had to fix every board myself as the tunnel advanced.

> In the second season the state of matters was still more dangerous; falls of the sides and roof continually took place, even three times in twenty-four hours. . . . One of these falls would bring down tons of bricks from the sides and roof, along perhaps 20 feet in length. . . . Turning everybody out— sometimes at night—I used to re-prop the sides without any interference. The need of listening acutely all the time to detect any sand running down—the prelude to a fall—and the need of having the narrow way quite clear to retreat in half a second if need be, made it necessary to work quite alone.

Dr. Margaret Murray, Petrie's first pupil, told me that throughout his archaeological career Petrie would never allow one of his workmen to take a high risk. If any risk had to be taken—as in the case of the Hawara pyramid-tunnel—he took it himself, alone. Among other qualities, he had resolute courage; the possibility of the tunnel collapsing, at night, and suffocating him before his men could reach him, could not have been absent from his mind.

Petrie the grave, bearded professor with his long black cloak, lecturing his respectful pupils on the technique of sequence dating provides one picture. The other is an active, resourceful, thirty-year-old man, soaked in mud, groping his way on his stomach through apertures barely two feet wide, deep within the water-logged galleries under the pyramid of Amenemhat III.

On the twenty-first day . . . a boy ran down with the welcome news of a hole found. I had just been all the morning at work in the water of Horuta's tomb, and had come out for a wash and breakfast; but I went up, as I was, to see to the matter. There was a black hole in the floor of the mason's cutting. . . . Soon I managed to squeeze through, and found that I was in a little forced passage cut by the ancient treasure-seekers, which led to the superchamber. Searching around it I saw the top of the entrance passage on the north side, on a level with the floor I was on. Jumping down, I found the passage was blocked; but there was a hole under the stone I had been standing on. Into this I squeezed, sloping head downwards, on the mud which partly filled it, and managed to see that there was a chamber beneath with something in it, and a great deal of water.

Petrie, failing to find the cunningly concealed entrance to the pyramid, had tunneled his way through to the burial chamber of the Pharaoh, but now he found himself in one of those intricate "puzzle-passages" which the architect of Amenemhat III had designed to foil the tomb robbers.

Being too big to enter the burial chamber, he sent in "a thin and active lad" who found the sarcophagus of the king, rifled in antiquity and empty. But on a piece of an alabaster vase he found the cartouche of the king, and that satisfied him. This was indeed the pyramid of Amenemhat III "as I had expected."

But now, with typical intrepidity, he tried to find his way out, not along the artificial tunnel he had made, but if possible along the maze of passages made by the original architect, and thus find the true entrance to the pyramid. This was even more dangerous than the initial tunneling-in because the Nile had risen since Amenemhat's time and had partly flooded the galleries and Petrie had to squeeze himself under half-blocked trap doors of stone.

Up the east passage the muddy earth rose nearly to the roof, and we had to crawl through. At the south end of this there seemed to be no exit, but a slight gap under the S.E. trap-door showed that there was a way; and clearing out some earth I got in far enough to stick tight, and knocked the candle out. Matches had to be fetched, as we were streaming with the heat, so that nothing could be kept dry in the only garment I had on. Under the stone I got into the S.E. chamber and then the south passage was so nearly filled with mud that we had to lie flat and slide along it propelled by fingers and toes.

At last I reached the S.W. chamber. The blind passage being level did not promise a way out; the lean lad got up on the top of the first trap-door . . . and waded through the water to the ante-chamber. There at last I found a passage sloping considerably upward, and knew that we were in the entrance passage.

Read out of context this sounds almost like cave exploration, but in fact Petrie did not perform these feats for adventure—although he obviously enjoyed them. Like all true archaeologists he was searching for facts, in this case to discover who built these pyramids, and to learn as much as he could about their construction. No two are alike, and the construction of Amenemhat's pyramid, in particular, reveals a subtle and brilliant intelligence.

Then Petrie moved on to explore more pyramids. One of these was that of Senusret II at Illahun, also of the Twelfth Dynasty. Petrie began his excavations in 1887, found his way inside, but discovered that the king's burial chamber was empty, as he had expected. But many years later he returned, accompanied by his wife and a number of students including Rex Engelbach. Another student was Guy Brunton, who had been a bank clerk in South Africa, until he was drawn to follow Petrie. Near the main Illahun pyramid were several subsidiary ones belonging to the royal family, and Brunton was responsible for investigating these. The tomb shafts (under the small pyramids) were, as expected, empty, having been robbed at the same time as the large pyramid of the Pharaoh. However, one afternoon, at 4:30 P.M. Brunton received a message from his head workman that some gold beads had been found. He hurried to the site and revealed a marvel. In very ancient times, before the first tomb robbers entered these sepulchers, they had been partly flooded during Egypt's infrequent rain-storms. At one side of the empty sarcophagus chamber was a small recess which had been choked by dried mud left by the flood water. It was in this mud that one of Petrie's loyal "Qifti" (work-men he had recruited and trained, mostly from the village of Qift in Upper Egypt) had found the gold beads.

Brunton then set to work, alone, to remove the dried mud with a small penknife and his fingers, which, said Lady Petrie "were long and delicate." The job took him eight days. Brunton himself wrote in his report:

> I found the recess so low that I could not even kneel in it but had as a rule to work lying flat—resting on my elbows. Of course, the continued succession of finds, day after day, was amazing and utterly unequalled. . . . The work of picking out the small beads [there were over 9,500 of them] was so laborious that eventually any detached scraps of mud were examined in the camp . . .

Of this find Lady Petrie told me:

> For eight days and nights Brunton hardly ever left that cham-ber. At night he slept near the recess, and whenever he was awake he kept probing away in the dried mud, removing object after object; a golden crown, with feathers and streamers of gold, eight hundred and ten gold rings, a pectoral [breast-orna-ment] with the name of King Senusret II; another with the name of Amenemhat III; golden lions' heads, golden *couchant* lions, amethyst ball-beads, gold and turquoise ball-beads, brace-lets and anklets of gold, a silver mirror, toilet vases containing perfumed ointment, and even copper toilet razors.

The discovery of the famous jewelry of Princess Sit-Hathor-Unet was made in 1914 and does not, therefore, properly belong to this section of the book, but as it follows on logically from Petrie's earlier pyramid work in the 1880's, I have seen fit to men-tion it here.

However, we must now go back to Petrie's early days, and see how he progressed from pyramid excavation, first to search for the monuments of the Early Dynastic kings (from the First to the Second Dynasties, before the first pyramid was built) and thence further and further back into Egypt's past to discover the primitive ancestors of the historical Egyptians. By the mid 1890's he was no longer a lonely pioneer. Other embryo archaeologists, from many walks of life, were drawn by the power of his personality to work with him, practically for nothing. And in 1893 he had been appointed the first Professor of Egyptology at University College, London, a post he held down to 1935.

It was one of Petrie's younger colleagues, J. E. Quibell, who found evidence of the first known Pharaohs at a place called Hierakonpolis. Although nothing much to look at compared with, say, the jewelry of Sit-Hathor-Unet or Tutankhamen's treasure, these finds were of far higher archaeological importance than either. One was a ceremonial macehead inscribed, in primitive hieroglyphs, with the name Selk, "the Scorpion." The other was a large slate palette bearing the name Narmer and carved with scenes showing the king defeating his enemies. Although primitive in style, the scenes on the palette (now in the Petrie Collection, London) are very like those on Egyptian royal monuments of fifteen hundred years later; we see the king wearing the tall crown of a Pharaoh, striding forward, one upraised arm wielding a mace, the other grasping the hair of a crouching captive; at the top of one side of the palette is the falcon god, Horus, and near the bottom scenes of the king's enemies running away.

The macehead also depicted the triumphs of the Pharaoh, but the style is so like that of early Sumerian art as to leave no doubt that there was a link with the culture of southern Mesopotamia in these early days. Both objects can be confidently dated to before 3000 B.C.

Why was this discovery so exciting to Egyptologists? You will remember that the Ancient Egyptians, assiduous record keepers, preserved king lists; but none of these has come down to us in perfect condition. Egyptologists knew the names of the early Pharaohs who reigned before Joser (2800 B.C.) but until Quibell's discovery at Hierakonpolis, there was not a single piece of material evidence to prove that they had ever existed. They could have been entirely mythical, as some scholars believed. To put the situation in a nutshell, when Petrie published the first edition of his *History of Egypt* in 1894, he wrote: "The first three dynasties are a blank, so far as monuments are concerned. They are as purely on a literary basis as the kings of Rome or the primeval kings of Ireland . . . We cannot regard the first three dynasties as anything but a series of statements made by a state chronographer, [Manetho], about three thousand years after that, concerning a period of which he had no contemporary material . . . "

Yet *only eight years later,* in the 1902 edition of his *History* Petrie gives solid material information about eighteen kings who ruled before Snofru—last king of the Third Dynasty or first ruler of the Fourth, we cannot be sure. Not only this, but Petrie was equipped to describe their tombs, furniture, inscriptions, and art. What had happened in those eight years?

First there had been Quibell's discovery of the macehead of Selk (the "Scorpion King") and the slate palette of Narmer, who might possibly have been Menes, the first unifier of Egypt. Later Quibell found relics of two Second Dynasty kings, Kha-sekhem and Kha-sekhemui, who are recorded in the king lists. Then in 1896 an archaeologist named de Morgan, who had succeeded Maspero as Director of the Antiquities Service, unearthed an enormous mud-brick tomb at Nagada, in Upper Egypt. It was not a pyramid, but of rectangular shape, like the tombs in which the nobles of the Fourth and Fifth Dynasties were buried, only much larger. It had, inevitably, been robbed in antiquity, but was rich in small objects, among which was a small ivory label bearing the name Hor-aha, another name on the king lists.

On the label, beside the name Hor-aha, appeared the hiero-glyphic symbols for the word "men". As we know, each Pharaoh bore several names. Could Hor-aha have been the great Menes who conquered Egypt before 3000 B.C.? (In the light of later research, this Early Dynastic tomb is now generally believed to have been that of Nithotep, Hor-aha's mother.)

The next dramatic discovery was made by a Frenchman, Amé-lineau, who had been financed by collectors to dig for Egyptian antiquities. This man decided to investigate a mound near Abydos called by the Arabs Umm el Gaab (Mother of Pots) because of the vast accumulation of potsherds on the site. In later Pharaonic times this had been regarded as the sacred tomb of Osiris, god of death and resurrection, hence the mass of votive offerings brought by worshipers. Amélineau had no idea of what he was to find, but he had obtained a concession from the Egyptian Government and began to dig.

With hardly any training in archaeological method, concerned only with finding portable objects, he burrowed into the mound, and discovered a series of very large mud-brick tombs of a type similar to the great mastaba at Nagada. By accident he had tumbled on what Egyptologists had sought so long in vain, the tombs or cenotaphs (empty tombs in honor of a dead person) of a number of kings of the Archaic period. One of them, that of King Zer, had been rediscovered in antiquity and regarded as the tomb of Osiris. With the coming of Christianity the fanatical Copts, determined to wipe out pagan worship, had smashed every object of beauty within it. The rest of the tombs, covered by driftsand, had survived, though partially robbed; but a great many valuable antiquities remained, especially large numbers of beautiful stone vessels similar to those found under Joser's pyramid.

Much more valuable historically were the number of royal names found in the tombs, names such as Kha-sekhemui, Udimu, Semerkhet, and Ka'a, all of whom are mentioned in the king lists as belonging to the First or Second Dynasties. But Amélineau was little interested in these, except as proof of the antiquity of stone jars and other vessels. He made no attempt to identify each tomb with its owner, and establish their chronological order.

Four times Petrie sought permission to dig at the site but each time was told that his concession would not be granted until the Mission Amélineau had finished with the site. And "finish" it they did, or nearly so. Petrie wrote afterward, "In the royal tombs there had been not only the plundering of precious metals and the larger valuables by the wreckers of earlier ages; there was after that the systematic destruction . . . by the vile fanaticism of the Copts . . . and worst of all, for history, came the active search in the last four years for everything that would have value in the eyes of purchasers . . . a search in which whatever was not removed was deliberately and avowedly destroyed in order to enhance the intended profits of European speculators."

What Petrie then did is best described by Professor Walter B. Emery, one of the world's most eminent authorities on Archaic Egypt:

> Petrie immediately reopened the excavations and in two seasons of brilliant research rescued every scrap of evidence that his predecessor had not completely obliterated. By his painstaking work, he was able to trace the architectural development of the funerary structures and to identify their royal owners. From the mass of disordered evidence, he established the order of succession of the kings of the First Dynasty so soundly that with small modifications his reconstruction of the chronological position of each monarch still stands at the present day and is confirmed by discoveries made at Sakkara forty years later.

It may seem strange that Quibell's discovery of yet another royal cemetery of the First and Second Dynasties at north Sakkara in 1912 was not immediately followed up. But it was not, partly, perhaps, because preliminary investigation showed that these big mud-brick tombs had been severely plundered and burned, but mainly due to difficulties in interpreting the very primitive hieroglyphs. For at the time when these tombs were built, Egyptian writing was in its very early stages of development.

Archaeologists often use the term "the historical horizon" which means the point beyond which all written records cease. This "horizon" varies from area to area. In Egypt the historical "day" shades into darkness round about 3400 B.C. In southern Mesopotamia it is a little earlier in date; Sumerian writing seems to have come first.

But in other parts of the world it is much more recent, for example in China the "oracle bones" mentioned earlier have been dated approximately between 1500 and 1700 B.C. In Crete writing began somewhat earlier, but in Western Europe, apart from the Greek colonies along the Mediterranean coast, there appears to have been no writing system until the Roman conquerors introduced Latin and Greek. In the Americas there were great civilizations, like that of the Incas, which never produced a written language. The Mayas of Central America had one, but its earliest examples date from long after the beginning of the Christian era.

Until recently, once you descended below the "historical horizon" you could use only comparative methods of dating, by studying changes and developments in the style of artifacts, especially pottery, though even that fails when you enter the ages before pottery was invented. In the last two decades the physicist has come to the archaeologist's aid with his carbon-14 method, though this has a limited application and works only with material that has once been alive, for example vegetable and animal matter. Other techniques, are *dendrochronology*—tree-ring dating—and, most extraordinary of all, the dating of certain types of pottery or other earthenware by determining the position of the earth's magnetic field on the day the clay was put in the firing kiln. This technique is still in its experimental stage and is of value only under certain conditions.

Despite the addition of these new, experimental methods, the modern archaeologist still has to learn and apply the now-classic techniques of stratigraphy and sequence dating invented respectively by General Pitt-Rivers and Flinders Petrie. Petrie, having pushed back the time frontier six hundred years, to the beginning of the First Dynasty and the birth of Pharaonic Egypt, decided to probe even further back into Egypt's past. Now he was in unknown territory far beyond the historical horizon.

He had traced the origins of Egyptian civilization before the pyramid age. But what lay behind that? Had Egyptian civilization been introduced to Egypt by a more highly developed people from outside? Or had it grown up on Egyptian soil? Or had there been a combination of both foreign and native elements? This point has still to be settled; for instance Professor Emery believes that there was a mass invasion of a foreign race, which he calls "The Followers of Horus," and which established control of the indigenous inhabitants of the Nile Valley and ruled as a military aristocracy. This may perhaps turn out to be true, but at the time of writing Emery has many opponents, most of whom still accept Petrie's view that Egyptian civilization originated on Egyptian soil, though perhaps with some foreign influence.

Petrie did not think this at first. He seems to have believed that the founders of Egyptian civilization invaded Egypt from the Red Sea, crossing the desert via the Wadi Hamamat in southern Egypt and entering Upper Egypt at Koptos (modern Qift, where he obtained his workmen.) At Qift he unearthed, in 1893, parts of three large statues of the god Min, who preceded Amen-Ra as chief deity of Upper Egypt. Near the statues was pottery of an unfamiliar pattern. In the following year he and his assistant Quibell decided to dig in the desert fringe on the west bank of the Nile, between Ballas and Nagada.

Some two miles to the south Petrie noticed a slight depression in the sand and began to dig. He unearthed the first of some three thousand pit graves, each containing a skeleton in a crouched position and usually accompanied by a small slate palette (for grinding eye paint) and pottery of a hitherto unknown type. On some of the clay vessels there were marks reminiscent of the hieroglyphs; a cross, a crescent, a palm tree, and a scorpion. The graves were not all of the same size, and in the larger ones the excavators found objects which reminded them of the art of the Archaic period; ivory combs and bracelets, small statues of painted clay, stone maceheads, and in a few graves, objects of copper. Most significant was the fact that in nearly every grave there was a slate palette, carved in the form of a fish, an antelope, or a tortoise, clearly reminiscent of the great ceremonial palette of King Narmer, but on a much smaller scale.

Notice that this discovery was made three years before de Morgan found the royal tomb at Nagada, which contained objects very similar in style to those unearthed by Petrie and Quibell from these little pit graves, and four years before the Mission Amélineau had torn open the First and Second Dynasty tombs at Abydos, which contained objects of similar style. At first Petrie assigned the pit graves at Nagada to what he described as a "New

Race" of foreigners which had entered Egypt during the period of the Sixth and Seventh Dynasties (circa 2400 B.C.). He imagined them as one would imagine American Indians who were permitted to live near a frontier settlement. But as soon as he recognized, from his close study of "typology" that the objects found in the pit graves were akin to, *but earlier than,* those discovered in the mighty royal tombs of the Archaic period, he abandoned his "New Race" theory, and concluded that these people, primitive though they were, must have been the ancestors of the civilized, pyramid-building Egyptians.

In a number of these little graves Petrie discovered something which may, or may not, be sinister. Sometimes, instead of a complete, crouched skeleton, the bones had been separated and piled up in neat little heaps, with the skull placed some distance away. In one grave the spine was perfect, but all the ribs lay in a recess of the grave at the back, as if the ribs had been cut off the spine. It looked as if some of the bodies had been dismembered before burial, but why? In another grave a number of bones, broken and split, lay together in a heap. "Not only were the ends broken off," writes the excavator, "but in some bones the cellular structure had been scooped out forcibly . . . and beside this were grooves left by the gnawing of the bones."

It could be that jackals or hyenas had found the bodies and partially eaten them, after which the relatives of the dead had collected the bones, rearranged them in heaps, and reburied them. This may be the explanation; on the other hand the myth of the god Osiris (who may have been a very early king, subsequently deified) states that Osiris reclaimed the Egyptians from cannibalism. It is a fact that among primitive peoples of much more recent times the ritual eating of the dead—to absorb the power of his spirit—is known to have been practiced. A more scientific examination of the bones, to establish whether the tooth marks were human or animal, might have solved this problem.

Here is another fascinating point. Earlier, I quoted some obscure texts found in Sixth Dynasty pyramids by Maspero, which he conjectured must date from prehistoric times, since they bore no relation to funerary rituals of the pyramid-building period. One read "cast the sand from thy face." Could this have been a survival of a time when even the important dead were buried under sand, with perhaps a small tumulus or mound above them? Again, another text describes the king "devouring the gods," perhaps a reference to primitive cannibalism. And in a third we have the words "the bricks are removed from thee from the great tomb." The pyramids in which these texts were found were of stone, not brick, but, as we have seen, the Pharaohs of the First and Second Dynasties *were* buried under brick tombs. And remember that Maspero had no knowledge of this when he made his conjecture. These and other facts convince most Egyptologists that the civilization of Ancient Egypt did arise in the Nile Valley, and was not imposed by an incoming people.

Since the end of World War I, other prehistoric Egyptian sites have been excavated which are even older than those discovered by Petrie. The earliest date to the Neolithic (New Stone Age) stage of development: people ignorant of metals, who used stone tools, but who had already learned the arts of farming and stock rearing. They grew barley and harvested it with wooden sickles inset with flint blades; they stored their grain in underground silos made of coiled basketry; they kept domestic animals such as oxen, sheep, and goats but they also hunted wild animals such as the antelope, gazelle, and hippopotamus. There are two main points to be noted here: *a)* the conditions favorable to the development of a civilization can only occur where large numbers of human beings are enabled to live for long periods in one place; the invention of farming alone made this possible, and *b)* notice how archaeologists who had adopted and improved on Petrie's methods were able to establish how people lived, what crops they grew, what animals they had domesticated, what tools they had used, at a period some two thousand years before the invention of writing, All these archaeologists had to guide them were small, intrinsically valueless objects such as the treasure hunters of the nineteenth century would have ignored.

Archaeology is an evolving science, or art (call it what you will), and the methods of even its most outstanding exponents may eventually come under criticism. This is as true today as it was one hundred years ago. But what distinguishes the great archaeologist from the mere plodder is just this quality of daring and imagination. When, in 1942, Petrie lay dying in Jerusalem (he is buried on the Mount of Olives), Wheeler visited him and paid this tribute: "When I last visited him, on his deathbed in Jerusalem . . . his restless brain was still hovering over a multitude of problems and possibilities which extended the smaller minds of his listeners, and I left him for the last time with a renewed sense of devotion which he inspired in his pupils and friends."

But Wheeler adds: "It is almost with a feeling of guilt that I now, after considerable experience of his work and of the tradition which he established widely over the East, find myself compelled to deplore an influence which in much of its technique so long outlasted its scientific usefulness."

Sir Flinders Petrie was eighty-nine when he died, and had continued excavating until a few years before his death. Beginning as an iconoclast and a reformer, he ended as the Grand Old Man of archaeology, too inflexible in mind to modify or improve on the techniques he had invented. Sometimes, alas, one can go on working for too long. But he stands head and shoulders above most of his contemporaries, not only as an excavator but as a teacher. The lessons he learned and subsequently taught to others transformed archaeology from mere antiquity hunting to a search for facts.

Linked Civilizations

IN AN EARLIER CHAPTER I stated that the work of individual archaeologists could be likened to stones dropped into a pool. At first there is only a local splash, but gradually, as the ripples expand and touch each other, scholars begin to realize that they are dealing, not only with localized manifestations of civilization in one country but with a number of separate and distinct cultures which drew from, and interacted upon, each other.

Thus a number of archaeologists began to ask themselves the question, If the earliest civilizations on earth grew up in two areas, the valley of the Nile and those of the Tigris and Euphrates, why was this so? What had the two regions in common? And to what extent did they influence others at a time when communication was difficult and dangerous?

One interesting answer came when a succession of distinguished archaeologists—Vyse and Perring, the German Karl Lepsius, the Englishman Cecil Firth, and the French scholar J. P. Lauer investigated the mysterious, much-damaged pyramid of King Joser, which overlooks the Nile at a point some twelve miles south of

Cairo. This place, Sakkara, was the royal and noble cemetery of the capital Memphis, not long after the southern conqueror of Egypt, Menes (3200 B.C.), subdued the inhabitants of the wide-spreading Delta, the richest agricultural area of Egypt. By establishing their new capital at a point where the Nile breaks from its imprisoning cliffs and desert and begins to flow freely across the fertile plain, these Early Dynastic Pharaohs could keep a vigilant eye on the southern valley, from which fresh invaders might come.

At first no one could be certain how old the Step Pyramid was. It had many strange features not found in other pyramids. Under it lay a maze of underground galleries, from which the archaeologists extracted some twenty thousand stone vases of archaic pattern. The granite-lined burial chamber of the king lay ninety feet deep in the rock, directly under the peak of the pyramid, surrounded by a suite of rooms decorated with bright greenish-blue tiles and "false" (blocked) doors. The alabaster sarcophagi, and in one case the actual body, of members of the royal family were found in the labyrinth of rock-cut corridors surrounding the main sepulchral chamber. This was unlike any other pyramid then known in Egypt, both in regard to its unique stepped shape, the multitude of subterranean galleries and the remains of a vast enclosure surrounded by a high wall with a paneled façade, an entrance colonnade consisting of tall fluted columns, and the remains of a number of "dummy" buildings within the enclosing wall.

The building was studied first by Vyse in 1836, later by Lepsius in 1843, who found the frame of a door inscribed with the name Neter-khet. At that period no one had heard of a Pharaoh named Neter-khet so the pyramid could not be dated. Generally it was thought to be later than the Giza pyramids, largely on account of the subterranean rooms lined with tiles of greeny-blue faience. Then, in 1890, at a place called Sehel in Upper (south) Egypt, an inscribed stele or tablet was found with the name Neter-khet in association with the name Joser (the Pharaohs always had several names). It now became clear that Neter-khet was none other than Joser, who was known from the king lists to have been the first

Pharaoh of the Third Dynasty which began about 2800; therefore the Step Pyramid was older than those at Giza; indeed it is—so far as is known—the oldest pyramid in Egypt and the first stone monument to be erected anywhere in the world.

Much more interesting was the fact that, when archaeologists began to clear and examine the structures around the pyramid— the courtyard with its "dummy" buildings, the colonnaded entrance, and the enclosing wall— it was realized that *their design and construction was not characteristic of stonemason's work.* The stone blocks were needlessly small, hardly bigger than bricks. Some of the columns, instead of being free standing, were "engaged," that is, attached to the wall behind. The stone-enclosing wall was built in a series of recessed panels with projecting bastions, highly pleasing to the eye, but it is doubtful if the effect was merely intended as decoration. It was far more likely that these structures reproduced, in stone, the mud-brick and timber buildings of the king's earthly palace, which had disappeared.

Proof of this came when it was noticed that at the entrance to the colonnade through which the courtyard was approached stood a reproduction, in stone, of a wooden door, complete with bolt. The "door" was quite useless. It was solid, fixed to the ground. Like the buildings within the courtyard, which were partly of solid masonry and unusable as rooms for the living, it was a dummy. Next the archaeologists noticed that the roof which had been supported by the columns was not of flat stones, as would have been expected, but blocks of semicircular sections, like palm-logs. The flutings of the columns themselves, charming though they are in artistic effect, were probably reproductions of the bundles of reed which the primitive, predynastic Egyptians used to support the roofs of their dwellings.

You now see the exciting point at which we have arrived. When Maspero read the *Pyramid Texts,* he guessed that some of these religious rituals must refer to a period long before the Egyptians became civilized. Other archaeologists, notably Petrie, were moving toward the investigation of the Archaic period before the building of the first pyramid. Here, at Sakkara, for all to see, was a reproduction in stone of the mud-brick and timber buildings in which the Pharaohs had lived in the Archaic or Early Dynastic period, and doubtless they incorporated features which had been in use in predynastic times.

Later, when royal tombs of the Early Dynastic period were excavated, this proved to be true. Egyptologists would eventually be able to answer the much-vexed qustion, Was this glorious civilization introduced to Egypt by more highly developed peoples from beyond her borders? Or had it grown up on Egyptian soil? That there had been outside influences became clear when it was noted that the paneled façade type of building was very like those discovered by Sumeriologists in far-off Mesopotamia. Here is an example of the links between civilizations. Of course it did not prove that the Sumerians had civilized Egypt, but when, in addition to the resemblances between buildings, it was noticed that the most primitive forms of Egyptian writing, which Petrie found scrawled on bits of potsherd, included symbols like those of Sumerian writing, it became obvious that a link existed. Later, when Petrie found, at the ancient capital of Hierakonpolis, works of art which used Sumerian motifs, there could no longer be any doubt about it.

Let us consider what archaeologists were discovering, at the same time, in western Asia and Europe. Take Mesopotamia first. You will remember how such pioneers as Layard and Botta discovered and unearthed the Assyrian palaces at Khorsabad, Nineveh, and Nimrud. At Nineveh Layard found twenty-six thousand baked-clay tablets, part of the royal library of the Assyrian king Sennacherib; these precious records, written in the cuneiform system, were in the main copies of much earlier documents inherited, through the Babylonians, from a very ancient people called the Sumerians, whose cities were flourishing in southern Iraq more than two thousand years before the time of Sennacherib.

Other investigators such as the American Hilprecht then began to explore these buried cities in the south—mere mounds of mud brick between the Tigris and Euphrates—and at one of them, Nippur, Hilprecht found another huge collection of Sumerian documents. Then there was an Englishman, W. K. Loftus, who worked

Layard at Nineveh.
These drawings appeared in his book
Nineveh and Its Remains.

Wall panel found by Layard at Nimrud.

Alabaster wall panel in the Palace of Ashurnasirpal II, King of Assyria

*This winged lion was guardian of
the gate in Ashurnasirpal's palace*

An artist's reconstruction of the Hanging Gardens of Babylon

The eyes in this Sumerian statuette are characteristic

*The Hittites. The stela of a
Hittite king (below) was found
in a burying ground near Mar'ash,
Asia Minor*

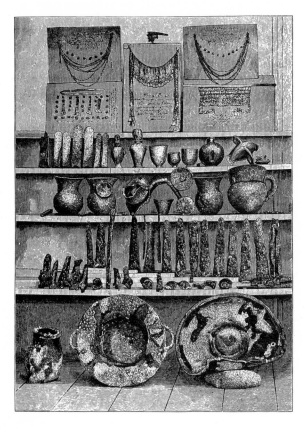

A view of Troy, showing the great trench cut through the whole hill, and the treasure of Priam. Both drawings are from Schliemann's book Troy and Its Remains.

The Lion Gate at Mycenae and (below) the royal tombs within the circle of the Agora. Both drawings are from Schliemann's book Mycenae.

at Erech (Uruk) and Susa; J. E. Taylor who investigated a city called by the Arabs Muqaiyir—which turned out to be the Biblical Ur of the Chaldees; and a Frenchman, Ernest de Sarzec, who from 1877 onward explored the hills of Telloh. Each of these helped prove that there had been a civilization and art quite distinctive from that of Babylon and Assyria (which were later) and which could only be attributed to an earlier people; these were the Sumerians of the Biblical Land of Shinar. All these pioneers did valuable work, especially in discovering written tablets and superb works of sculpture. But their excavations, like those of the pioneer Egyptologists, were primitive and in their search for antiquities and tablets they undoubtedly destroyed much valuable evidence.

Among those whose caution and conscientiousness in excavation merit the highest praise was the German scholar Robert Koldewey, whose researches at Babylon, carried on painstakingly over a number of years, produced a recognizable plan of this great city from an inchoate mass of ruins. Koldewey, one of that rare band of scholars who not only worked brilliantly but wrote vividly and with imagination, produced a book *The Excavations at Babylon* which should be read by all who want to know how true archaeology *should* be conducted, but all too often isn't.

But the Babylon which Koldewey excavated was relatively late. It had been seen and described by Greek visitors when it still retained much of its former glory. Indeed Greek mercenaries fought in Nebuchadnezzar's army. With Sumer the situation was different, and as excavators laid bare the mud-brick cities of Lagash, Eridu, Ur, Nippur, and Erech, they revealed a lost civilization of which hardly a memory survived, save for a few names in the Old Testament.

In fact there had been two neighboring kingdoms, Sumer to the south and Akkad to the north, Sumer being the older of the two. They resembled each other closely; the Akkadians worshiped Sumerian gods (whose names could be identified from the cuneiform tablets) and followed many Sumerian customs. But the two peoples had been racially distinct, the Akkadians being Semitic, like the Assyrians, Hebrews, and Arabs, whereas the Sumerians were non-Semitic, their racial origins obscure and mysterious.

In some respects their cities resembled those of the later Baby-lonians and Assyrians: a maze of mud-brick buildings, with narrow streets, a tiered tower called a ziggurat surmounted by a temple, and numbers of other temples, usually standing high and sur-rounded by concentric rings of walls. But they themselves were quite unlike the Semitic races, and their art—especially their sculpture—was unique. Stone, which had to be brought from a great distance, was rarely used, except for sculpture and in some cases for tombs. The common building material was mud brick, either sun-dried or baked in kilns. Yet with this simple material, which the very early Egyptians also used, they created superb buildings which even in ruin showed the skill and artistry of their designers.

For instance mud-brick columns of substantial girth were often ornamented with baked-clay cones stuck into the columns, the broad ends then being colored in brilliant reds, greens, and blues, giving a jeweled, mosaic effect. But the objects for which the nine-teenth-century excavators sought with the greatest avidity—usually destroying valuable archaeological evidence in the process—were the magnificent Sumerian sculptures, portraits of gods and men, some of them inscribed with their owners' names, such as the famous Governor of Lagash, Gudea, of which examples exist in the Paris Louvre and elsewhere. These strange, obese statues with their huge, staring eyes, dumpy, static figures, and long woolen robes, fascinated nineteenth-century art historians, especially the French. Ernest de Sarzec's wonderful finds at Telloh (ancient Lagash) attracted wide interest among contemporary artists of the French school.

As in Egypt so in Mesopotamia the art historian and collector all too often became a burden upon archaeology. Archaeological excavation, even at its best, is destruction, but in the case of the Sumerian cities the friable mud-brick walls were destroyed, no proper records kept, and there was little or no understanding of stratification and of sequence dating by changes in pottery styles. All too often the sites were mined rather than dug in a single-minded search for works of art and written documents.

True, these documents were of immense value and interest.

There were poems and chronicles, letters and trading accounts, proverbs and "wisdom literature," mathematical and astronomical calculations, religious rituals, hymns to gods and goddesses, of which some of the most interesting examples have been translated and published by Stanley S. Kramer in his book *History Begins at Sumer.*

But during the nineteenth century few people tried to establish just how old Sumerian civilization was, and how it arose. No system of comparative dating existed and it was left to a later, twentieth-century generation of archaeologists to re-excavate the cities, to establish their position in the time scale, and to inquire into their antecedents.

There were a few inquiring minds, however, which pondered on the significant fact that both the Egyptian and Sumerian civilizations had grown up along the banks of annually flooding rivers, and reflected that if one dug deep enough, and with patience and care, into the foundations of cities which had obviously been occupied for long periods of time, it might be possible to discover remains of the very earliest settlers, and perhaps discover whence they came. But archaeologists capable of doing this would have to be more than antiquity hunters. They would be people with broad, imaginative minds who accepted Wheeler's trenchant doctrine: "The archaeological excavator is not digging up *things,* he is digging up *people;* however much he may analyse and tabulate and desiccate his discoveries in the laboratory . . . Of our scraps and pieces we may say, with Mark Antony in the market-place, 'you are not wood, you are not stones, but men'."

Extending our view a little, but still remaining in western Asia, let us consider what other archaeologists of this period were doing in Syria and Turkey. Once again the first clues were found in the Bible, and in written inscriptions. Everyone who has read the Bible, or attended church or chapel, knows the story of King David and Uriah the Hittite. The Old Testament refers to the Hittites on several occasions.

Abraham, seeking a burial place for Sarah his wife, bought the cave of Macphelah from "the sons of Heth" (another name for the

Hittites). Esau had Hittite wives. And the Book of Numbers states that: "Amalek dwell in the land of the south; and the Hittite, and the Jebusite, and the Amorite, dwell in the mountains . . . "

Now the Amorites, Amalekites, and Jebusites were small Semitic tribes like the Hebrews themselves at that time. But the Hittites (or the Hatti or the "sons of Heth") were much bigger fry. This was recognized by nineteenth-century scholars who examined and translated the inscriptions on certain Egyptian temples. The Pharaohs were fond of depicting, on temple walls, their military triumphs over their enemies, among whom the traditional foes were the Nubians (a Negroid race) from the south, and the "Asiatics" from the northeast.

These "Asiatics" probably included the Hebrews (the "Habiru" are mentioned once in a long list of conquered tribes), the hill peoples of Jordan, and those occupying what are now Lebanon and Syria. Egypt established colonies along the Lebanese and Palestinian coast and was frequently obliged to send punitive expeditions there. On one occasion, after the collapse of the Middle Kingdom in about 1700 B.C., Asiatic tribes called the Hyksos or Shepherd Kings actually established a temporary dominion over Egypt until thrown out by the Pharaohs of the Eighteenth Dynasty.

In the Egyptian bas-reliefs the Nubians are instantly recognizable by their Negroid features, and the Asiatics by their beards (the Egyptians were clean-shaven). But there was one race which was singled out for especial hatred, at least during the early days, and that was the "abominable *Kheta*." Now the ancient Hebrew name for the Hittites was the *Khatti*, and linguists noted the resemblance between this and the Egyptian word *Kheta*. When the Kheta are shown on the Egyptian inscriptions they are not a bit like the "vile Asiatics"; they are clean-shaven, with long hair and rather prominent noses. Their dress too was not like that of the Asiatics.

They must have been formidable foes, since the Pharaohs covered hundreds of square yards of masonry with bas-reliefs depicting historic battles between the Egyptian armies and those of the Kheta. Of these perhaps the most famous was the battle of

Kadesh, fought by Ramses II in the valley of the Orontes in Lebanon. Every visitor to Thebes soon becomes familiar, even bored, with Ramses II and his alleged victory at Kadesh. It seems to have been an obsession with him, and although he praises his own superior generalship and valor in battle and claims total victory, we know now that this was in fact a drawn fight.

Later, in the reign of the same Pharaoh, a treaty was drawn up between Ramses II and the Hittite king Hattusilis, the terms of which were inscribed on a stone stele found at Thebes. The two kings agree not to encroach on each other's territory, and to aid each other if attacked. Ramses then married one of the Hittite king's daughters to cement the bond and congratulatory letters were exchanged.

Archaeologists asked themselves, Who were these mysterious Kheta or Khatti? Where did they come from? We know from the Bible that they were neighbors of the Israelites, but here a difficulty arose, because the period of the Book of Kings, of Numbers, and of King David, was long, long after the time of Ramses II (1290–1224 B.C.). The situation was very aggravating. Archaeologists had discovered the capitals of the Assyrians, the Babylonians, and the cities of Sumer. But of the Hittites not a trace remained, except for a few Biblical references and the Egyptian temple-reliefs. Yet a nation capable of meeting on equal terms the armies of Egypt, the greatest power in the world at that time, must have had a homeland, with cities and a civilization. They were obviously no mere congerie of tribes like the "Asiatics."

The first clue came from the linguists. In 1812 a Swiss traveler, Johann Ludwig Burckhardt, noted a block of basalt at Hamath in Syria, inscribed with an unkown form of writing. Later, at Aleppo, also in Syria, a similarly inscribed stone was found embedded in the wall of a mosque, though it was clearly of earlier date than the Moslem building. Some European scholars attempted to copy the inscriptions, whereupon the local people removed the stone and hid it. Still later reports began to circulate of similar inscriptions being found, not in Syria, but much further north in the Taurus mountains of Asia Minor (modern Turkey).

In 1876, a few years before Petrie first went to Egypt and some

thirty years after Layard had unearthed the Assyrian palaces of
Nimrud and Nineveh, a British scholar, Professor A. H. Sayce,
pronounced that in his opinion these inscriptions were probably
Hittite. His reasons would take too long to explain here, but the
result was that from 1880 onward a number of intrepid European
explorers made the dangerous journey into the little-known hinterland of Turkey in search of more inscriptions.

They came back with glowing reports not only of inscriptions
in the now-familiar "Hittite hieroglyphs" but of sculptured bas-
reliefs cut out of the mountainside, figures of soldiers in procession, wearing tall conical hats, woolen clothing, and boots with
turned-up toes. There were also massive remains of buildings. "At
Alaja Huyuk was a gateway flanked by huge sphinxes leading to
a mound of debris which clearly covered an ancient city or large
building. Farther west were the rock-reliefs at Gavur Kalesi . . .
and in the hills above Smyrna were other rock-sculptures known
since the time of Herodotus."

But the most impressive site of all was at a place called Bogazköy, where explorers discovered massive walls built on a steep
escarpment, with remains of buildings within. A few miles away,
in a cleft in the hillside, was carved a double procession of figures,
some of which appear to have been kings and gods, in high relief.
And in the center of the city area of Bogazköy was a huge weath-
ered slab of stone covered with "Hittite hieroglyphs."

All the same, though the conjecture was strong that these were
the remains of Hittite cities and sanctuaries, there was yet no
proof, since the inscriptions were in an unknown writing system.
Meanwhile further tantalizing clues turned up in Egypt, at a
deserted site called Tell-el-Amarna, roughly midway between
Cairo and Luxor. In about 1350 B.C. this had been the capital
city of the Pharaoh Amenophis IV, later called Akhenaten.
Akhenaten, unlike most Pharaohs of whom we have knowledge,
appears to have been a pacifist, a poet, and a dreamer. Revolting
against the entrenched priesthood of the god Amen-Ra, chief god
of Thebes, he built himself a new capital on a virgin site at Tell-
el-Amarna, and founded a short-lived new religion based on the
worship of one god, called "the Aten." His reign was marked by

a steady decline in Egyptian military power, and on his death
the court moved back to Thebes; the old pantheon of many gods,
with Amen-Ra at the head, was re-established, and Tell-el-Amarna
was never occupied again.

Over three thousand years later, in 1887 A.D., a peasant woman
was digging in the buried foundations of Akhenaten's city for
sebakh, a fertilizer produced by the decay of ancient mud-brick
buildings. The Egyptian peasants spread it on their fields. During
her digging the woman found, not far from the surface, a large
number of inscribed baked-clay tablets. Recognizing that these
might have some value to an antiquities dealer, she put the lot
in a sack, mounted her donkey, and made for the nearest town.
Dealer after dealer turned her down, so that by the time she found
one who would buy the tablets for a modest sum, more than half
had crumbled to dust owing to their rough treatment. The remainder turned out to be letters from the files of Akhenaten's
Foreign Office. They were his diplomatic correspondence.

Some of the letters were from the hard-pressed Governors of the
Pharaoh's provinces in Palestine and Syria; among them are some
of the most poignant documents which have come down to us from
the ancient world of Egypt and western Asia. Here is one from
the loyal Governor of Tunip, a city near the Libyan coast:

> My lord, Tunip, thy servant speaks, saying; who, formerly,
> could have plundered Tunip without being plundered by
> Menkheperre, [the great Tuthmosis III, Akhenaten's warlike
> ancestor]. The Gods of Egypt, my lord, dwell in Tunip. May
> our Lord ask his old men if it is not so.
>
> Now, however, we belong no more to our Lord, the King of
> Egypt. If his soldiers and chariots come too late, then the King
> of Egypt will mourn over the things which Aziru has done, for
> he will turn his hand against our land. . . . . And now Tunip,
> thy city, weeps, and her tears are flowing, and there is no help
> for us. For twenty years we have been sending to our Lord, the
> King of Egypt, but there has come to us not a word, no, not
> one. . . .

What was happening at that time? And who was Aziru? Gradually, after examining the rest of the correspondence, linguists were able to form a pattern. The Pharaoh's Syrian provinces were being threatened by the Kheta, the Hittites under their king Shub-biliuma. Aziru appears to have been a quisling or traitor who, under the pretext of protecting the Pharaoh's cities from the advancing Hittites, was annexing Egyptian territory on their behalf.

Perhaps the most moving letters are those from the Governor of Gebal, on the Lebanese coast, another vassal-city which, in former days, had been well protected by the Pharaohs. The name of this Governor was Ribbadi, and his letters breathe the spirit of a tough, loyal, resolute officer, probably well on in years, driven almost to desperation by the indolent young Pharaoh's failure to send reinforcements.

> Grievous is it to say what he hath done, the dog Aziru. Behold what has befallen the lands of the King on account of him, and he cried peace unto the land, and now behold what has befallen the city of Simyra—a station of my Lord, a fortress . . . and they spoil our fortress . . . ah, the cries of the place . . . a violent man and a dog. . . .

And Ribbadi goes on to say, in another letter:

> . . . march against him and smite him . . . the land is the King's land; and since I have talked thus and you have not moved the city of Simyra has been lost. There is no money to buy horses, all is finished, we have been spoiled . . . give me thirty companies of horse with chariots, men, men . . . there is none of this for me . . . not a horse . . .

These letters were written in Babylonian cuneiform, which Rawlinson and his successors had translated some thirty years before this discovery It seems that this writing system, invented originally by the Sumerians, had become the language of international correspondence throughout western Asia, and no doubt among Akhenaten's Foreign Office staff there were scribes who could read and write this script. And the conclusive proof that central Turkey was indeed the original home of the Hittites came when a German archaeologist, Hugo Winckler, dug at Bogazköy and found a cache of tablets, many of them in cuneiform, which included correspondence between the kings of Hatti and Egypt, and a copy of the very treaty which Ramses II had signed with Hattusilis, and which the Pharaoh had caused to be inscribed on a building in Thebes. The mystery was solved; the mysterious Hittites had been tracked to their homeland. But the "Hittite hieroglyph" on the rock carvings were still undecipherable.

Civilization
Spreads Westward

THIS IS NOT A BOOK about the growth of world civilization but about the development of archaeological methods which have enabled us to trace that growth. I shall try, as far as possible, to correlate the two, but it is necessary to recognize that the progress of archaeology was not a steady growth. Sometimes it went in a series of leaps, from point A to point B, and thence to points C and D, all being logically linked. The discovery of the Hittites was a case of this kind. At other times it groped and fumbled, reached false conclusions, and had to retreat from them. Again there were vast differences between the ability, imagination, and working techniques of archaeologists operating simultaneously in different parts of the world. In the mid-nineteenth century there was no standard "grammar" of archaeology, as there is today. There was no regular system of regular communication between archaeologists, such as exists now. So we find that in 1784 Thomas Jefferson, later to become President of the United States, excavated an Indian burial mound in Virginia in an intelligent, scientific manner and published his findings in a report of which a modern excavator would

not be ashamed; whereas one hunderd years later so-called archaeologists were brutally destroying archaeological evidence in Egypt
and Mesopotamia in a search for portable antiquities, which were
all they cared about.

Again, in 1880 General Pitt-Rivers, whom many experts claim
to be the founder of scientific archaeology, was excavating British
burial mounds on his Wiltshire estate with a precision and attention to detail far in advance of, say, Heinrich Schliemann who
began unearthing the shaft graves at Mycenae only a few years
earlier. In 1887 Pitt-Rivers published words which should be
learned by heart by everyone aspiring to be a true archaeologist:

> Excavators, as a rule, record only those things which appear to
> them important at the time, but fresh problems in Archaeology
> and Anthropology are constantly arising, and it can hardly fail
> to have escaped the notice of anthropologists . . . that, on turn-
> ing back to old accounts in search of evidence, the points which
> would have been most valuable have been passed over from
> being thought uninteresting at the time. *Every detail should,
> therefore, be recorded in the manner most conducive to facility
> of reference, and it ought at all times to be the chief object of
> an excavator to reduce his own personal equation to a mini-
> mum* [my italics].

It should also be remembered that even if valuable and beautiful funerary equipment had been buried in Britain, northern
France, the Low Countries, or Germany, for instance, the damp
soil of northern Europe would have rotted it, unless it happened
to be gold, silver, or precious stones. Whereas in Egypt such objects as beds, chairs, cabinets, and other things made of wood and
fabric could survive for five thousand years. Archaeologists working in Egypt, the eastern Mediterranean, and western Asia were
influenced, to some extent, by the Bible, by the writings of Greek
and Roman historians who had known and visited these countries,
and even by the myths and legends surrounding them. But, as for
northern Europe, including the British Isles, the only references
by classical authors were to the "tin islands" which lay beyond the
Strait of Gibraltar and may have been the British Isles, and such

comments as the poet Homer puts into the mouth of his hero
Odysseus:

> Thus she [Circe] brought us to the deep-flowing River of Ocean
> and the frontiers of the world, where the fog-bound Cimmerians
> live in the City of Perpetual Mist. When the bright Sun climbs
> the sky and puts the stars to flight, no ray from him can pene-
> trate to them, nor can he see them as he drops from heaven and
> sinks once more to earth. For dreadful Night has spread her
> mantle over the heads of that unhappy folk.

This sounds suspiciously like the British Isles in winter. Or it
could have been northern France or the Low Countries, as seen
some three thousand years ago by Mediterranean seafarers who
had ventured beyond the Pillars of Hercules (the Strait of Gibraltar) and cruised along the coast of the north Atlantic. For the
Greeks of preclassical times—before 700 B.C.—believed that the
earth was flat and bounded by "the river of Ocean." To them, as
to the Egyptians and the peoples of the Levant and Asia Minor,
the hub of the world was the Mediterranean Sea, or as the Ancient
Egyptians called it "the Great Green Sea."

The ancestors of the classical Greeks who entered Greece about
1100 B.C. knew the Mediterranean best of all. Their mainland
home was hard and stony, divided by high mountain ranges and
penetrated by deep bays and inlets. Pressure of population, and
the downward thrust of fresh immigrants from the north, forced
them to become seafarers, traders, and colonists. When Ancient
Egypt was in decline, and Assyria little but a name, the Greeks
were founding colonies in the Aegean islands, in North Africa,
Sicily, France, and even Spain.

Among the greatest products of their civilization were two great
epic poems, the *Iliad* and the *Odyssey*, believed to have been
written by an Ionian poet named Homer in the ninth or eighth
century B.C. These poems looked back to a period when an earlier
generation of Greeks, called the Achaeans, were ruled by kings
such as Agamemnon, Menelaus, and others. Though they did not
rule a closely integrated kingdom or empire as did the monarchs
of Egypt, Babylon, and Assyria, these Greek overlords could, in

times of emergency, call on the services of other princes such as
Achilles, Nestor, and Odysseus to wage war. According to tradition the greatest of these wars was fought against the Trojans,
whose city of Troy guarded the entrance to the Black Sea. There,
for nine years the Achaeans under Agamemnon of Mycenae,
assisted by his brother Menelaus of Sparta, Odysseus of Ithaca,
Achilles from Ptheia in Thessaly, and other rulers laid siege to
Troy, capital of King Priam. Eventually, through the well-known
subterfuge of the Wooden Horse, Priam's city was entered and
sacked.

The nominal reason for the war was "the rape of Helen" the
most beautiful woman in Greece, who had been stolen from her
husband, Menelaus, by Priam's son Paris. Homer's *Iliad* describes
only one episode in the war, the "wrath of Achilles." The *Odyssey*
describes the homefaring journey of one of the Achaean heroes,
"the wily Odysseus" who was persecuted by the sea god Poseidon
and forced to endure many hardships and adventures before he
reached his homeland in Ithaca.

This long and romantic preamble may appear to have little or
nothing to do with archaeology, but it has. Because it instilled in
the mind of a German parson's son, Heinrich Schliemann, a passionate determination to excavate Troy, Mycenae, and other
places mentioned by Homer and find out whether or not these
stories, which most scholars believed to be mere legends and folk
tales, had any basis of truth.

Heinrich Schliemann was quite unlike Layard, or Botta, or
Maspero, or Petrie. As a young man he had never visited the
countries in which he proposed to excavate. He had not seen Troy,
or Mycenae, or Tiryns, or Sparta. His inspiration and determination came entirely from having, as a child, read *Jerrer's Universal
History* containing pictures of the sack of Troy, and later, when
Schliemann was a romantic adolescent, hearing a drunken miller
named Niederhoffer, who had been in his youth a Greek scholar,
recite passages from the *Iliad* and the *Odyssey* in the original
Greek, which at that time the young Schliemann could not understand.

Disgusted by his dissolute father, Schliemann ran away from home, worked for a time in Amsterdam, embarked on a ship and was shipwrecked, lay perilously ill in a hospital for weeks, then got himself a job with a firm of indigo merchants in Amsterdam. His business sense was so acute that within a short time the directors of his firm sent him to St. Petersburg (now called Leningrad) as their representative. Before he was thirty he had taught himself seven languages and was practically a millionaire.

It was not until he was nearly fifty, when, having made a vast fortune, he gave up his business activities entirely, and sailed to Greece for the express purpose of digging up the Homeric cities which had so excited him as a child.

He was entirely without training or scholarship. He knew the poems of Homer almost by heart and regarded them as literal truth. He was also familiar with the works of such classical authors as Pausanias, who had visited and described the sites in the second century A.D. As an excavator he could tell a spade from a wheelbarrow but that was about all. He knew nothing about stratigraphy and sequence dating, nor was he familiar with the techniques of measurement and recording. This was the man who, in 1871, accompanied by his new, eighteen-year-old Greek wife, Sophia Engastromenos, addressed himself to the mound of Hissarlik, near the Dardanelles, which Schliemann believed concealed Homer's "city of Priam."

During the autumn of 1871, eighty workmen drove a deep trench into the face of the mound on its steep northern slope, and dug down to a depth of thirty-three feet below the surface of the hill. The workmen sang, and Schliemann's heart was joyous. Six months later he was back at Hissarlik with an augmented force, including "three overseers and an engineer, to make maps and plans." This is significant, since it shows that despite his inexperience in excavation, Schliemann had recognized the importance of surveying and recording.

His young wife was at his side during the long days when he toiled in the trench; and at night, in their hut on top of the mound, her delicate fingers helped him to sort out and classify the fragments of pottery, clay idols, fragments of weapons and tools, which they had sifted from the soil. It was a far more difficult, perplexing and unrewarding task than Schliemann had dreamed of, nor did the climate make it easier. Summer brought dust, flies, and a sultry heat; snakes slid down from the roof of the hut and had to be killed; mosquitoes put Heinrich down with malaria. [In] winter, he wrote, "a freezing blast from the north blew with such violence through the chinks in our house-walls . . . that we were not able to light our lamps in the evening, and although we had fire in the hearth, the thermometer showed nine degrees of frost."

Although Greek scholars had scoffed at the very idea of there having been a historical Troy, Schliemann's childish faith was vindicated. As his workmen trenched into the mound they disclosed the foundations of not one city but many. Schliemann, though delighted, was also puzzled and dismayed. Among this tangle of stone walls, evidently frequently rebuilt, where was Priam's Troy that had been sacked by the Greeks several thousand years ago? And was there any hope of finding the golden treasure of King Priam, which the German amateur was convinced must be there?

He had, of course, no means of dating, except by comparison. Obviously the highest layer of ruins must be the latest, and the lowest the oldest. With the aid of overseers, Schliemann was able to trace seven separate cities, but as he had no means of establishing the true age of the ruins he naturally concluded that the Homeric city would lie near the bottom. He was distressed at finding that among the upper layers, parts of which he had to demolish to get at the lower, were buildings far more like his imagined Trojan city than those he found further down.

When he reached the lowest layers he was disappointed. Surely this small, cramped settlement with its primitive walls could not have been "Priam's royal town"? It was not, of course. The city which the Achaeans had sacked was far higher up in the mound and was eventually established by the American scholar, Professor Carl Blegen, as being Troy 7A. What Schliemann had grubbed out of the lower layers was a prehistoric settlement at least one thousand years older.

In 1873 he wrote to his brother: "We have been digging here for three years with a hundred and fifty workmen . . . and have dragged away 250,000 cubic metres of débris and have collected in the depths of Ilium a fine museum of very remarkable antiquities. Now, however, we are weary, and since we have attained our goal and realized the great ideal of our life, we shall finally cease our efforts in Troy on June 15th."

Notice the date, June 15, 1873. *One day* only before Schliemann had decided to pay off his workmen and cease excavation, he was standing, with a few of his men, close to a building which he believed, wrongly, to be Priam's palace. His keen eyes suddenly noticed a large copper object embedded under a layer of burned ruins, above which stood a fortification wall.

He glanced surreptitiously at his Turkish laborers. Clearly they had not seen what he had seen. Calling for Sophia he told her to announce to the workmen that it was his birthday. "Call the *paidos*" (time of rest), he instructed her. "Tell them they'll get their wages today without working!" Sophia obeyed, the delighted workmen trooped off, leaving the site deserted. Then Schliemann pointed out to Sophia what he had found. She stood beside her husband as he crouched at the foot of the wall, digging from the earth object after object gleaming in the sunlight. The copper object which he had first noticed turned out to be a chisel, but because of its shape Schliemann thought it was the key to Priam's treasure chest.

Near it was a whole mass of lovely things, evidently a hoard of treasure hidden under the wall by someone, probably at the time the city was being attacked. The signs of burning showed that a sack had taken place, and Schliemann naturally assumed that this must have been the historic sack of Troy. Eventually the two excavators, like excited children, carried their finds up to the hut and laid them on the table. The sight was truly astonishing. There were six gold bracelets, a gold goblet weighing 601 grams, a goblet of gold-and-silver alloy (electrum), a large silver vessel containing two magnificent gold diadems, sixty gold earrings, and 8,700 small gold finger rings. There were also gold buttons, perforated gold bars, and other vases of silver and copper.

Then follows the famous scene which, to me, typifies the essentially romantic approach of most nineteenth-century archaeologists. Schliemann had, in three years, shifted 250,000 cubic meters of debris, and "collected a fine museum of very remarkable antiquities." He had done his fumbling best to interpret the tangle of ruins for the benefit of future archaeologists. But at heart he had been weary and disappointed, until he found the treasure. He took out the two lovely diadems from the silver bowl. The largest consisted of fine gold chain intended to encircle the wearer's head, and from this chain hung seventy-four short, and sixteen longer, chains of gold. The shorter chains formed a sort of "fringe" for the brow; the longer ones had hung down to the wearer's shoulders. There were no less than 16,353 separate gold pieces in the larger diadem, of the most exquisite workmanship.

He looked across the table at his lovely young wife with her coils of dark hair, and her hands still grubby from digging out the treasure. For Schliemann, at that moment, she was the reincarnation of the "white-armed Helen" whose beauty had brought Troy to ruin, the very Troy on which he was now standing. Through the doorway he could see the burning plain upon which Greeks and Trojans had fought for nine long years, and beyond gleamed the "wine-dark sea" across which the Greeks had sailed in their black ships. With trembling hands he lifted the largest diadem and gently placed it on the head of his wife. . . . Surely, he thought, these must be the jewels of Helen.

Schliemann was now completely convinced that his instinct had been right. Homer had written of "windy Troy" and the treasure of Priam. He, Schliemann, had unearthed Troy and found what he confidently believed to have been Priam's treasure. Homer had also described "golden Mycenae," the capital of Agamemnon, in southern Greece, and Pylos, the home of the "sage Nestor." To Schliemann the poet's writings were a guidebook to the past; he accepted them literally, and having proved triumphantly that there had been an actual Troy, he decided to devote the rest of his life to digging up other Homeric sites. But he was wise enough to enlist the aid of more experienced scholars, such as Rudolf Virchow and young Wilhelm Dörpfeld, to help him in his researches.

There is something extremely attractive about Schliemann. Naive, impulsive, hot-headed, romantic, he was at the same time shrewd enough to realize that he had taken on a bigger job than he could handle alone. Treasure hunter though he was (someone called him "the goldseeker") and passionate in his belief that the Homeric myths were true, he had the instincts of the true archaeologist. As he grew older he became more cautious and painstaking, so that his published works still have value to his successors in the same field.

After his triumph at Troy, Heinrich Schliemann went to England where he was rapturously acclaimed by thousands who attended his lectures. The Prime Minister, Gladstone, wrote a Foreword to his book, and though some of his German fellow countrymen still regarded him with suspicion and even contempt he was accepted by most of the Western world as an archaeologist of genius. Three years later he obtained permission from the Greek authorities to dig at Mycenae, the capital of King Agamemnon, and Sophia went with him.

Like Troy, Mycenae was a city of legend. The ruined walls of the citadel, built of massive stone blocks weighing several tons, were regarded by the Greeks of classical times (roughly between 600 and 300 B.C.) as the work of giants. Homer had described Mycenae as the home of Agamemnon; he and later poets and dramatists had told the story of how Agamemnon, on his return from Troy, had been treacherously murdered by his wife Clytemnestra and her lover Aegisthus.

But most scholars of Schliemann's time regarded this as nothing more than a myth, even though Pausanias, a Greek traveler of the second century A.D., had left a detailed report of his visit to Mycenae, describing the tombs of Agamemnon and his companions "within the citadel" and those of Clytemnestra, Aegisthus, and others outside the city boundaries. There were, indeed, enormous *tholoi* or beehive-shaped tombs cut out of the hillside surrounding the city, one of which was attributed to Clytemnestra and another to Agamemnon. But these had been robbed in remote antiquity, and as Pausanias had stated that the tomb of Agamemnon was "within the citadel," Schliemann sought and obtained permission to excavate the narrow space between the "Lion Gate" and the "Cyclopean" walls. The terrain was highly unpromising, a narrow rock-strewn slope between the walls of the palace and the outer ramparts, not far from the "Lion Gate" with its rampant beasts above the stone lintel. Yet Schliemann, disregarding the sneers of some archaeological authorities, was determined to dig there and nowhere else.

He was rewarded by the discovery of a sacred circle of hewn stones with grave-stelae under which lay five deep shafts cut out of the rocky soil, containing rich burials. Some of the bodies, of both men and women, were laden with gold. Two of the men wore golden masks, and on their chests were golden breastplates. There were bodies of two children encased in sheet gold. The women, gorgeously adorned in gold, had worn long-skirted dresses ornamented with golden disks, spirals, rosettes, bees, and cuttlefish. This rich art, quite unlike that of prehistoric Troy or classical Greece, was called Mycenaean after the site at which such objects were first found.

Schliemann concluded that these shaft graves were those of Agamemnon and his slain companions, but we now know that they date from at least three hundred years before the Trojan War, and the funerary raiment could not possibly be that of Agamemnon and his companions. The graves belong to a much earlier period of Mycenaean history, of which hardly a record remains. But they do prove that there had existed on the Greek mainland, before 1500 B.C., a European civilization contemporary with that of Egypt.

From the strictly archaeological standpoint Schliemann proved that significant discoveries could be made, not only through studying artificial irregularities on the earth's surface or historical records kept by the official archivists of Egypt and Mesopotamia, but also through what are commonly called myths. In the nineteenth century a myth was a fairy story, a romantic expression of a poet's fancy, in which there might lie buried some fragment of historical truth.

Since the time of Schliemann and his distinguished successor, Sir Arthur Evans, scholars have been less skeptical. Very often clues derived from the so-called "myths" have led to important archaeological discoveries—the Palace of Nestor at Pylos, the Artemisian sanctuary at Brauron in Attica, and the homes of Jason at Iolcus and Achilles in Thessaly (only recently identified).

As a distinguished Greek archaeologist said to me in 1962, "Mythology, properly understood is folk-history; the history of things . . . before historical documentation existed." So Schliemann may have been partly right after all.

MAN'S
EARLIEST KNOWN
ANCESTORS

Remote Prehistory

THE FIRST PART of this book has been an attempt to show how archaeology began, and how it was practiced by the great pioneers of the nineteenth century. Later I shall try to demonstrate how archaeology has developed from about 1900 down to the present day. There is, of course, no such arbitrary dividing line between ancient and modern. A few nineteenth-century pioneers, such as General Pitt-Rivers, were using methods which a modern excavator would regard as almost up to date; indeed his principle of accurate stratigraphy—making a section through a site like a "layer cake" and accurately observing and recording the layers—is practiced by all competent modern excavators. He also laid emphasis on full and accurate publication of his finds, another principle which is universally accepted today.

Again, Petrie's rejection of mere treasure hunting, and his revelation of how the past of mankind could be interpreted not only through works of art but through small and intrinsically valueless things as well, was a vital contribution to archaeological technique, as was his method of comparative or sequence dating.

But Petrie made mistakes. In his role of salvage man he often worked through sites too fast; he paid too little attention to the stratigraphic method, and his rapidly produced and frequent publications, though valuable, contain gaps which a modern scholar would prefer to see filled.

However, this present chapter, and that which follows, is not confined to either early or modern archaeology but spans the entire period. There is a reason for this. The archaeologists whose work we have been studying confined themselves almost entirely to the civilizations which grew up in Egypt, Mesopotamia, Asia Minor, and southeastern Europe. These, together with that of the Indus Valley (which was discovered only fairly recently) and ancient China, are the oldest known to have existed. But, to recall the simile of the hunderd-page book of man's history, they all belong to page 100. The oldest goes back a mere five thousand years, whereas there have been men living on earth for one hundred times that span of years.

But from the early nineteenth century onward another kind of archaeologist—the prehistorian—has been exploring these hitherto uncharted regions of man's history: long before the days of cities and towns, long before the invention of agriculture which made civilization possible, back through the times when our ancestors lived in caves or rock shelters and hunted their food, to the period when man was evolving from his apelike forebears. These archaeologists, in many countries—but mainly in Europe—have no ruined buildings to guide them in their researches because early man did not erect buildings. They have no pottery either, because primitive man did not know how to make it. He used baskets made of perishable material which has, of course, disappeared. Nor are there any metal tools and weapons, let alone elaborate jewelry.

Yet despite these handicaps, scholars specializing in remote prehistory have managed, over a period of more than one hundred years, to chart a rough map of man's progress over some 500,000 years, until their work has begun to link up with that of their colleagues who have concentrated on man's *immediate* prehistory—the predynastic Egyptians and the forebears of the Sumerians, and the civilizations to which they gave rise. How has this been done? By the study of the stone tools and weapons which are practically the only artifacts which primitive man has left, by exploring the cave dwellings and rock shelters in which he lived, by examining his bones and those of the animals he hunted, and, perhaps the most valuable of all, by discovering the mysterious cave paintings—some of them between fifteen and twenty thousand years old—which provide a faint clue to his social life and religious beliefs.

In this vast field of research other specialists have helped: the geologist who understands rock formations and can sometimes approximately date the strata in which remains are found, the zoologist who can identify the types of animals hunted by early man, the geobotanist who can sometimes establish the kind of climate in which he lived and the type of flora and fauna existing at the time. There is also the anthropologist who, from a study of contemporary peoples who are still at a Stonge Age level of development, can often throw light on the habits and beliefs of people who lived more than twenty thousand years before our epoch. For archaeology is, or should be, the study of people, not things, and as Dr. Margaret Murray has said, "archaeology is only anthropology in the past." And she was both an anthropologist, "a student of man as an animal," and a distinguished archaeologist.

In the eighteenth century A.D. most Europeans, if they thought about the matter at all, believed that the world had been created by an act of God in 4004 B.C. When fossils were found, and curious minds began asking questions and forming deductions, one authority solved the problem by stating that the Almighty had planted these forms in the rocks *after* the Creation, some six thousand years ago. There were skeptics even in the eighteenth and early nineteenth centuries, but Archbishop Ussher's chronology fell to pieces when Charles Darwin proved, in his *Origin of Species* (1859) that man had evolved, by a process which he called "natural selection," from an ancestor whom he shared with the great apes; that man was, in fact, a part of, and not apart from, the rest of animal creation.

Another great intellect of the same epoch was Thomas Henry Huxley who, like Darwin, was not an archaeologist but a biologist and naturalist. For nearly a century before his time the possibility of organic evolution had been discussed; he and his fellow naturalists had been stirred by the presence, in ancient rock strata, of fossilized animal and vegetable forms which clearly belonged to a remote period of the earth's history. But as for the daring theory that man had also evolved in the same way, Huxley was, in his own words, "inclined to say to Mosaists and Evolutionists 'a plague on both your houses' and disposed to turn aside from an interminable and apparently fruitless discussion to labour in the fertile fields of ascertainable fact." That was until Darwin's *Origin of Species* appeared. After that Huxley came down on the side of Darwin, accepting the evolutionary theory and all its implications.

Some of the archaeologists working in Egypt and Mesopotamia at this time stayed within the framework of Archbishop Ussher's chronology. They were looking for the Assyrians or the Babylonians or the Egyptians, who had been mentioned in the Bible, and that was good enough for them. But there were others, like Petrie, whose minds were profoundly influenced by the far-flung vista of man's past dramatically revealed by Darwin and Huxley. This may be why some became more interested in the origins of civilization than in civilization itself. This interest has persisted and developed down to the present day, so that the modern archaeologist is able to relate the epoch he is studying, which could be the Bronze Age, with the Neolithic (New Stone Age) and Paleolithic (Old Stone Age) which preceded it. The old distinction between the prehistorian who was concerned only with the relics of early man, and the archaeologist who dug up buried cities, is much less precise today. Specialization still exists, of course, but the two studies have joined, at least at a superficial level.

A problem arises from the fact that our knowledge of prehistory is not spread uniformly throughout the world. The scientific study of prehistory began in Europe; many of the Stone Age "cultures" identifiable by certain stone tools are named after tiny villages and hamlets in one small area of France, where they were first noted and classified. Yet these artifacts are spread over an immense area, from the Atlantic Ocean to southern Russia. But because Europe has been for over a century the center of prehistoric studies, far more is known about European prehistory than that of Africa, Asia, or America. This fact is bound to influence anyone trying to make a survey of world prehistory. In Europe scholars have thrown light in many dark places, so that the picture is a little clearer than elsewhere. In Africa great and important discoveries have been made and will be made, as in eastern Asia and the American continent. But compared with Europe these regions show only a few bright patches of light in surrounding darkness.

Before we start, here is a simplified time chart which should help you to recognize the technical terms which geologists and prehistorians use, and trace the successive stages in the story of the earth, of animals, and finally of man.

AGE OF THE EARTH	*approximately* 3,000,000,000 years
TIME DURING WHICH MAN HAS LIVED	500,000 years
TIME DURING WHICH MAN HAS BEEN ABLE TO FARM, DOMESTICATE ANIMALS, AND LIVE IN SETTLED COMMUNITIES	10,000 years
CIVILIZED MAN	5,000 years

By a simple arithmetical sum you can relate these figures to a twelve-hour day. Thus, if man's existence over 500,000 years could be crammed into twelve hours, beginning at noon, he would not begin to farm, make permanent buildings, and live in settled communities until ten minutes to eleven, and his earliest civilizations, those of Egypt and Sumer, would not appear until thirty-five minutes to midnight. During the whole of the remaining time he would have been a wandering hunter and food gatherer, using primitive stone tools and weapons and living in shelters.

Now consider the following chart, which might be called the History of the Rocks. By studying and classifying these according to age, and observing the evolution of the fossil plant and animal forms found in them, geologists have been able to show the development of life on earth.

TYPES OF ROCK	TYPES OF LIFE
PRE-CAMBRIAN	Practically no life.
PALEOZOIC Cambrian, Ordovician, Silurian, Devonian, Carboniferous, Permian	Living organisms, but no mammals. Man had not appeared.
MESOZOIC Triassic, Jurassic, Cretaceous	Huge reptiles existed. Mammals begin to evolve. During the last (Cretaceous) stage chalk cliffs laid down.
TERTIARY Eocene, Oligocene, Miocene, Pliocene	This is where prehistory begins, during the Pliocene period. In the Miocene period man had left behind his purely animal state and the history of humanity begins.
QUATERNARY Pleistocene	Development of human species.

This is how the geologist charts the background to man's appearance and progress. But how are we to define man? How do we distinguish him from the hominids or man-apes who preceded him? Perhaps the best definition of man is "a tool-making animal." His predecessors *used* tools, but the human species alone learned to *make* tools. Why? Why, despite his physical weakness compared with many other animals, did he become superior to them?

First, he learned to walk upright. His feet and legs became so strong that he could walk on two limbs instead of four. This left his hands and arms free. Second, he developed a fine pair of eyes, able to see close-up and long-distance, and examine things picked up by his hands. Third, his jaw had many tongue muscles; he could learn to speak and communicate with his fellow men. Fourth, and most important of all, man became *specialized* (in the genetical sense) in his brain, whereas other animals were specialized in bone and muscle. Man has *consciousness*. As Professor

Miles Burkitt has commented, "Man is the only animal which can stand outside the window and see himself talking" and "Consciousness is the mistletoe on the apple-tree." Another, much earlier scholar, Fernando Galiani, put it this way: "Man is the only animal which takes an interest in things which don't concern him."

The development of man's ancestors, the sub-hominids or ape-like men, does not belong properly to archaeology. Suffice it to say that several parts of the world have yielded fossil remains of creatures which, though not fully human, have certain human characteristics, such as an upright posture and superior brain. Among the earliest known are *Australopithecus* (meaning "the southern ape") and his successors *Paranthropus* and *Telanthropus;* all three species came from Africa, which some prehistorians believe was the birthplace of the human race. Then in Java was found *Pithecanthropus erectus,* who walked like a man, and in China came *Sinanthropus,* who could make quartz tools and used fire. These creatures walked the earth scores of thousands of years before our own species, Homo sapiens, was evolved.

On the American continent no remains of these submen have been discovered; indeed the earliest human remains and tools found so far cannot be dated earlier than about twelve thousand years ago and these of course belong to Homo sapiens. It is generally believed that the first human beings to enter America were of Mongoloid stock, and they crossed over from Asia via the Bering Strait to Alaska at the end of the last Ice Age, when the crossing was easier. The pre-Columbian inhabitants of America, from the North American Indian to those of Tierra del Fuego, are the descendants of these people.

Now from geological terms—Miocene, Pleistocene, etc.—we pass to a few archaeological terms, such as Upper and Lower Paleolithic, Mesolithic, and Neolithic. These are not as alarming as they sound. We know that man—true man—began to develop during the Pleistocene period, which is the term geologists use to describe the most recent geological period. Now it was in part of this period that men were making stone tools. Therefore archaeologists call it the Paleolithic or Old Stone Age. And as it lasted a very long time—upward of 400,000 years—prehistorians divide it into Upper and Lower Paleolithic; the difference shows itself partly in the types of stone tools which man made.

If you examined an Upper Paleolithic tool—and there are many on exhibit in museums—you might find it difficult to believe that it was a man-made object. In appearance it is just a rough piece of flint, sharper at one end than the other. How do prehistorians *know* that this bit of stone was worked by human hands? Could it not be shaped by nature, say by being flung about on a rocky river-bed? The answer lies in the method of "flaking," that is chipping off small slivers of flint to give the tool a cutting edge. If the flaking had been produced by accident the flakes would have been knocked off in any direction. But the Upper Paleolithic "hand ax," a pear-shaped lump of stone, reveals that the chipped parts are all flaked in certain definite directions.

The hand ax is a product of human intelligence. A very skillful workman has shaped it. Sometimes he pressed the flakes off until he got the right shape. At other times he used percussion—he hit the flint with a harder piece of stone and flaked it to the shape he required. In either case, it took great skill. (If you find this hard to believe, try taking a piece of flint yourself and making a hand ax like the original. You will find it impossible.) Some prehistorians, like Louis B. Leakey, who has devoted a lifetime to the study of early man, have learned the technique by repeated experiment, but it took them a very long time.

Many thousands of these hand axes have been found all over the world; occasionally they have been discovered near the skeletal remains of early man. We believe they were used as axes or picks, for felling trees, chopping wood, or as a weapon for killing an animal or an enemy. They are not much to look at, but if you use your imagination they can be as exciting as an Ancient Egyptian pyramid or a Greek temple. Because here, in the palm of your hand, is something made by man, our ancestor, a human being like ourselves, but living at a distance of time which makes the pyramids seem as if they were made only yesterday. Here is a *tool*, one of the first steps which our ancestors took on the long road to civilization.

If you think about it, that shaped piece of flint is the ancestor of all the tools which man has on his long march from the cave dwelling to the skyscraper, from the dug-out canoe to the ocean liner, from the stone-tipped wooden spear to the hydrogen bomb.

The March of
Mankind

FROM THE BEGINNING the prehistorians of the nineteenth century approached their work in a much more scientific spirit than did the men who, at the same period, were unveiling the civilizations of Egypt and Mesopotamia.

Among the pioneers was an Englishman named John Frere of Hoxne, in Suffolk. In 1790 he found chipped stone implements in proximity to bones of extinct animals. The implements, he reasoned, must be contemporary with the animals, suggesting a remote antiquity for mankind. These views were regarded by most of his contemporaries as irreligious, and were ignored. Then in 1847 a Frenchman named Boucher des Pérthes, Chief Customs Officer at Abbeville in northern France, found, in the Somme Valley, worked stones which he believed were very ancient and made by human hands.

Meanwhile, in Norway and Sweden, two men, C. V. Thompson of Copenhagen and Sven Nilsson of Lund revived the classical idea (found in the poems of Hesiod twenty-seven hundred years ago) of the "Three Ages of Man"—a Stone Age, Bronze Age, and

Iron Age. Hesiod, a contemporary of Homer, may have been expressing, in poetic myth, a dim folk-memory from far-distant times. But in Scandinavia these two nineteenth-century scholars had found ancient implements of all three materials which provided a useful basis for classification.

All this was taking place before Darwin and Huxley propagated the theory of evolution. But from the moment this bombshell exploded the floodgates were opened, and scholars began exploring drift deposits and limestone caves for any evidence they could find of early man and his tools. John Evans, father of Sir Arthur Evans who excavated the Minoan culture, went to the Somme Valley with his colleague, Prestwich, met Boucher des Pérthes, and examined the implements he had found. They were soon convinced of their great antiquity. Other explorations were carried out in England where, in a cave at Brixham in Devon, explorers found humanly worked flints with remains of the woolly rhinoceros and mammoth; these were in a cavern sealed by stalagmite. The same was true of another Devonian cave, Kent's Cavern near Torquay, where as a boy I remembered seeing the fang of a saber-toothed tiger still embedded in the stalagmite; presumably it is still there.

But the greatest of the early discoveries were made between 1863 and 1864 in the Dordogne Valley in central France. If Egypt is, in Glanville's words, "a unique National Park of ancient life," the valleys of the Dordogne and its tributary the Vézère are a "National Park of prehistoric man." It was here, in gravel terraces above the river and in adjacent caves, that two scholars, Edouard Lartet and Henry Christy, made a whole series of fascinating discoveries. Today thousands of visitors come every year to the quiet, verdant, tranquil valley of the Dordogne to see the sites at which these finds were made and the stone tools, carved bones, and rock shelters of early men who lived there over a vast period of time, more than fifty thousand years ago.

Even the tiny hamlets and villages near which these remains were first found are recalled by the names given by prehistorians to the paleolithic cultures found near them. For instance the "Mousterian" culture is named after Le Moustier, in the valley of the Vézère; the "Magdalenian" culture comes from La Madeleine, and so on. Other paleolithic cultures, identifiable by particular types of stone tools, are named after places—mainly in France—where the first examples were found: Acheulean, from St. Acheul, a suburb of Amiens; Chellean, after Chelles-sur-Marne near Paris; and Aurignacian, after Aurignac in the Haute-Garonne.

It is important to realize that these cultures did not necessarily originate at these places, or were confined to them. Examples of such tools are found scattered over a large area of the Old World and Asia, and similar types are found in Africa. The systematic classification of these various types of tools owes much to that great prehistorian, Gabriel de Mortillet, and his remarkable successor, the Abbé Breuil. Breuil became a prehistorian in his twenties, investigated sites all over Europe, founded the Institut de Paléontologie Humaine at Paris, and held several professorships. The most distinguished prehistorian of this century, he traveled to many countries, including Ethiopia, South Africa, and China, and probably did more than any man to correlate these bewildering classifications and sub-classifications and produce a *world* view of prehistory.

So far the newcomer to prehistoric studies might be excused for thinking this a dull subject compared with the archaeology of more recent times. Flint tools and bits of inscribed bone, carefully arranged and ticketed in museum cases—of what interest are such things to anyone but the specialist? This view is understandable, but quite wrong.

Everything depends on the degree of knowledge and imagination one brings to the subject. The tools themselves are interesting, once one has learned to recognize the type of man who made them, how they were made, and what they were used for. Do not be put off by the chilling designations—Aurignacian, Mousterian, Chellean, etc. The objects so designated were made scores of thousands of years ago by human beings like ourselves, and from them you can learn a lot about the way of life of these early men, who lived in an environment which would be hostile and frightening to most of us.

I have mentioned the hand axes, among the earliest tools known. These belong to the category called core-tools; a lump of flint was flaked to the desired shape, and the core used as a tool or weapon. But there were other types of tools made from the flakes, and these, it is believed, were manufactured by a different group of men from those who made core-tools. It is obvious from the geographic distribution of these Lower Paleolithic tools, that, whereas east of the Rhine as far as China the "industries" (to use a prehistorian's term) are predominately of the flake-tool type, west of the Rhine, in the main, one finds predominantly core-tools.

Remember, too, that even the simple hand-ax did not remain the same shape and size for scores of thousands of years. It evolved, as other tools have done. At first it was roughly pear-shaped, pointed at one end and rounded at the other. In what are called Acheulean times the tool became neater, with sharper and more regular edges. At the same period there was an oval type of hand-ax called the "ovate."

Most of us would probably recognize a hand-ax if we found one. But when one comes to the flake-tools made by detaching a flake from the core or nucleus, only an expert can guide us to the meaning and purpose of these odd-shaped lumps of stone. But once recognized they immediately become interesting. A "side scraper" with a sharp convex cutting edge along one side only was used for removing the tissue from the inside of animal skins to make them softer. Immediately a whole picture rises before us, of men (or more likely women) sitting outside their rock shelter, scraping the animal skins which were their only form of clothing. The spinning and weaving of cloth were not to be invented until some fifty thousand years later.

When we arrive in Upper Paleolithic times the variety of tools becomes bewildering. Besides scrapers we find knife blades, spearheads, arrowheads, "points" (for drilling holes in skins), and a number of other tools made from the bones of animals. A piece of animal bone with a hole drilled through it was, it is believed, an arrow straightener. Beside it are a number of harpoons, with barbs, made from reindeer antler. At this period, too, appear wonderful works of art; a Magdalenian carving of a trout, an engraving on a reindeer antler of a spirited wild horse, a carving of a horse's head in bone, and a carved ivory pendant—one of the early examples of ornament.

Most interesting of all is a strange, obese figure of a woman with enormous breasts, carved in stone. This, known as the "Willendorf Venus," was found at Willendorf in Germany. It may be the prototype of the Mother Goddess or Earth Mother who we know was worshiped by prehistoric peoples of the eastern Mediterranean and western Asia.

To examine, study, and classify the tools of early man helps us to understand his way of life. We know that the men of the Dordogne Valley lived in a harsh, bitter climate, quite unlike that of today; theirs was the time of the last Ice Age, when glaciers had moved down over northern Europe and North America. That was why he took refuge in caves and rock shelters at the mouths of caves which gave him protection against the bitter climate. He was a hunter living almost entirely off the flesh of wild animals, many of them much larger and more powerful than himself, but which, with his superior intelligence, immense courage, and simple stone weapons, he had learned to kill. He also used traps. His relationship with these wild creatures must have been two-sided. On the one hand he hunted and killed them, because without their flesh he would starve, and without their skins he would freeze. On the other hand he may not, as we do, have regarded them as an inferior species; he must often have been awestruck by their power, or swiftness; perhaps even by their beauty.

It is highly significant that the earliest examples of art, scratched on a piece of bone or painted on the walls of a cave—always depict animals. Human beings hardly ever appear. It is also significant that many of the Ancient Egyptian gods such as Horus, Anubis, Hathor and even the king of gods, Amen-Ra, were animal-headed, relics of a time when animals were regarded with religious awe. And this brings us to a most important point. The tools of paleolithic man can tell us something about his technical accomplishments, and indirectly of his way of life. But they tell us nothing of how he felt and thought about the world around him, and if he had any conception of a supernatural power outside himself.

If you look at the earliest remains of any mature civilization—whether it be the Incas of Peru, the Mayas and Aztecs of Mexico, the Ancient Egyptians, the Hittites, the Sumerians—you will invariably find that the most important structures are temples or other centers of religious ceremonial. If you go back even further, to a period when permanent buildings did not exist, or have disappeared, still you will notice that the dead were buried in a ceremonial way, and accompanied by objects, be they only tools or pots, and a few clay statuettes of gods or goddesses, suggesting that these people had some belief in a life beyond this one.

Just how far back did this belief go? No one knew, until they began to find and examine the relics of early man. I mentioned the valleys of the Dordogne and the Vézère in central France. On either side of the flat valley floor are limestone cliffs, not very high, and forming steps or terraces, one above the other. Sometimes these cliffs hang right over the road, and if you look carefully you will see, every now and then, the black mouths of caves in the limestone. These, and the terraces in front of them, were the homes of generation after generation of paleolithic men.

One of these caves is near the village of Le Moustier, in the Vézère Valley. Here the French archaeologists of one hundred years ago found the dwellings, not only of Homo sapiens, our own ancestor, but of Neanderthal man. These human creatures (the name comes from a valley called the Neanderthal in Germany) lived more than fifty thousand years ago. They had enormous jaws without chins, their foreheads sloped back more than that of Homo sapiens, they had deep ridges over the eyebrows, their heads were set well forward of their shoulders, and they must have walked with a stoop. Also they were probably hairy. We can deduce these facts from an examination of their skulls and bones. We are not certain whether or not they evolved before Homo sapiens, but we can prove that for a long period both species lived at the same time.

Neanderthal man appeared during the last warm period of the Ice Age; there were successive warm and cold periods—cold when the glaciers advanced, warm when they retreated. In caves near Le Moustier were found relics of Neanderthal man: remains of his fires, the half-burned bones of the animals he hunted and ate, and thousands of his stone tools.

As the climate grew colder with the last advance of the glaciers, he had to find shelter in the caves, and so did the animals. Bones of such animals as bears and hyenas have been found in these caves. When one emerges from the dim caverns onto the terraces, and looks down on the tranquil valley, it is difficult to imagine what this region must have been like in the last cold spell of the Ice Age when the ice sheets were again spreading south across Europe and the climate grew steadily colder.

In one of these caves the explorers found a Neanderthal burial. The skeletons were lying in a bent-up position, and beside the bodies lay tools and the bones of animals. Above each grave a great rock had been lowered into place. So even at a remote period of time, ten times as remote as that of the Egyptian pyramids, creatures whom we would hardly recognize as human were already thinking about life beyond the grave. They imagined, and they worried, as we do.

Nor was this an isolated instance. Similar Neanderthal graves have been found in other parts of the world; in some cases the bodies were of small children. They too were accompanied by food placed near the mouth, and by flint tools.

Remains of our own species, Homo sapiens, have also been found at Le Moustier. The curious fact is that in some of the caves, at the lower level, were things which Homo sapiens had left behind. Above this layer, and therefore later, were things which Neanderthal man left behind. And above that layer were more evidences of Homo sapiens. Since the deposits had never been disturbed, it is obvious that there was a period when both species existed at the same time. Yet today every member of the human race—American, European, Negro, Chinese, Polynesian, Kalahari bushman, and Australian aborigine—is descended from Homo sapiens. Neanderthal man died out completely. One wonders why. One theory is that he was not as well equipped as our own ancestors to survive. There may possibly have been some intermarriage between the two stocks, and some anthropologists claim to recognize "Neanderthaloid" features among people living today.

But on the whole the two types of men must have remained apart, and one wonders if the legends of "ogres" in the folk tales of many peoples are a race memory of those hairy, powerful, stooping creatures who would surely have been abhorrent to our own ancestors. The Greeks had the myths of the Titans and the Cyclops; the Norse folk tales tell of the trolls—malignant but stupid monsters; the Arabs have their jinn, who sometimes appear as men of appalling hideousness; and giants figure in many Teutonic and Celtic folk tales. This is, of course, romantic speculation, but, to me, the similarities in the folk tales of peoples separated by vast distances, even among peoples who could have had no communication with each other in historical times, only reinforces the scientific evidence of the prehistorian.

All mankind has a common ancestor, who was a hunter. For scores of thousands of years he wandered the earth, impelled by changes of climate and the need for following the wild herds which were almost his only source of food. Could it not have been during this time, long before the migrations of civilized peoples, that some of the most ancient myths were carried to the ends of the earth?

But to return to paleolithic man; we have noted that he practiced ceremonial burial, with "grave goods" for the dead, suggesting a belief in, or hope for, an afterlife. Did he practice other ceremonies, perhaps of magic and propitiation? For what we call magic and superstition gave birth to the earliest known religions; the magician came before the priest. Did paleolithic man have sacred places or sanctuaries, ancestral to the temples of civilized peoples? There is every indication that in Upper (later) Paleolithic times he had.

In several parts of France and Spain there are caves, the walls of which are covered with marvelous paintings of now-extinct animals. The first of these to be discovered was at Altamira, near Santander in Spain. In 1868 a hunter was digging out a fox and found the cave, but not the paintings. However, as the place showed evidence of having been inhabited in prehistoric times, a local archaeologist, Señor Marcelino de Sautola began investi-

gating the archaeological deposits; this was in 1880. While de
Sautola was working not far from the mouth of the cave, his little
daughter wandered further into its recesses, carrying a candle.
Suddenly the father heard his child's excited cry, "*Toros! Toros!*"
(Bulls!) Following his daughter into the cave de Sautola came
upon an astonishing, awe-inspiring sight. On the roof of the
cavern, lit by the flickering candles, were paintings of animals,
which the little girl, being a Spaniard, thought were bulls. In fact
they were bison, vividly colored in red ocher shaded with black
manganese. There were also pictures of other animals, including
a deer-hind and a beautifully executed wild boar.

We know that during the warm period following the last Ice
Age bison inhabited the coastal plains of Europe between the
mountains and the sea. This was the first time, so far as is recorded,
that modern man (or in this case modern small girl) had seen their
representations. They were at least twenty thousand years old,
but at the time few people took any interest. It was not until 1895
that another painted cave was found at La Mouthe in the Dordogne Valley, and the discovery published. Then people remembered de Sautola's discovery of fifteen years earlier. In 1902
the Abbé Breuil and his colleague Cartailhac examined the Altamira paintings and on the basis of deposits found in the cave
mouth pronounced them to be of Magdalenian date.

Thus a search began for other examples of cave art, and several
were found in both France and Spain. Usually they were deep
underground, far from the entrance to the caves near which men
had lived. They were not dwelling places. The paintings were
always of animals which Upper Paleolithic man had hunted:
bison, wild horses, wild boars, reindeer. In some caves explorers
found remains of the oil lamps the artists had used to give them
light to do their work, and even remains of the coloring material
they had used, such as ocher ground into a powder and mixed
wth animal fat. As works of art there is nothing in the world more
compellingly alive than these superb animal studies. Only a
people who had very close relationships with animals could have
made them; they reveal that man's artistic impulse was as strong
twenty thousand years ago as it has ever been. Even sophisticated

twentieth-century man can feel something of the fear and excitement of those paleolithic hunters.

Fear, excitement, and something else which is difficult to describe. Poetry, perhaps? There *is* a poetic intensity in the way the ancient artists have depicted the beauty, power, and movement of these beasts; heavy bison with their huge shoulders, young wild horses at the gallop, a herd of reindeer swimming across a river. But there is something else, a sense of deep-felt magic and mystery which is almost religious. One is reminded of the wonderful evocations of animal power in the Old Testament:

> Hast thou given the horse his strength?
> Hast thou clothed his neck with thunder?
> Canst thou make him afraid as a grasshopper?
> The glory of his nostrils is terrible. . . .

Why, one asks, should primitive men have penetrated to these dark, damp caverns, the entrances to which were so narrow that they became blocked with fallen rock and remained sealed for two hundred centuries? Why should they paint on roofs and walls these brilliantly colored figures which could rarely be seen, and then only by the dim light of oil lamps? We don't know, but there are strong reasons for believing that they were sanctuaries, primitive temples in which religio-magical rites were performed.

One of the most remarkable of these caves is at Les Trois Frères, in the Ariège Department of France. As in other similar caverns the walls are covered with engravings of reindeer, horse, and bison. But at one end, near a sort of natural pulpit in the rock, is a human figure. It is of a man wearing a mask and a crown of antlers. He dominates the chamber and is all the more impressive, indeed frightening, because human beings were so rarely depicted in these times.

Now, leaving Les Trois Frères for a moment, let us consider certain other cave paintings. In one there is a bison with darts or spears sticking in the animal's sides. Other paintings, of mammoth and reindeer, also show these spears, but hardly ever, at this period of cave art, do we see a man throwing them. Again, close examination of some of the animal figures shows that they have been painted over again and again, sometimes with different species of animals.

You may be wondering why prehistorians believe that these paintings are of such early date? Could not they have been painted later? The answer is simple. First, in many cases the caves were found completely blocked until the pictures were discovered. Second, some of the walls were hidden under layers of loose rock and earth and each layer contained flint tools and the bones of animals. If you know the period when the tools were made and the kind of animal which existed at the time, you have a clue to the age of the paintings behind those layers of earth.

When the excavators reached the dried mud at the original floor level of the cavern of Les Trois Frères, they found the footprints of a number of people who had evidently been running, or perhaps dancing. The theory is that this and similar caves were used for magical practices connected with successful hunting. The masked figure was probably a magician or sorcerer wearing the horns of the animal the hunters wished to find and kill. Very probably the spears depicted sticking into certain animals were drawn by the sorcerer himself. The African bushmen paint pictures on the walls of caves to this day, and among American Indians there was a practice of dressing up as buffaloes and dancing before a buffalo hunt. And one Indian tribe had a custom in which the chief medicine man drew a picture of an animal, and then chanted:

> I shoot thee, O beast, in the heart,
> I smite thy heart,
> My friends, every beast
> I smite truly.

As for the footprints of running or dancing feet, these could be those of hunters performing some magical ritual, probably accompanied by wild drumming and chanting, so that the participants were worked up into a frenzy. Similar dances are performed today by the aborigines of Australia, who still live at a Stone Age level of existence; when game is scarce they dress in animal skins, sometimes with animal horns, and go through a dance which imitates the movements of the animals they are going to hunt.

Thus the anthropologist, who studies contemporary peoples, comes to the aid of the archaeologist, who studies the life of people long dead.

Before we look at the most recently discovered and most glorious cave paintings, I would like to quote the statements of two distinguished men personally known to me, but who are unknown to each other. One, Dr. William Sargant, is a famous London specialist in mental and nervous disorders, and Director of the Department of Psychiatric Medicine at Guy's Hospital, London. The other is Professor Miles Burkitt, one of the greatest living prehistorians and a pupil of the late Abbé Breuil. The gist of Dr. Sargant's statement, in conversation with me this year, is as follows: "The methods used in brainwashing political prisoners, of inducing certain types of religious conversion, as for example during the Spanish Inquisition and some Revivalists' hell-fire sermons, and the methods which psychiatrists sometimes have to use in discharging nervous tension in battle-shocked troops—by inducing them to re-live their experiences under drugs or hypnosis —are basically the same, although the aims may be either good or bad. The method is to work upon the patient's or victim's fears, anxieties, and hopes to such a degree that at last resistance is broken and a new thought pattern can be imposed."

Shortly after hearing this thesis (which is set out at length in Dr. Sargant's recent book *The Battle for the Mind*), I suddenly recollected what Professor Burkitt has said to me several years ago about the cave of Les Trois Fréres. Fortunately I had kept notes of the conversation so I can quote, almost verbatim, what this famous prehistorian said:

Delay between perception and reaction causes a growth of nervous tension. When man depended for his very existence on the presence of animals which he hunted, the nonappearance of those animals, due to climatic conditions, caused intense nervous and emotional strain. Man had no means of storing and preserving food at this time. If the animals did not appear, he starved. He may have found relief in ritual dancing, or by taking part in ceremonies which induced a trancelike state and so increased suggestibility.

Caves are frightening places, even today, but much more so to primitive man. At Les Trois Frères the medicine man, wearing antler horns and the tail of a horse, stood in the natural "pulpit" which can still be seen. All round the walls are paintings of animals in movement. He may have intoned a ritual spell in a monotonous, trance-inducing voice, and then, after ritually "killing" the pictures with his spear, suggested to the worshipers that next day's search for game would be successful, or that they must travel even further in search of their prey. Thus the excess of emotion and strain was canalized and released. It was necessary, in those days as in ours, to have people who could control the emotional and spiritual side of humanity.

Having read these notes I then remembered something else which Dr. Sargant had said to me; that he believed primitive tribes induce, by exciting drumming and dancing, intense emotional states which may end in partial collapse—and this I have seen myself in Haiti and Trinidad.

Having checked that Burkitt and Sargant have never met or exchanged ideas, I am more than ever impressed by Burkitt's qualities of imaginative reasoning. Like Petrie and other great archaeologists he looks for facts, but he brings imagination to the interpretation of those facts. Those who wish to become archaeologists might well ponder on this.

Undoubtedly the most glorious cave paintings known in the world are those at Lascaux, in France, and these were discovered as recently as 1940. On the morning of September 12 of that year, when France was partly occupied by the Germans, and British and Allied pilots were fighting the Luftwaffe over the English Channel, a party of boys from the district of Montignac were out hunting. Their names were Ravidat, Marsal, Queroy, Coencas, and Estreguil. There was also a dog, named Robot, who is the most important individual in the story.

To the south of Montignac there is a hill called Lascaux and here the boys wandered about with their guns and their dog. On the ridge of the hill was a place where, twenty years earlier, a tall pine tree had been blown down in a storm, leaving a hole where its roots had been. Twelve years before the boys arrived, a donkey had stumbled into the hole, broken its legs, and died. This time Robot went down the hole, and after frantic searching, calling, and whistling, the boys stood around the dark, narrow aperture, listening to the muffled barks of Robot from the depths below. Ravidat, whose dog it was, decided to try to rescue Robot, and after widening the hole sufficiently to allow him to slip through, he descended, followed by the others.

Twenty-five feet down they found themselves in a dark, damp cave. Robot came up, licking his master. Then the lads lit candles and looked around them. On every side, gleaming on the damp rocky walls, were painted vividly colored animals. They were bulls, the largest being seventeen feet long. Groping through narrow passage, candles in hand, the boys came upon more painted caves. In one there was a frieze of stags' heads and a pair of male bison, tail to tail. In yet another cavern was a frieze of little horses over which a cow appeared to be jumping. And there was a deep pit, at the bottom of which was a picture of a bison with lowered head, transfixed by a spear. In front of the animal a roughly drawn man with a head like a bird was falling backward. Nearby was a picture of a rhinoceros.

Robot had discovered the best-preserved example of paleolithic cave art in the world. Unlike most other caves, those at Lascaux were not clogged with earth and rock. They, and the paintings, are as clean as on the day the ancient artists left them some fifteen thousand years ago. By some happy chance the original entrance had become blocked and this sealing-off of the air, plus the fact that the caves are so far below ground as to be unaffected by frosts and changes of temperature, had left them intact.

In eastern Spain there are other paleolithic paintings of a somewhat later date, about eight to ten thousand years ago. These are painted in rock shelters, not in caves. They are mainly lively hunting scenes, in which not only animals but men appear, although the animals are still carefully drawn whereas the human beings are mere caricatures. At this period no one seemed to think that man was sufficiently interesting or important to draw in detail. All we see are "pin men" firing arrows at their prey, and also occasionally at each other—the earliest known representations of men fighting each other with weapons. No doubt there were tribal quarrels over hunting and fishing rights, the embryonic form of large-scale warfare. The fact that these men were archers, not spearmen, indicates a further advance in technique. The bow was one of the first machines, as distinct from tools. With it men could kill at a distance.

At the end of the Upper Paleolithic period, when the northern icecaps had retreated and the climate of Europe became warm again, a period began which prehistorians call Mesolithic or Middle Stone Age. Forests and lakes appeared, many animals moved northward, and those men who remained behind had to adapt themselves to a different kind of life. We know, from excavations, that many of these men lived on the swampy ground beside great lakes or at the edge of the sea. They lived partly by fishing, partly by hunting. They still made and used stone tools, of course, and wooden ones too. They could make dug-out canoes, and they fished with both nets and hooks. They also tamed and used a domestic animal—the dog.

There are no cave paintings or cave shelters to prove this. The evidence we possess has been dug out of bogs in Denmark and eastern England. Later we shall describe how one of these sites— Star Carr in Yorkshire, England—was discovered and excavated by modern archaeological methods. But for the fantastic advance in archaeological technique since the days of Layard, Maspero, and Petrie such sites would not have been recognized, let alone excavated and interpreted.

And now we come to the most revolutionary advance in the history of the human race. As stated earlier, the progress of man throughout the length and breadth of our planet has not been uniform. For example, at the time when the Egyptians were building their pyramids and the Sumerians their ziggurats, and when both peoples had learned the art of writing, the rest of humanity was illiterate and few members of it were capable of making permanent buildings. A thousand years after the peoples of the Nile, Tigris, and Euphrates valleys had learned the art of metal working in copper and bronze, the inhabitants of Western Europe, including Britain, were still using mainly stone implements. In the Americas, as recently as the sixteenth century A.D., the Aztecs, who had inherited a high civilization, faced their Spanish enemies with wooden swords inset with flint blades. Even at the present day the aborigines of Australia and the bushmen of South Africa are still living in the Stone Age.

Yet, at a time when the Upper Paleolithic inhabitants of northern Spain, despite their newfangled bows and arrows and fishhooks, were living much as their ancestors had lived for some half-million years—by hunting wild game—there were other people in western Asia who had already learned—or were beginning to learn—to grow crops, to domesticate animals, and free themselves for the first time of the compulsion to travel incessantly in search of their food.

These people—we still have no idea where they came from—introduced what archaeologists call the Neolithic (New Stone Age) some 10,000 years B.C. They were the first farmers. They still used stone tools but of greatly improved design and workmanship. Any amateur, after a short period of study, can distinguish between a paleolithic and a neolithic tool. But they were of the same basic human stock, neither more nor less intelligent than the rest. Why was it then that certain members of the Homo sapiens family, living somewhere between the Syrian desert and the mountains of Afghanistan, leaped ahead of all the rest?

The obvious answer seems to be "an accident of climate and geography," but no one can be quite certain. Geologists tell us that during the last Ice Age—when the ice sheets were spread over northern Europe, America, and Asia—the climate of central Europe was intensely cold, that of southern Europe less so, while to the south what are now Egypt and the Sahara desert enjoyed a temperate climate. It is difficult to imagine the Sahara desert and the Nile Valley blooming with verdure, but geological evidence proves that this was so.

Then, as the northern icecaps retreated, the climatic conditions of North Africa, western Asia, and Europe changed. What had been forest, steppe, or tundra began to dry out, and animals accustomed to such conditions began to migrate northward, followed by Homo sapiens. Europe became a temperate zone, as it is today, whereas Egypt, Syria, and Mesopotamia became virtually deserts. Under such conditions both animals and men would tend to congregate around the main water supplies, rivers, and oases.

So those members of the human race who remained behind would be forced to live near each other, and the wild animals would congregate near their camps. Eventually (according to the late Gordon Childe) man (or more likely woman) tamed and domesticated certain of the animals, such as wild cattle, sheep, goats, and asses. These became, in Childe's words, "living larders and walking wardrobes." The cows and goats provided milk and flesh, the sheep produced wool (hence the invention of weaving), and the asses both milk and transport. The wild horse was not domesticated until thousands of years later.

At about the same time a much more important development took place—the invention of agriculture. Nowadays we are so accustomed to seeing farms with fields of wheat and barley and vegetables, and orchards laden with fruit, that we take them for granted. But in the history of the human race these have existed for only a minute fraction of the time during which man has walked the earth. As far as we can tell, farming was invented somewhere in the Middle East. Ingenious theories have been advanced to account for its introduction. Some authorities have suggested that neolithic man used to supplement his scanty food ration by gathering wild grasses, and that one day, returning to a camping site, he noticed that the surplus grain he had thrown away had germinated in his absence. Then it would occur to him that if he planted the seeds of wild grasses they would grow again each season; then there would be no need to travel in search of them.

This may well be true. The discovery of agriculture, like the discovery that one could make fire, may have been an accident.

But once the lesson was learned, man's retentive, reflecting brain could transmit the information to his successors, which mere animals could not. The upshot of these discoveries—the domestication of certain animals and the planting, growing, and reaping of grain—set man's feet on the path to civilization, which can occur only when a sufficient number of people can live permanently in one spot. Hence, in time, would arise settled communities, kings, and chief priests, a social system more elaborate and complex than that of the tribe.

Then would follow another important development. A wandering hunting community could not afford to employ specialists. The shortage of food was such that every man was expected to play his part. A man might be a hunter, a skin dresser, and a toolmaker at the same time. But once there was a sufficiency of surplus wealth—in the form of food and clothing—then it was possible to support specialists, such as artists, craftsmen, architects, scribes, poets, and priests. And thus it was that the earliest civilizations grew up in Sumer and Egypt, and nowhere else. But the technical inventions which made these developments possible came from elsewhere; just where we do not yet know, except that it was in western Asia.

Childe calls this development the "Urban Revolution," the period of the first cities. Yet even when the Ancient Egyptians, Sumerians, and Babylonians built their first cities, they inherited beliefs which stemmed from their far-off, hunting ancestors. Prehistorians have proved beyond doubt that there is a continuous thread binding paleolithic man with the mature, metal-using, civilizations of Mesopotamia, Egypt, Crete, and elsewhere.

THE
NEW WORLD

Archaeology
in the Americas

Now we must consider the archaeological discoveries in North, Central, and South America. This subject must be dealt with separately because, apart from the late prehistoric period, about twelve thousand years ago, there were hardly any links between the cultures of what are now called the Old and New Worlds until the time of Columbus. Geologically, of course, the American continent is as old as those of Europe, Africa, and Asia. Similar types of plant and animal life were in existence millions of years ago, long before the evolution of man, and it is obvious that the continents of the two hemispheres must have been joined; there is also clear geological evidence of this fact.

There is, however, no evidence that species of sub-hominids or man-apes evolved in America as they did in Africa and Asia; and as for our ancestor Homo sapiens, there appears to be no reason why, in theory, he could not have crossed over to North America via the Bering Strait during either of the last two warm interglacial periods of the Ice Age. But all the evidence collected to date suggests that the first men to enter America arrived *after* the final retreat of the icecaps. The date has been variously estimated at between 12,000 and 10,000 B.C., long after the date of the Lascaux Caves and some time before the hunting scenes in the rock shelters of northern Spain. It is essential to bear in mind that long before this period, Homo sapiens, though of one species, had split up into differing racial groups with widely varying physical characteristics. Some of his skulls found in Europe resemble those of modern Europeans. On the other hand at Monaco in southern France skulls have been found which look Negroid.

The first men to enter America were of Mongoloid stock, like the Chinese, the Malays, and some East Russian people of the present day. The descendants of these first Americans and those who followed them in successive migrations are the Indians of North, Central, and South America. Their resemblance to the modern inhabitants of southeast Asia are obvious: high cheekbones and sometimes slanting eyes. Their yellow or yellowishbrown coloring is another indication. Nevertheless they are of the same basic species as the European-descended Americans, and indeed of every inhabitant of our planet.

Once arrived, however, they began to differentiate again; there is a distinct difference between the North American Indians and those of South America, just as in Europe there is an obvious physical difference between the inhabitants of Scandinavia and those of Spain, Italy, and southern France. But in biological terms we are speaking only of yesterday. These physiological differences are superficial, probably produced by climate and environment; among all races the structure of the body, and the average brain capacity, are the same.

As in Europe, Egypt, and Asia, much of American archaeological research has been concentrated on civilized epochs, such as those of the Aztecs, the Mayas, and the Incas. Before we go on to examine these, it is worth pondering on the fact that there were human beings in America at least ten thousand years before the earliest American civilizations were born, and that these people brought with them the cultural traditions, the religious (or magical) beliefs, and the technical skills—such as toolmaking—inherited from their paleolithic ancestors who had been wandering over Europe, Africa, and Asia for some 400,000 years. Bearing this fact in mind, we shall not fall into the trap of thinking that superficial resemblances between, say, the Mayas and the Ancient Egyptians were due to direct contact.

Let us see what some of these resemblances were. The Mayas and the Aztecs built pyramids. So did the Ancient Egyptians. The Ancient Egyptians and Sumerians worshiped a sun god. So did the Aztecs, the Mayas, and the Incas. Both the Ancient Egyptians and the Minoans of Crete worshiped a snake deity. So did the Aztecs. The Ancient Egyptians had a calendar, as had the Mayas. The Incas of Peru erected great buildings from stone monoliths weighing many tons. So did the Mycenaeans and the Egyptians.

These are not the only parallels; the peoples of the ancient East and of America buried their important dead in well-built tombs and accompanied them with offerings. Faced with such an impressive assembly of facts, people whose imaginations cannot stretch beyond an obvious (though false) explanation, have been tempted to say that there must have been some direct contact between peoples separated not only by some ten thousand miles of land and sea, but by scores of centuries. More than four thousand years separate the builders of the Egyptian and Aztec pyramids. As for sun worship, snake worship, and monumental stone building, these practices have existed, and some still exist, among many of the earth's peoples.

The reason I have attacked this completely untenable theory is that not only is it false but that it diminishes the wonder of these great Amerindian civilizations, the earliest of which began only a few centuries before the birth of Christ, and the latest of which was contemporary with the European Middle Ages. The comparative lateness in the time scale does not matter at all. What is absorbing is that here we find human beings separated by vast distances of time and space, who nevertheless developed along broadly similar lines.

There were great differences, of course. The Sumerians had the wheel before 2700 B.C.; the Egyptians had it by 1500 B.C. The Mayas never had it at all. The Egyptians, Hittites, and Mycenaeans had the horse and chariot in 1500 B.C. The Amerindians of Mexico never saw a horse until three thousand years later. The civilizations of the ancient East had bronze weapons before 2500 B.C. The Aztecs, four thousand years later, fought the Spaniards with wooden swords although metalworking was known. The Mayas had an elaborate calendar superior to that of Ancient Egypt, and both civilizations could measure and predict the course of the sun, moon, and stars. But whereas the Egyptians had an accurate system of weights and measurements which they applied to their commercial transactions, the Maya peasant could not even weigh a sackful of his corn.

Yet all these civilizations had sun gods, earth gods, grain gods, animal gods, and moon deities. All labored to build temples which, as dwellings of the gods, were more important than those of human beings. All were dominated, at various times, by priests or priest-kings. All practiced animal sacrifice and some human sacrifice. All drew their wealth from the tillers of the soil and used that wealth mainly for the building and adornment of temples or the earthly dwellings of their great men and women. All knew the art of war and possessed drilled, disciplined armies for attack or defense. With a few exceptions, such as the horse and chariot, all made and used the same types of weapon: the sword, the shield, the spear, the bow, and the club.

To explain these similarities between civilizations which could never have been in contact, it has been suggested that all human beings, faced with the same problems, tend to solve them in the same way, which is broadly true. But I think the matter goes much deeper than that, and this is where prehistory comes in. We now know that more than fifty thousand years ago human beings were burying their dead with ceremony and in a way which suggests a belief in an afterlife. If they were capable of this they must also have pondered on the mysterious forces—sun, rain and storm, the earth itself, and the superhuman powers of the animals they hunted—the swiftness of the reindeer, the size and strength of the mammoth and the bison, the bird with its power of flight, the snake with its secret, furtive life. We know too that at least twenty thousand years ago and probably earlier, men assembled in cave sanctuaries to carry out ceremonial acts of magic.

These human creatures, whom we would no doubt regard as savages, already carried in their minds, and could transmit through their tongues, technical knowledge, traditional lore, social and religious customs, ideas about the meaning of life, death, and the significance of what we call "natural forces" more than sufficient for their remote descendants to create a civilization. Some accomplishments they would have to learn for themselves, such as agriculture, pottery-making, and eventually metalworking. But I see nothing surprising in the fact that when, after some nine or ten thousand years, some of their descendants created civilizations, they would express similar religious conceptions whether they had settled in America or Asia, Egypt, and southeastern Europe.

As with the earliest civilizations of the Old World, so with those of the New; they followed on the invention and development of farming which made permanent settlement possible. By contrast the North American Indians of the Western plains lived by hunting the buffalo (descendant of the ancient bison) while others, for example, those of the North Pacific coast, lived by fishing, gathering edible wild plants, and by hunting such animals as the deer and otter. Sometimes these peoples were able to encamp for a while at hunting or salmon-fishing grounds, but essentially they were all wanderers. But they had elaborate religious rituals presided over by shamans (magicians); some were sun worshipers and they believed in good and evil spirits.

Spread over large areas of what are now Canada, the United States, Central and South America, were thousands of these primitive tribes, differing widely in customs, from the inhabitants of the North American plains to those of the Andean mountains and the Amazonian jungles. But all were descended from the same basic stock which began to enter America from Asia some twelve thousand years ago. It has been argued that some might have made the sea-crossing to South America from the Pacific Islands during much more recent times, but few archaeologists and anthropologists accept this theory. Until much more positive evidence is forthcoming it is wisest to assume that all pre-Columbian Americans—those who were in the Americas before Columbus—

were descended from those tribes who crossed the Bering Strait.

Traces of these Stone Age primitives have been found at several places, notably in southeast Wyoming, southwest Nebraska, eastern New Mexico, and western Texas. They made beautifully fashioned flint implements, of which the most typical is the Folsom Point, a thin pressure-flaked blade probably used as a spearhead but small enough for use with a bow. They get their name from a place called Folsom in New Mexico, where they were found with the bones of extinct animals, and they have been dated by what is called the Varve method (to be discussed later) to between ten and twelve thousand years ago. But so far no human remains of this period have been discovered in America. This does not mean that they didn't exist. Stone Age men were few in numbers, and the accidental preservation of their bones is a rare miracle. Some day, somewhere, someone may find the bones of these first Americans; that discoverer could be you!

To return to the invention of agriculture and the rise of the great American civilizations; the earliest of these developed in what are now Peru and Bolivia. It is named Inca after the tribal aristocracy which ruled it before the coming of the Spaniards. Inca simply means "king" or "ruler." Using modern techniques, archaeologists have traced how it developed over many centuries until one powerful tribe successively overcame its neighbors and founded a great empire which the Spaniards discovered and overthrew in the sixteenth century A.D. But as in Egypt and Mesopotamia, we will try to show how first explorers and then archaeologists penetrated by degrees from the historical to the prehistoric periods, and begin with the Inca civilization in its full maturity.

The Spanish conquistadores under their leader Pizarro were the first Europeans to see it. They of course were not archaeologists but adventurers looking for gold, and not overscrupulous in their methods of acquiring it. But in the wake of their conquest came priests who, while their main concern was converting the heathen to Roman Catholicism, were sufficiently interested to study and record the customs and history of the Incas before their civilization perished. As the Incas themselves had no writing system of their own, we owe much of our knowledge either to Spaniards such as Don Diego Rodriguez de Figueroa, Father de Lancha, Friar Diego and Friar Marcos, and Pedro Sancho (one of Pizarro's secretaries); or to Incas of royal or noble birth who learned Spanish and dictated what they knew of their country's history to Spanish secretaries. These are the only written records we have of one of the greatest civilizations known to have existed. Beyond these the archaeologists who later began to investigate this civilization had nothing to guide them; no hieroglyphs, no cuneiform, nothing but the remains of Inca settlements and the objects the Incas made and used.

From these writings we know that at the height of their power the Incas ruled not only Peru, but also territory extending over what is now Bolivia and Ecuador. The principal city was Cuzco, where you can still see remains of magnificent Inca masonry; huge blocks of stone weighing many tons have been fitted together with an accuracy which would not have shamed the Ancient Egyptian pyramid builders, and there can be no higher praise than that. From Cuzco thousands of miles of roads linked the capital with other Inca cities such as Vitcos and Vilcabamba, high up in the Andes. Since the Incas had no wheeled vehicles, the roads had only to be the width of a man. Sometimes they passed through tunnels, and when a river had to be crossed huge suspension bridges were made from ropes of twisted lianas —woody vines which grow in the Peruvian jungles.

One Spanish traveler in 1548 wrote of these roads:

I believe since the history of man, there has been no other account of such grandeur as is to be seen on this road which passes over deep valleys and lofty mountains, by snowy heights, over walls of water, through the living rock and along the edges of tortuous torrents. In all these places, the road is well constructed, on the inclining mountains well terraced, through the living rock cut along the riverbanks supported by retaining walls, in the snowy heights built with steps and resting places, and along its entire length swept cleanly and cleared of debris— with post stations and storehouses and Temples of the Sun at appointed intervals along its length.

I have emphasized the Inca road system because, apart from that of the Roman Empire, there is nothing like it on earth. To the Egyptians and the Mesopotamians, roads were less important than the river which provided the main means of travel and transport. Fragments of Mycenaean and ancient Cretan roads have been found but are not extraordinary. None of these peoples had to face the difficulties of building roads over terrain which ranged from hot, fetid jungles to an Alpine landscape of glaciers, and mountains over twenty thousand feet high. Nor did they have to bridge roaring, torrential rivers hundreds of feet wide. Like the Romans of Imperial times, the Incas had to control a diversity of peoples throughout their empire. Having once conquered these peoples the only way to control and unify them was by establishing permanent communications. Without their engineering skill the Incas could not have created a civilization and an empire.

The Inca Empire resembled that of Rome in one other way. Whereas many ancient peoples, when they conquered territory merely looted it, carried off prisioners, and then levied tribute, the Romans absorbed them into their own system and gave them the benefits of their own civilization. So did the Incas. From what we can learn from the Spanish and Inca writers, the Inca Empire at its highest development was despotic but benevolent.

No one was hungry or homeless. The idea of individual property—each man having a bit of land which he called his own—was unknown. Land was held in common, though each inhabitant had his own allotment. When he had children his allotment was increased but food was distributed in such a way that—in theory at least—no individual had more than anyone else. Since property was communally owned, theft was hardly known; the Inca peoples had no locks on their doors. Yet this system could be imposed only by strong laws and regulations backed up by force. The Inca rulers were evidently realists; they did not believe that all men, left to themselves in a condition of equality, would wish to remain so. There were regulations governing every aspect of life, and multitudes of officials, among whom the senior ranks did not have to pay taxes.

But nearly everyone was taxed in one way or another. The farmer gave up some of his produce to the government; others paid tribute in the form of labor, on the roads and other public works, and in the mines. Those with special skills, such as metalworkers and tapestry weavers, paid tribute by employing their skill in the service of the state. Then there were the runners posted along the imperial roads to carry messages by relay, and at great speed. Although they had no system of writing, the Incas had what they called *quipus,* a system of knotted strings in which the arrangement and positioning of the knots conveyed a message. These *quipus* were carried by the runners. Not that they carried only messages. There is a story that fish caught in the Pacific were carried across the mountains to arrive at the royal table in Cuzco, still fresh enough to be eaten.

Apart from human beings, the only means of land transport were the llama and the alpaca (an Inca word which survives as the name of a cloth). Beautiful garments and tapestries were woven from the wool of the alpaca, but apart from these (which they bred from the native American camel, the guanaco), and the guinea pig and the dog, they had no other domestic animals; no cattle, no sheep or goats, none of the animals bred by the prehistoric ancestors of the Egyptians and Sumerians. But they were superb agriculturalists.

Over a period of perhaps two thousand years, long before the coming of the Spaniards, long before the time of the first Inca rulers, the tribes of this area of South America had done, independently, what the neolithic ancestors of the Middle Eastern peoples had done: taken native wild plants and bred domestic crops from them. From the wild potato, which still grows in the Andes and has tubers the size of a pea, they bred twelve varieties of the potato we know today. They did the same with tomatoes, beans, cassava, corn, and many other plants. Unlike the Ancient Egyptians and the peoples of Mesopotamia, the Incas had no slow-moving, mud-bearing rivers, the annual flooding of which would refertilize their soil. Undeterred by their mountainous land with its few plains, they built artificial terraces to hold back the soil, and fertilized them artificially.

Without the inventiveness, skill, and labor of these unknown generations of Indian farmers, the Inca civilization could not have come into existence; the same is true of the other Amerindian civilizations, and indeed of all civilized societies.

The Incas mined gold and silver which their craftsmen fashioned into lovely objects which were stored in the royal treasure house. A Spanish traveler, Hernando de Soto, wrote of his first sight of their principal city Cuzco: "Cuzco, grand and stately, must have been built by people of great intelligence. The city is certainly the richest of which we have any knowledge in all the Indies . . . Neither gold nor silver, they tell me, can be taken out of here on the pain of death, and there are many goldsmiths here and workers in silver."

It was this gold, of course, which had lured the Spaniards to Peru, and as de Soto was carried around the streets of Cuzco in a gold-plated litter, he was already making a military estimate of its defenses and communications, noting, for instance, "the four roads which led to all parts of the empire." As is well-known, Spanish gold lust led to the conquest of Peru in a campaign during which a combination of armed violence and treachery (for at first the Incas welcomed the Spaniards) brought the Inca civilization to an end.

This tragic and painful story has no place in this book except in one respect. From the writings of the Spaniards and in particular of a certain Captain Garcia who pursued and captured the last Inca king, Tupac Amaru, we know that when the last Inca rulers realized they had been betrayed, they fled to their other fortified cities high up in the Andes mountains. If they had stayed there and cut their bridges they might have resisted the Spaniards far longer, but Tupac Amaru was induced to leave his fortress at Vilcabamba and was eventually captured deep in the Amazon jungles to which he and a few faithful followers had fled.

But there is no record in these chronicles of the Spanish army ever having found Vilcabamba, though two missionary friars, guided by the Incas, appear to have been allowed as far as its gates. Had the Spaniards, or indeed *any* European, ever seen this mysterious mountain fortress? It seemed doubtful; and it was this mystery which led the distinguished American explorer Hiram Bingham, accompanied by Professor Isaiah Bowman, geologist and geographer; Professor Harry W. Foote, naturalist; Dr. William G. Erving, surgeon; Kai Hendrikson, topographer; H. L. Tucker, engineer; and Paul B. Lanius, to mount an expedition in the hope of finding it. This was in the year 1911.

Bingham was not, in the strict sense, an archaeologist, but neither were the explorers who had preceded him in the area—men such as Castelnau, Marcou, Squier, and Raimondi. As long ago as 1834 the Count de Sartiges had made an adventurous journey through the Andes, and both he and Raimondi, who traveled there in 1865, had left descriptive accounts and the latter a map which was of great assistance to Bingham (since much of the territory he was to explore was literally "off the map"). The history of archaeology in Central and South America has been molded by the fact that many of the more important archaeological sites were buried in jungles or hidden in high mountains. Therefore the scientific explorer—botanist, naturalist, geologist—has usually come before the professional archaeologist. Another scholar whose writings stimulated archaeological exploration was Sir Clements Markham who not only traveled widely in Peru but wrote a history of the country and translated some of the most important Spanish chronicles relating to it.

Bingham had soaked his mind in these chronicles and carried them with him on his travels. Those who wish to read his story in full detail should consult his *Lost City of the Incas*. I know of no more gripping and romantic true story of discovery. At first he was unsuccessful; the clues in the writings were so vague that he was sometimes led along false trails. In his search for Vilcabamba he examined a mountain fortress called Choqquequirau, in the upper valley of the river Apurimac, an Indian word meaning "Great Speaker." To reach the fortress Bingham had to cross a suspension bridge 270 feet long and three feet wide, slung across the "Great Speaker," the roar of whose rapids is so powerful as to drown all speech. Bingham dryly comments, "No one bothers to learn to swim in the Andes."

Unsatisfied that the fortress was indeed Vilcabamba, he decided that "the chronicles contained enough evidence to show that the last Inca capital was not at Choqquequirau but probably over the ranges in the region where I had seen snow-capped peaks." He and his colleagues traveled down the valley of the Urubamba River, looking for "a great white rock over a spring of water" as described by one of the Spanish chroniclers. He found Inca terraces, towns, and forts; he questioned people in villages and isolated farms, he consulted again and again the descriptions left by Raimondi and other explorers, and eventually, after repeated disappointments succeeded in identifying at least one Inca city, Vitcos, which had been described by a Spaniard named Ocampo. The description fitted the site, and Bingham's heart rose again.

But still there was Vilcabamba, of which no description existed, since no Spaniard had ever been inside it. The account by Father Calancha of the two friars who had reached its gates was of little value, since they suffered much on the circuitous and painful route which the Incas made them take, and were in no state to describe it, even had they been interested. Eventually Bingham and his colleagues returned to the great canyon of the Urubamba. At a place called Maquina they came on "a little open plain called Mandor Pampa. Except where the rapids roared past it, gigantic precipices hemmed it in on all sides." Near this place a local Indian mentioned that there were some fine ruins not far away. "Where?" asked the explorers. "On top of that mountain opposite," came the reply.

"That mountain" was of formidable height and could be approached only up slopes so steep that in Bingham's words:

A good part of the distance we went on all fours, sometimes holding on by our fingernails. Here and there a primitive ladder made from the roughly notched trunk of a small tree was placed in such a way as to help one over what might otherwise have proved to be an impassable cliff. In another place the slope was covered with slippery grass where it was hard to find handholds or footholds. . . . The humidity was great. We were in the belt of maximum precipitation in Eastern Peru. The heat was excessive, and I was not in training!

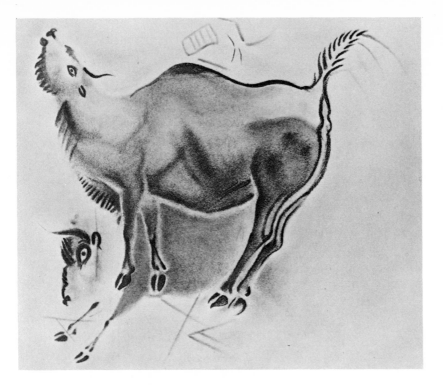

Paintings found in the caves at Altamira. These drawings are from Abbé Breuil's book The Caves of Altamira.

A cave painting at Lascaux

Machu Picchu, in Peru

*Inca art. The group in silver (above) may represent a funeral procession.
The bib, or collar, is made of shell and stone beads; the alpaca is silver.*

The Aztec Calendar Stone

Aztec sacrificial knives;
(below) The Temple of Quetzalcoatl at Teotihuacán, Mexico

*Typical Mayan decoration. This is a detail of the north side
of the Palace of the Nuns at Uxmal, Yucatán*

Two thousand feet above the foaming river, Bingham, who was accompanied only by the Peruvian Arteaga, and an Army sergeant named Carrasco, came upon terraces which he recognized as being of Inca date. Here two Indians, Richarte and Alvarez, greeted them. They were farmers who had begun to cultivate the terraces again.

> They said there were two paths to the outside world. Of one we had already had a taste; the other was "even more difficult," a perilous path down the face of a rocky precipice on the other side of the ridge. . . . Tremendous green precipices fell away to the white rapids of the Urubamba below. Immediately in front, on the north side of the valley, was a great granite cliff rising 2,000 feet sheer. . . . Beyond them cloud-capped snow-covered mountains rose thousands of feet above us.

He stumbled on, following the Indians up the slope, scrambling through thickets of bamboo until, quite suddenly he found himself among mighty buildings of hewn stone; there was a semicircular building the outer wall of which reminded him of the Inca "Temple of the Sun" at Cuzco. Bingham lingered, swaying with the fatigue of his climb, staring fascinatedly at this building which in his own words "surpassed in attractiveness the best Inca walls in Cuzco, which had caused visitors to marvel for four centuries. . . . It fairly took my breath away." But the Indians were calling, "Come up higher, Señor! This is nothing!"

They led him to a huge granite stairway which ascended to two buildings of shining white stone, of which the larger blocks must each have weighed from ten to fifteen tons. Each block, higher than a man, was beautifully fitted to its neighbor. These buildings were temples, each with only three walls, the fourth side having been left open. Nor had they even been roofed, as if to welcome the sun. Within one were niches which had been made to receive the mummies of dead Incas. Then came a spacious stone-paved courtyard, on the eastern side of which was what appeared to be another temple containing three great windows looking out over the canyon to the rising sun.

The discoverer writes, "Nothing like them in design and execution has ever been found. . . . This was clearly a ceremonial edifice of peculiar significance." And then he remembered having read that a Peruvian chronicler named Salcamayhua, writing in 1620, had stated that the First Inca, Manco I, had "ordered works to be executed at the place of his birth, *consisting of a masonry wall with three windows.*" The First Inca had reigned at about 1000 A. D., five centuries before the Spaniards arrived in Peru.

Bingham then had to return to the United States, but he went back to Peru in the following year, 1912, and formed an expedition to survey and excavate these ruins, most of which were smothered in a hardwood forest. As more and more splendid buildings were revealed, the hundred stone stairways leading from terrace to terrace, the stone conduits which led water under the city wall to a series of stone reservoirs, more and more temples, houses, remains of garden plots, a sacred plaza flanked by two of the largest temples, the archaeologists realized that they were uncovering one of the wonders of the world. They worked with a sense of dedicated purpose, high up on the rocky crest called Machu Picchu, where the roar of the Urubamba could still be faintly heard.

They found cemeteries in caves on the rocky slopes; within each tomb skeletons lay on the floor where they had fallen when the mummy wrappings decayed. Near them lay bone and sometimes bronze implements, together with some pottery. The tombs had not been robbed, although some had been disturbed by jaguars and bears. In another cemetery skeletons of fifty women were found. These were almost certainly the Virgins of the Sun mentioned in the ancient chronicles; they lived in buildings which might be compared with nunneries, and were always associated with the worship of the sun god. Probably some of the marvelous woven and embroidered cloths for which the Incas were famous came from their hands.

Bingham believed that he had discovered the home of the First Inca, but it was not until later that he realized that it could well have been the final sanctuary of the last. There is now little doubt that this was Vilcabamba and that it was chosen as the last refuge of the Inca Tupac Amaru because of its inaccessibility and the strength of its defenses. You may disregard the fact that an American explorer who admits he was "out of condition" could climb up to it from the valley of the Urubamba. It might still have remained undiscovered (unless observed from an airplane) if a road had not been made along one side of the river, not long before Bingham made his discovery. Before that road was made it would have been quite impossible to approach Vilcabamba from that side, which was defended by the rapids of the Urubamba and the precipitous heights above it. They protect the city on three sides. The fourth side could only be approached along a razorlike spur, the eastern edge of which is impassable, and on the western edge there is a mere footpath clinging to the side of a precipice. A few score men could hold it against an army, as the Greeks checked the Persians at Thermopylae.

With what cunning the Incas chose this site! And with what labor must they have quarried and transported the huge stones with which they built their city! Within its walls they had everything they needed; there were terraces on which they grew their crops, and an ample water supply, though here lay one weakness; there seem to have been no springs within Vilcabamba and the water had to be brought in conduits from a mile away. Was this why the Incas chose to desert their impregnable fortress?

Finally one might ask why it was that this city, built possibly about 1000 A.D., was never seen by a white man until nearly five hundred years after the Spanish conquest? One reason was supplied by Alfred H. Bumstead, chief topographer to the expedition. He wrote, "Our surveys opened an unexplored region, *1,500 square miles in extent,* whose very existence had not been guessed before 1911. It proved to be one of the largest undescribed glaciated regions in South America. Yet it is less than a hundred miles from Cuzco . . ."

And Bingham explains that

this ridge is in the most inaccessible corner of the most inaccessible section of the central Andes. No part of the highlands of Peru is better defended by natural bulwarks—a stupendous canyon whose rock is granite, and whose precipices are frequently a thousand feet sheer, presenting difficulties which daunt the most ambitious of modern mountain climbers. Yet here, in a remote part of the canyon, on this narrow ridge flanked by tremendous precipices, a highly civilized people, artistic, inventive, well organized . . . at some time in the distant past built themselves a sanctuary for the worship of the sun.

The People
Before the Incas

Pure archaeologists who had been trained in stratigraphy, the evolution of pottery styles, and the interpretation of artifacts were naturally interested in finding out how the Inca civilization had originated. All its elements existed long before the conquering Incas arrived. What could be discovered concerning the diverse tribes who had settled in Peru, Ecuador, and Bolivia centuries before the Incas became dominant? What kind of life had been created by such peoples as the Aymaras and the Chimus before the Incas? Their history, if it could be known, would depend mainly on the digging out of unexciting sites and the examination of pottery, tools, weapons, and grave goods. How far back did the pottery go? When was metalworking invented? When was agriculture introduced? Like the archaeology of Egypt and the Middle East, that of America has proceeded from the latest manifestations of civilization to its beginnings.

Obviously one of the first steps was to establish some kind of chronology for the pre-Inca period. A German scholar named Max Uhle began this in the 1890's and conducted a long series of excavations. After his death A. L. Kroeber worked over Uhle's notes at the University of California and published accounts of the collections he had made from various "digs." Then, in 1925 and 1926, Kroeber himself dug in Peru, sponsored by the Field Museum at Chicago, and an Ecuadorian archaeologist Jacinto Jijon y Caamano, excavated sites near Lima. Another great pioneer of Peruvian archaeology was Julio C. Tello, who from 1913 onward explored some of the remotest places and excavated widely and indefatigably.

As a result of the work of these and other men we can now say, with some confidence, that the first people to settle in Peru were a hunting folk, classified as the Early Hunters. Then came the Early Farmers who dwelled along the coast, and lived by fishing, gathering wild plants, and by primitive agriculture. The invention of agriculture in Peru has been dated approximately to about 3000 B.C.; the Early Hunters, descendants of those Stone Age immigrants who crossed over from Asia via the Bering Strait some twelve thousand years ago, have been roughly dated to between 3000 and 7000 B.C.

At Huancayo, in the central highlands of Peru, rock shelters have been found containing flaked stone "points" such as blades and scrapers. There is no pottery with these deposits, although plenty in the surrounding region. Archaeologists therefore suggest that these may be relics of the earliest men to reach Peru. Other Early Hunter sites have been found near the coast and doubtless more will be discovered. The Early Farmers seem to have been a different kind of people. Their relics have been found near the coast and we know about them through the mounds of debris they left near the sites of their homes. Modern Peruvian grave robbers, looking for ancient pots to sell to antiquity dealers, have left these middens alone since they hardly ever contain pottery; this has been beneficial to archaeologists. From the contents of the middens it is clear that the Early Farmers (or Early Gardeners as Bushnell prefers to call them) lived principally by fishing and collecting shell fish. They used seine nets with floats and sinkers, and among the shellfish were deep-water mussels.

These people also gathered wild plants, some of which, such as beans, gourds, squash, and chili peppers, were cultivated. They also used cotton, which may or may not have been cultivated. But they did not hunt on land, since no hunting weapons or land-animal bones have been discovered. As much of the material found was organic, that is had once been alive, it was possible to apply the radiocarbon or carbon-14 method of dating, and this has yielded an earliest date of about 2500 B.C.

At higher levels primitive handmade pottery has been found which has been dated to 1200 B.C. Before that the Early Farmers cooked by roasting on hot stones, or by putting hot stones in gourds and boiling the water. They lived in pit-dwellings roofed with mud and stones resting on wooden beams of pieces of whale-bone. These dwellings have been found intact within one of the middens, that of the Huaca Prieta, when excavated by Junius Bird, who also found graves in it. The Early Farmers also put a few simple offerings beside their dead, suggesting a belief in an afterlife.

Like Petrie's discovery of the pit-graves of the predynastic Egyptians, the finding of this forty-foot-high mound, containing so many material relics of Americans who had died nearly five thousand years ago, was as exciting in its own way as the discovery of great stone monuments. Yet of the millions who must know about the Inca cities of historical times, how many have heard of Huaca Prieta? It even contained such fragile objects as fishing nets, fabrics made from cotton and fiber, and fragments of dyed cloth which may have been parts of shawls. These perishable stuffs had been preserved by the dry climate and the lack of ground water.

There is no space here to give a detailed account of the successive periods which mark the growth of Andean civilization—Cultist, Experimenter, Mastercraftsman, Expansionist, City Builder, and Imperialist (Inca). The names themselves, given to these periods by archaeologists, are sufficiently evocative. The broad picture is of a large number of separate tribes, at first living along the coast, then, with expansion, gradually moving eastward, higher and higher up the valleys. During what is called the Formative period (about 800 B.C. up to about the first and second centuries of our era), the Andean peoples became more and more skilled as farmers. Their tools were the digging stick, hoe, and clod breaker; the plow did not exist, and in any case would have been of little use in terrace cultivation. Bushnell makes an important point when he writes: ". . . the water supply of a valley all came from a single source, the river, and that this, of necessity, imposed a high degree of unity on the inhabitants as soon as the population increased . . . As irrigation developed, *it became necessary to organize the people* [my italics] not only to construct and maintain the ditches but also to see that the water was fairly distributed. The consequence was, in several instances, the emergence of a highly centralized type of state."

This would help to explain why the Inca civilization, when it arose, was so highly organized. The many peoples who were absorbed by it were already accustomed to a high degree of co-operation and control. The same problems had arisen along the banks of the Nile, the Tigris, and the river Indus in India; each of these societies was bureaucratic, that is, tightly governed by a hierarchy of officials so that there was little individual liberty. But the Inca bureaucracy must have been one of the sternest and most rigid the world has ever known—until quite recent times.

As the population increased and more and more land had to be formed, the pre-Inca tribes of the Formative period had to make terraces higher and higher up the mountainsides, and make irrigation channels, fed by the melting snows of the Andes. They grew maize up to an altitude of twelve thousand feet and above that level they planted a hardier kind of grain called *quinoa*. They learned to preserve food by freezing and drying it, and even dehydrated potatoes over two thousand years ago!

They also bred the llama and alpaca in large numbers; the llamas were used as pack animals and from the wool of the alpaca they wove wonderful fabrics. One can trace the evolution of these, from the primitive examples found in the middens of the Early Farmers, made by twining, to the much finer and more elaborate types made on hand looms.

Early religious centers have been found, the ancestors of the great stone temples of the Inca period. In about 900 B.C. these people were building massive rectangular buildings of dressed stone, arranged around a central court. There are stairways and ramps, chambers and galleries, and sculptured human heads with feline tusks. Stone carvings found at the finest of these sites, that at Chavín de Huantar, show animal-headed gods, mainly felines, or other animals such as the snake and condor, but equipped with feline fangs. "The principal object of worship," writes Bushnell, "was a feline god, of which the prototype must have been either the puma or the jaguar."

This early Peruvian art is instantly recognizable, even by an an amateur, as that of the southern Amerindians. To the non-specialist it is hardly distinguishable from the later art of the Inca period, or indeed of the Mayas of Central America. But notice the faint resemblance it bears to the primitive art of south-east Asia—China for example—and it is obvious that these early American settlers were not only Asian in appearance, but that their minds were accustomed to looking at things, and drawing them, in a manner we associate with Asia. Compare them with, say, the paintings and engravings of paleolithic man in Europe and you will see what I mean.

The period which archaeologists call Classic (roughly between 250 B.C. and 750 A.D.) saw the full flowering of Andean culture. Wonderful works of art, in pottery, metalwork, copper, silver and gold, vigorous painting on pottery (often depicting warlike scenes), massive stone buildings, and powerful stone sculpture, suggest strong, skillful, self-confident, aggressive people. It is significant that at this time begins the period of war and conquest. Tribe fought against tribe, the inhabitants of one valley against those of another. For it should always be remembered that Peru at this time was not a unified state like Ancient Egypt or Mycenaean Greece, but a conglomeration of independent petty states, some powerful, some weak. The division of the landscape by high mountains and deep valleys, by deserts and coastal plains, made this inevitable. Yet, though they spoke different languages and followed different customs, they were sufficiently alike in race, social customs, and religious beliefs to make it possible for one more powerful state to unify them; this, as we know, is what the Incas eventually did.

The Classic was followed by what scholars name the Expansionist period (roughly between 700 and 1000 A.D., the time when

England was being fought over by the Vikings, Saxons, and Danes), at the end of which three important states had arisen on the coast. The greatest was that of the Chimú in the north. All three states were notable for their powerful cities, hence this period is called that of the City Builders. The Chimú capital at Chan-Chan covered an area of eleven square miles. When it was excavated there were found within it "ten or more large, walled, rectangular enclosures. . . . Each of these could have been the dwelling, or at least the headquarters, of some such division of the nation as a clan."

Between them were canals, reservoirs, and areas which had been irrigated. The mighty defensive walls, some of which still stand to a height of forty feet, were evidently built to protect these irrigation works and the people who worked there. Even some of the canals were guarded by strong posts. Within the compounds were palacelike buildings with numerous smaller rooms, perhaps for servants, and usually a small pyramid. Pyramids have also been found dating from the Classic period, before the first century A.D. They were associated with the religious cult, and at a much later date became the principal architectural monuments of the Mayas of Central America.

Perhaps the most exciting aspect of archaeology in Peru, Bolivia, and Ecuador is that far more sites await discovery and excavation than have so far been found. The remoteness of the country, the difficulties of travel in a mountainous land where good roads are few, have prevented intensive investigation and left much to be discovered by present and future generations. Quite recently an archaeologist named Henri Reichlen has found other great walled cities in the valley of the Marañon in the Department of Amazonas. Reichlen reports monumental walls with mummies built into them, and peculiar gabled houses—sometimes of three stories—built into rocky clefts which are difficult to reach. These were evidently tombs, and similar to the "houses of the dead" at Palmyra in the Syrian Desert, half a world away from Peru.

The powerful state of Chimú arose in the Moche Valley on the northern coast. It began to expand, absorbing neighboring states such as Virú, until by the middle of the fifteenth century A.D., about the time Columbus was born, it controlled an area stretching almost as far south as Lima. It was, in fact, an empire, and it is more than likely that the rulers of the greater Inca Empire learned much from it.

No one knows where the Incas came from, but it was probably from the highland country around Cuzco which eventually became their capital. Excavations there have brought to light remains of rough stone buildings and objects such as slate knives and bone tools, together with pottery which, though more primitive in design and decoration, is clearly of Inca character. These may well have been made by the ancestors of the formidable Incas of later centuries, a tough mountain folk, short and stocky, with powerful shoulders and broad faces and noses slightly hooked.

Why did the Incas, and not one of the other more civilized peoples such as the Chimú, come to dominate the entire land? No one can be certain. When the Incas took over the Chimú and other coastal states with their elaborate, highly civilized, but vulnerable system of agriculture, they did not destroy them but left them in working order—as the Romans had done when they conquered their empire. So, after a succession of battles they eventually became overlords of one of the richest and most productive areas in the world, populated by races which, over two thousand years, had developed the skills and techniques which make a high civilization possible. But, unlike that of the Romans, the Inca Empire lasted only ninety years. Then the Spaniards destroyed it.

Discoveries
in North and Central
America

In THE LAST CHAPTER I tried to sketch, very briefly, how one of
the three major civilizations of pre-Columbian America developed,
and how this development was revealed by archaeologists of various nationalities, at various times, working at various sites in
Peru, Bolivia, and Ecuador.

One could do the same with the development of the Maya, the
Toltecs, and the Aztecs, but I shall not repeat this method for two
reasons. First, it would tend to be repetitive, because these civilizations too went through their Early Hunter, Early Farmer, and
Classic periods culminating in civilizations which bore some
resemblance to that of the Incas. Second, because this is a book
about archaeology and how it works, not about the growth of civilizations. And archaeology does not, in fact, work in this neat
orderly way, from A to B, from B to C, and so on.

What actually happens is far more like one of those games in
which you begin with a jumble of assorted pieces and have to put
them into their correct order—dominoes for instance. Perhaps a
better example is a simple card game in which you have to collect
a complete suit of cards from, say the 2 of Clubs to the ace. Put

into archaeological terms it would be ideal if Professor A. first discovered the 2, then Dr. B. discovered the 3, Mr. C. discovered the 4, and so on. But of course it does not happen like that, or very rarely so. As the Bible says, "Time and Chance happeneth to them all."

Meanwhile, before we return to the Old World, I would like to pinpoint just a few of the many interesting and important archaeological discoveries which have been made in Canada, the United States, and Mexico. These will be arranged in no chronological order, nor will they be confined to any one archaeological period. My object is to show how rich this vast land is in archaeological opportunities—and surprises.

How many people know that the first scientific excavation in the United States was made 180 years ago by the author of the Declaration of Independence? It was scientific in the sense that Thomas Jefferson made his excavation, not out of idle curiosity, but to verify the truth of certain common beliefs about Indian burial mounds found in Virginia. It was said that these were either the graves of warriors slain in battle, or alternatively, the inhabitants of a single settlement, who had been buried standing upright.

The barrow he chose was "on the low grounds of the Rivanna, about two miles above its principal fork, and opposite to some hills, on which had been an Indian town." Here is part of his report:

> Appearances certainly indicate that it has derived both origin and growth from the accustomary collection of bones, and the deposition of them together; that the first collection had been deposited on the common surface of the earth, a few stones put over it, and then a covering of earth, that the second had been laid on this, had covered more or less of it in proportion to the number of bones, and was then also covered with earth, and so on.

Jefferson also noted that a few stones from the mound were brought from a cliff a quarter of a mile off, and from the river, one-eighth of a mile off. And among the bones he noted some of infants—the jaw of a child which had not cut its teeth, and the rib of another infant. Notice that the excavator had observed the principle of stratigraphy—the careful examination of layers—over 130 years before it began to be applied as a matter of course by all competent archaeologists. He also took the trouble to find out where the stones had come from. Were they local or had they been brought from a distance? He is careful to describe where the mound was discovered and relate it to natural features of the landscape. And he demolished hearsay notions by establishing scientific truth about the way the bodies were buried. Not bad for a busy statesman whose principal concern was the creation of a new nation.

Compare the methods, a century later, of Schliemann, of whom one of the foremost modern archaeologists has written:

> We may be grateful to Schliemann for plunging his spade into Troy, Tiryns, and Mycenae . . . because he showed us what a splendid book had in fact been buried there; but he tore it to pieces in snatching it from the earth, and it took us upwards of three-quarters of a century to stick it more or less together again and read it aright, with the help of cribs from other places.

This is not entirely a fair comparison, of course, because Jefferson was dealing with a small mound, whereas at Troy, Schliemann was attacking a large hill.

Haste and overexcitement are fatal to sound archaeology. Take the example of the disputed "Tepexpan Man" found at a place of that name in Mexico. Near this little town, which is on the road between Venta de Carpio and Teotihuacán, workmen were digging a ditch when they came upon some huge bones. The engineer in charge was able to recognize the bones as part of the skull of an imperial mammoth, *Archidiskodon imperator*. Archaeologists hurried to the site and found near the skull a man-made implement, a "flake-tool" of obsidian. Next a geologist, Dr. Helmut de Terra, appeared on the scene. Since a paleolithic tool had been found near the fossil, he wondered if by any chance there were other remains in the vicinity.

With the aid of Dr. Hans Lundberg of Toronto, Canada, he probed the area with an electrical device brought by Lundberg—something like a mine detector. Electrodes were placed in the ground, and by measuring resistance to the current flowing from one to the other, Lundberg could establish points of resistance which might indicate the presence of unusual formations or perhaps foreign bodies. (This apparatus is often used in field archaeology today.)

Three such places were noticed. The first, on being dug, yielded nothing. At the second spot, four feet below the surface, they found the fossilized skeleton of a man in the same geological layer in which the mammoth had been discovered. There was naturally great excitement, for if the skeleton could be proved to belong to the same period as the animal it would be a historic discovery—the first example of paleolithic man ever to be found on the American continent. The discoverers were confident that it was indeed a Paleoindian because, they stated, some twelve inches above the skeleton was a layer of *caliche,* a deposit of calcium carbonate; the age of the earth containing the remains was estimated at between eight to ten thousand years.

But not all anthropologists were convinced. Some said that the excavation had been unscientific, and were disinclined to believe that there had been a sealing layer of *caliche.* Presumably the layer, if it had existed, had been removed before other investigators could examine the site; this, if true, is an example of bad archaeology because, in order to establish scientific fact, one must provide evidence which can be checked by other scholars. As for Tepexpan Man himself, he was just like any modern Indian. This in itself does not disprove great age, since, as we have seen, every American, ancient and modern, belongs to the species Homo sapiens. But the clinching evidence was lacking.

A hot dispute arose, without any definite conclusion being reached. Then, some time later, Dr. Pablo Martínez del Río, head of the Mexican Government's Department of Prehistory, began to investigate the remains of another mammoth found about two miles from Tepexpan. This time every scientific precaution was taken and before the main work of excavation was started many other scholars, such as Dr. Marie L. Wormington of the Denver Museum of Natural History, and Dr. Elias H. Sellards of the Universtiy of Texas, were called in.

The mammoth was four feet underground. Between its ribs one of the investigators, Luis Aveleyra de Anda, found a flint spearhead pointing inward toward the elephant's vitals. Nearby were found an obsidian knife blade, a stone scraper, and other implements. This time there could be no doubt about it. In paleolithic times hunters had killed the animal and then cut up its carcass on the place where it fell. Similar examples have been found in Europe and Asia.

Mr. Frederick A. Peterson, describing this discovery, writes: "So it was that in March 13, 1953, ancient man in Mexico was officially a fact and no longer a fancy. Dr. de Terra's Tepexpan Man was acceptable, and many other previous finds were reinspected. The search was over."

This is an example of "jumping the gun." Tepexpan Man is not acceptable by eminent prehistorians such as, for example, Dr. Grahame Clark whose book *World Prehistory*, published in 1961, does not even mention him; nor do a number of standard works of reference published ten years after the discovery. But the stone implements found near the Itzapan Mammoth *are* acceptable and given their due importance in these works. For all we know, Tepexpan Man may have been a genuine specimen of a Paleoindian, a near-descendant of the people who crossed the Bering Strait ten or more millennia ago. Or he may have been a comparatively modern Indian; lacking positive evidence we shall probably never know, although one would have thought that fluorine testing of the bones or the use of the carbon-14 dating technique would have established whether or not he has any claim to great antiquity.

Whoever eventually finds a true example of a Paleoindian, verifiable beyond the possibility of error, is going to make his mark on archaeological history. There is no doubt that Paleoindian men crossed Canada, the United States, and Mexico on their way south. Their implements, and the bones of the extinct animals they hunted, have been found in a number of places already; mostly, as one would have expected, in the region of the High Plains, which would be on their route after they had crossed Alaska and western Canada.

Many Americans living in the states of Arizona, Colorado, Wyoming, Texas, Nebraska, and New Mexico will know about these sites, of which there must be other examples waiting to be discovered. At Lindermeier in Colorado there is an actual settlement-site where archaeologists confirmed that at the time when these early hunters entered the region, the climate must have been very different from what it is today. Far from being an arid region, the High Plains must have had sufficient rainfall to produce vegetation on which animals such as bison, mastodon, mammoth, and wild horses could roam. Bones of these extinct species have also been found at the Sandia Cave, New Mexico, in association with a type of projectile head, called the Sandia Point which is even older than the Folsom type.

At the Horner site near Cody, Wyoming, investigators found the skulls of over 180 bison. In most cases the tops of the skulls had been removed to extract the brains, and nearby lay flint scrapers, tanged knives of an unusual shape, and other implements which have been dated to around 5000 B.C. But, up to the time of writing, no one has found one skeletal fragment of the human beings who made and used these tools. The same applies throughout the entire American continent, from Alaska to Tierra del Fuego. In fact the only known specimens of paleoindian men are living ones. When Charles Darwin made his historic voyage in the *Beagle* and visited Tierra del Fuego, he found, at this southernmost tip of America:

Lowly denizens of a miserable land [who] lived on a diet of shell-fish, supplemented by fish, birds, seals, whales, otters and wild vegetable food. Their dwellings were caves, windbreaks or primitive huts, and they wore little beyond a skin mantle thrown over their shoulders in cold weather . . . they were ignorant of pottery and used coiled baskets as containers. Their chipped stone projectile-heads . . . recall Paleoindian ones in many different parts of America, and their harpoon and barbed spearheads of bone recall in a general way those of many North American groups. . . .

The descendants of these people are still living in Tierra del Fuego today, and there could be no more positive affirmation of the truth of Dr. Margaret Murray's statement that "archaeology is only anthropology in the past." For these primitives, living near the southern limit of the American continent, must be the remote descendants of the first wave of Asian immigrants who crossed over to America between ten and fifteen thousand years ago, and then moved slowly southward through what are now Canada, the United States, Mexico, and South America until they could go no further.

On the way their descendants and successors had settled in many parts of the continent. Some had become nomadic hunters, roaming the western plains in search of the bison and its descendant, the buffalo. Some had thrust eastward and settled in what are now Virginia, Massachussets, North Carolina, and South Carolina. Some had moved west beyond the High Plains to a desert area between the Rockies and the Pacific and lived by hunting the desert fox, bobcat, coyote, or skunk. There they lived for intermittent periods in caves and under rock shelters where archaeologists have found the equipment they used—baskets, nets, cordage and matting, digging sticks, fire drills, darts, and spear throwers. These things have been found at such places as Danger Cave, Utah; Ventana Cave, Arizona; Leonard Shelter and Gypsum Cave, Nevada; and Roaring Springs and Fort Rock Caves, Oregon.

Still others had moved further south into Mexico and Guatemala, where some of them, who had learned the art of agriculture and bred maize from its wild ancestor, had created great civilizations—Maya, Toltec, Aztec, Inca—with shining white pyramids and temples of hewn stone, a hierarchy of rulers, nobles, priests and officials, a calendar, and in one case, even a writing system. But the rest had drifted further and further southward, until, just over one hundred years ago, Darwin found their descendants still living much as their remote ancestors had lived between ten and fifteen thousand years ago.

There are, on the American continent, archaeological remains of cultures much more recent than that of the Paleoindians, though still very old. When the first nomadic hunters moved down from Alaska, not all continued to move south into Mexico and beyond. Some settled in the region of the High Plains; others fanned out to west and east and adopted their customs to the differing climatic conditions of these areas. We have seen how those who settled in New Mexico appear to have bred maize from the wild plant; an invention of tremendous importance because maize, the cultivation of which spread to many other parts of the American continent, became the staple crop of the Indians of Mexico and Peru, where the earliest civilizations grew up.

In what is now the eastern United States the paleoindian immigrants had to adapt themselves to living in more forested ground. From their tools, belonging to what prehistorians called the Archaic period, we can see this happening; also from their deposits in Alabama, eastern Tennessee, North Carolina, Virginia, and Massachusetts we know that besides hunting they lived off wild plants and shellfish. Thousands of years later the inhabitants of the eastern United States had developed a much more sophisticated way of life. Between about 500 B.C. and 500 A.D. they were growing maize, making pottery, and constructing elaborate burial mounds; archaeologists call this the Woodland culture to distinguish it from the Archaic.

In southern Ohio, southeastern Indiana, northern Kentucky, and West Virginia, excavators have come across elaborate tombs with evidence of funerary customs reminiscent of Egypt and other Old World civilizations. To quote Professor Grahame Clark: "First the dead man was placed in a log tomb erected on the floor of his house, together with suitable gravegoods and the corpses of other people, probably retainers slaughtered for the purpose. After a while the bones were disinterred, painted and placed once again in the tomb which was now heaped over by a small mound. Finally a gigantic mound up to 70 feet high was erected to cover both the grave and the burned out remains of the house."

Other settlements and burial mounds of these folk have been found in Illinois and the Mississippi area, in New York State,

Louisiana, and Florida. Much later, about 1000 A.D. there was a further refinement of this eastern culture. It is called the "Middle Mississippi" culture, of which interesting remains can be found in northcentral Georgia, northern Alabama and Mississippi, western Tennessee, Kentucky, Illinois, and southeastern Missouri. There were great plazas or squares with rectangular temple mounds, sometimes built in tiers like the pyramids of the Aztecs and Mayas, and around the plazas clustered the larger villages of the group. The mound at East St. Louis covered 16 acres; it was 1,080 feet long, 710 feet broad, and about 100 feet high. The ground area of the building was, in fact, slightly larger than that of the Great Pyramid in Egypt, though the latter, of course, was over four times as high and built of hewn stone.

Finally we come to the great civilizations of Central America— the Mayas and the Aztecs. Just as the average Englishman tends to be less impressed by the antiquities of his own country than those of Greece, Egypt, and the Middle East, so, I imagine, the average American tends to overlook the fascinating remains of the Pueblo Indians, with their great cliff-house settlements and hill towns in Arizona, and fixes his gaze on the exotic civilizations of Mexico and Guatemala. On the other side of the fence the grass is always greener.

Here, as in Peru, archaeology begins where recorded history leaves off. We all know something about the Aztec Empire and its glorious capital, Tenochtitlán (now Mexico City), because the Spanish conqueror Hernando Cortez and his followers have described it. It was built around, and even on, the great lake in the hollow of the central valley of Mexico, 7,500 feet above sea level and overlooked by snow-capped volcanoes, surely one of the most magnificent sites in the world, and a fit dwelling for Montezuma, last of the Aztec kings. The population was between half and three-quarters of a million. Here is how Díaz del Castillo described it: Montezuma had led him, with Cortez, to the top of a pyramid.

This great accursed temple was so high that from the top of it everything could be seen perfectly. And from up there we saw the three causeways that lead into Mexico. . . . We saw the aqueduct that comes from Chapultepec to supply the town with sweet water, and at intervals along the three causeways the bridges which let the water flow from one part of the lake to another. We saw a multitude of boats upon the great lake, some coming with provisions, some going loaded with merchandise . . . and in these towns we saw temples and oratories shaped like towers and bastions, all shining white, a wonderful thing to behold.

The more one considers this scene, the more awe-inspiring it becomes. Think of it in terms of time, backed by the knowledge which archaeology has given us; knowledge which Cortez and his followers did not possess. Between ten and fifteen thousand years ago paleolithic men, living and thinking like the men who painted the Lascaux caves in Europe, had begun to enter America. Much later other members of the species Homo sapiens, living in the Middle East, had invented agriculture, stock rearing, metalworking, writing, monumental architecture, and systems of law. Their descendants had raised great cities, in Egypt, Mesopotamia, Europe, India, Russia, and China. Some of these civilizations, richer than that of the Aztecs, had passed away a thousand, two thousand, three thousand years before Cortez stood beside Montezuma on a pyramid overlooking Tenochtitlán.

Here, in Central and South America, human beings had also created civilizations, uninfluenced by—indeed completely ignorant of—those which their remote cousins had brought to being in the Old World. Names such as Constantinople, Rome, Babylon, Nineveh, Memphis, and Thebes meant nothing to them; yet there were features of their civilization which closely resembled those which had grown up beside the Nile, the Euphrates, and the Tigris. And here stood Cortez and his followers who, though they did not realize it, were Old World representatives of Homo sapiens meeting, for almost the first time, fellow members of their own species whose ancestors had left the Old World ten to fifteen thousand years ago.

Yet what they saw before them were not tribes of painted savages yelling war cries, but city dwellers as civilized as themselves;

in some ways considerably more so. Even the proud Cortez, writing to his king, had to admit that the Indians "live almost as we do in Spain, and with quite as much orderliness," and he adds, "it is wonderful to see how much sense they bring to the doing of everything." How much one regrets that this epochal meeting took place in the sixteenth century A.D. when, through religious fanaticism, ignorance, bigotry, and gold lust, the Spaniards destroyed these precious examples of New World civilization and left behind nothing except a few written records and the broken, disorganized remnants of a once-great people.

In fact, as we know now, the Aztec civilization was of new growth. Their real name was the Tenocha, and only three hundred years before the arrival of Cortez they had been barbarous nomads from the north. They conquered, assimilated, and ruled over peoples who had trodden the hard path to civilization over a period of some thousand years. All the familiar features of Aztec life—intensive agriculture, planned irrigation, disciplined communities of men and women co-operating in a common effort to produce wealth—had existed long before the Aztecs arrived. So had the elaborate religious ceremonial and the buildings needed for its performance—pyramids, temples, priestly colleges, ball courts, and so on.

Far to the south, in the tropical forests of southern Mexico, Guatemala, and Honduras, the mysterious, pacific Maya people had produced a true civilization seven hundred years before the Tenocha appeared in the valley of Mexico. It was their cities which the travelers John Lloyd Stephens (the pioneer of Maya archaeology) and his friend Catherwood visited over a century ago, and of which Stephens wrote: "Architecture, sculpture and painting, all the arts which embellish life, had flourished in this overgrown forest; orators, warriors, and statesmen, beauty, ambition and glory had lived and passed away . . ."

Largely due to Stephens' inspiration, more and more scholars, mainly American, have been drawn to the Maya civilization, to which the Aztecs owed so much. As in Peru, painstaking research and excavation over many years have gradually pieced together their history, although there are still many gaps. Perhaps the most puzzling question is this. Why did the Mayas, when they began to build cities in about 300 A.D., site them in some of the most inhospitable land in Central America? Archaeologists have shown that, in general, civilizations spring up in areas most favorable to permanent human settlement; this is true of Sumer, Egypt, Crete, India, and the banks of the Yellow River in China. But it is not true of the Mayas.

Excavations show that the ancestors of the classical Maya (300–900 A.D.) had lived in the same area in which the builders of Uax-actún, Palenque, and Copán raised their dazzling temples. Between 1500 and 300 B.C. they had learned to cultivate maize, cotton, agave, to make baskets and fine pottery, to spin fibers and weave them into cloth. But they were still living in villages. Then, it would appear, quite suddenly, mighty buildings of hewn stone, adorned with sculptured figures of gods, began to rise in the dense jungles of Guatemala, and in parts of what are now southern Mexico and British Honduras. Weather experts—climatologists —have established that the climate and vegetation of this region in 300 A.D. was very much as it is today—hot and humid, except during the rainy season. Then, as now, there would be low-lying marshlands and dense forests of quick-growing trees, some of which were of towering height. The Maya builders would have to hack down the trees with stone axes, or ring their barks, burn the dead timber, and use the ashes as fertilizer.

In the clearings, they grew their crops, principally maize (one of their most venerated deities was a maize god, just as in Ancient Egypt Osiris was the god, not only of death, but of ripening wheat), but when the land was exhausted and choked by weeds they moved on to another part of the forest and repeated the process. One can see this same primitive method of farming, called "slash and burn" in East Africa today.

The cities which appeared with such apparent suddenness were primarily religious centers. It is not even certain that they were inhabited by anyone except the rulers and priests. The common folk probably lived outside in roughly built shelters which have long since disappeared. Judging from their monuments the Mayas must have been among the most religious (or superstitious) people

who ever lived. The peasants labored for years to build these enormous temples and pyramids in the jungle, just as the Egyptians
raised their pyramids and temples, and the Sumerians and Babylonians their tiered towers or ziggurats. But there was a difference.
The peoples of Egypt and Mesopotamia, Asia Minor, India, and
China certainly paid due reverence to their gods. But that was not
all. They appear to have enjoyed a lively secular life, and they
used their writing systems not only to record hymns to their gods
and the wars and conquests of their rulers, but also for ordinary
commercial transactions, for correspondence, and for writing love
poems and stories. Also they used the system of measurement devised by their priests to parcel out land, to number flocks and
herds, to weigh sackfuls of grain and other produce.

Not so the Mayas. Their priests had also invented a hieroglyphic
writing system, the only one known to have existed in the New
World before the coming of Columbus. They set up huge stone
stelae in their temple areas inscribed with these signs, which modern scholars can only dimly understand. But it seems reasonably
certain that this writing system was used only by the priests, mainly
for the recording of time. The ordinary Maya peasant could not
even weigh a sackful of grain, let alone write love letters or draw
up legal documents. But his priestly rulers, upon whom he depended to interpret the wishes of the gods, or to tell him when to
sow and reap, were able to forecast the movements of the sun,
moon, and stars for millions of years ahead. They developed a
calendar which was far in advance of the Roman calendar we still
use today.

It seems that the minds of these Maya rulers, the thinkers and
planners, were almost entirely absorbed in recording the passage
of time. They seem to have believed that history repeated itself
again and again in endless cycles. Maya sculpture shows us that
each day was a deity, represented by the figure of a man with a
weight on his back. There were day gods, night gods, week gods,
month gods, and year gods moving endlessly from the past into the
future.

The priest-rulers taught their subjects that if the land was to
flourish and crops grow in due season they must obey their com-

mands, since only they knew the hidden secrets of the Universe. On the tops of their towering pyramids they observed and recorded the movement of the heavenly bodies. They recognized, of course, that there was a difference between the solar year—measured by the sun and called the *tun,* and what we call the sidereal year, the time taken by the earth to make one complete revolution around the sun. Today we know that the solar year is approximately 365.2422 days in length, whereas the sidereal year (measured by the stars) is a little under 365.2564 days. Again we know that the revolution of the planet Venus is not exactly 585 days but 583.92.

Modern, or relatively modern, astronomers have worked out these figures with the aid of mathematics. But the Maya priest-observers, who believed the earth to be flat, and who had no way of expressing fractions or decimals, were just as well aware of the discrepancy between the solar and sidereal years, and managed to accommodate these awkward figures within the framework of their own artificial almanacs. They did this, not by using "leap years" as we do, but by keeping precise records made over a period of hundreds of years, so that at any time they knew the exact inconsistency between the true solar year and their year of 365 days. Armed with this knowledge they were able to forecast eclipses of the sun so accurately that their forecasts were almost as good as those of modern astronomers.

But the mathematical and astronomical calculations of the Maya priesthood, as revealed by linguists, were far in advance of anything achieved by the Babylonians, the Egyptians, or even the Romans. Through these strange inscriptions we can enter into the minds of these long-dead people, and dimly understand the way they looked at life and the world around them. To us their view may seem strange, and the labors of their subjects in raising these huge monuments an exercise in futility. If we think thus we are wrong. Just as today most of us tend to accept the statements of scientists because they possess specialized knowledge beyond our understanding, so the Maya peasant, laboring in his maize fields, looked up to the pyramids reared high above the treetops, and believed that there lived superior beings—the priests—who could interpret between gods and men, who knew when to call for due sacrifice, and who guarded his livelihood and his destiny.

We know also that a time came, about 900 A.D., when the peasants apparently lost faith in their priests and these great "cult-centers" (to use an archaeological term) were quite suddenly deserted; the people moved away, and the buildings, many of them unfinished, were left to be swallowed up by the ever-encroaching forests. But over a thousand years later, in 1949, a Mexican archaeologist, Dr. Alberto Ruz, was examining the ruins of Palenque, deep in the dense vegetation of the Chiapas, when he made an astonishing discovery.

As at other Maya sites, such as Chichén Itzá, Tikal, and Uaxactún, the principal feature of Palenque is a steep-sided stone pyramid with a small temple on the top approached by a flight of steps. It was within such temples, and on the stone staircases, that the Maya priests occasionally offered human sacrifice, though far less frequently than the fierce Aztecs who sacrificed legions of prisoners.

On examining the floor of the pyramid-temple, Ruz noticed that one of the stone slabs had two rows of holes provided with plugs. Lifting the slab he found a shaft filled with large stones, which he laboriously removed. The rest of his story might well have come from the pages of Petrie who had explored the Egyptian pyramids some sixty years earlier. First Ruz descended a stone stairway with forty-five steps leading down into the interior of the pyramid. Then came a landing, where there was a U turn and another descending passage of twenty-one steps. Next came a corridor choked with stone and lime which had to be removed. This having been cleared, Ruz discovered the skeletons of six people, all young and one of them female, lying in front of a triangular block of stone which was clearly intended to block the entrance to another chamber.

This slab, which was six feet high, took some moving, but eventually it was displaced, leaving sufficient room for a man to enter. Ruz squeezed himself through, and found that he was in a large crypt. In the light of his lamp the investigator saw, shimmering on the walls, the figures of nine richly garbed men modeled in stucco relief, apparently Maya priests. And in the center of the chamber, which was seventy-five feet below the floor of the temple, lay a magnificently carved rectangular slab covered with remains of jadeite mosaic human heads. The slab, which weighed five tons, was sculptured to represent a young man lying on a hideous mask of some earth monster. It was inscribed with the Maya symbols of life and death, and on the sides was a hieroglyphic inscription giving the date according to the Maya calendar which, by comparison with ours, works out at about 700 A.D.

Ruz had great difficulty in raising the slab in the confined space of the chamber, but with the help of four jacks and wooden supports it was eventually lifted about seven feet. Then the archaeologist discovered, underneath, a huge cavity in the shape of a capital *omega,* into which had been sunk another slab of the same shape, exactly fitting it. When this was at last removed Ruz and his assistants stared down with astonishment and awe. The walls and base of the cavity were bright with cinnabar, and at the bottom lay the well-preserved skeleton of a man, so heavily laden with shining jewelry—principally jade—that at first glance the body seemed not dead but glowing with life.

There was a jade diadem on his head, a collar of jade beads around his neck, and his hair was divided into separate strands inserted into jade tubes. The skull wore ear plugs in the form of a flower, suspended from which was what at first seemed to be a huge pearl; it was actually two pieces of mother-of-pearl fitted together. A pectoral of jade lay on the breast; on each wrist were bracelets, and every finger of each hand wore a jade ring. Near the skull lay pieces of jade mosaic which, when pieced together in the laboratory, proved to be a realistic face mask, so that today one can see the very features of this priest-ruler of Palenque who died over twelve hundred years ago.

There was another strange feature of this burial. A plaster figure of a serpent is represented as emerging from the sarcophagus and undulating up the stairs leading to the threshold. At this point it becomes a tube which runs the length of the corridor and then ascends to the temple on top of the pyramid. The inference is that by this means the living priests were able to maintain contact with their dead ruler and interpret his wishes. This wonderful tomb, which seems to bring us into the very presence of one of those astronomer-mathematician priests revered by the Maya people, is, at the time of writing, unique. But who can tell whether, hidden within the tropical forests of Guatemala, another Maya ruler may lie, buried deep within his pyramid?

FROM THE
PACIFIC TO THE
MEDITERRANEAN

Archaeology in
China and Russia

O<small>UR</small> archaeological journey has taken us to the birthplace of the oldest civilizations in Mesopotamia, Egypt, and the eastern Mediterranean, to the relics of early man in Europe, Africa, and the Far East, thence to the great civilizations which Homo sapiens, independently of the Old World, created in Central and South America. Now we shall return to the area from which we started, Egypt and the Near East, and take a brief look at what has been happening there from the turn of the century down to the present day.

We make our return journey, not via the Atlantic and Europe, but westward, across the Bering Strait, following the track by which Upper Paleolithic man entered America, and then on across the vast steppes of Russia and southward, through Persia, into the subcontinent of India and Pakistan.

As we cross the Asian continent we have time for just a few glimpses at archaeologists at work in China and Russia. I have already mentioned the finding of *Sinanthropus*, one of the most ancient of the hominids or submen whose bones were found in a

199

cave near Peking. You will also remember how the so-called oracle bones at Anyang led to the discovery of a rich Bronze Age civilization which flourished near the Yellow River over thirty-five hundred years ago. Since World War II there has been a great resurgence of archaeology in China, although information about it is less easy to come by than that of the Middle East, Europe, and America.

The civilization discovered near Anyang, that of the Shang Dynasty, is now known to be a later development of this culture. Chinese tradition states that the Shang capital was changed several times, and it is now believed that the remains found at Anyang represent a city built about 1300 B.C. In 1950 Chinese scholars discovered a much earlier city at Chengchow; most of it lies under the modern town, but in the suburbs was found the craftsmens' quarter, which included bronze-casting workshops; there were earthenware molds for casting axes and arrowheads and bronze vessels; pottery kilns and potters' tools of various types. Most of the pottery found was hand-turned, but others show that the potter's wheel was known. (Curiously, it was unknown in the Americas until Columbian times.)

In 1955 further excavations were made at Chengchow, and this time the archaeologists were able to trace parts of the town walls. They were of beaten earth and enclosed a rectangle measuring one and a quarter by one mile, larger, in fact, than the present-day town. Graves were found, but none so far discovered equal those of the later Shang capital in magnificence—and gruesomeness.

At the village of Wu Kuan, not far from the later capital of Anyang, excavators unearthed a rectangular pit forty feet by forty-six feet with ramps on two sides for the descent of the funeral party. Fifteen and a half feet down was a platform and below this a still lower pit, eight feet deep. This, which had evidently contained the coffin, had been robbed, but in the floor below where the coffin had lain was the body of a soldier with a bronze halberd. Presumably he was put there to guard his master from spirits who might attack from below.

But although the body of the king, around which the most

precious objects had been laid, had disappeared, those of his retainers had been left undisturbed. There were skeletons of seventeen men and twenty-four women, placed on the platform which
was level with the roof of the burial chamber. And on the northern approach ramp lay four chariot teems of horses (sixteen animals in all), some dogs, and two men. On the opposite ramp lay a
similar array of skeletons.

Nor was this all. It was apparent that at the time of the funeral
thirty-four additional human beings had been decapitated. Their
skulls were found neatly piled in the corner of the pit, and some
distance away lay their headless bodies in four rows of graves. One
is reminded of the royal graves which Leonard Woolley discovered
at Ur in Mesopotamia; there too there were ramps with the bodies
of retainers, soldiers, and ass-drawn chariots (the Sumerians did
not have the horse). There too Woolley found musical instruments; at Wu Kuan there was a strange "musical stone," a large
piece of marble with a hole for suspending it. When struck it gave
out a musical note—a three-thousand-year-old example of a Chinese gong!

In Siberia, a Russian archaeologist, S. I. Rudenko, has made a
discovery unparalleled anywhere else in the world. He found the
great tombs of Scythian chieftains preserved in a deep freeze for
some twenty-five hundred years. The Scythians and their kindred
peoples were nomads who roamed the steppes of Russia and Asia
at a time when the civilization of classical Greece (roughly between 600–300 B.C.) was at its peak, and when Greek cities such
as Ephesus and Halicarnassus had already been established along
the coast of Asia Minor.

In fact mounted nomads had appeared on the Asiatic steppes
and the plains of Hungary as early as 1100 B.C.; such facts are
known through archaeological research. But it so happens that
that indefatigable Greek traveler and historian Herodotus actually
met the descendants of these fierce horsemen and described their
customs in some detail:

When the king dies, they dig a grave, which is square in shape
and of great size. When it is ready they take the king's corpse,

and, having opened the belly, and cleaned out the inside, fill the cavity with a preparation of chopped cypress, frankincense, parsley seed and anise-seed, after which they sew up the opening, enclose the body in wax, and, placing it on a wagon, carry it about through all the different tribes . . .

The Greek historian then describes the method of burial.

There the body of the dead king is laid in the grave prepared for it, stretched upon a mattress; spears are fixed in the ground on either side of the corpse, and beams stretched across above it to form a roof, which is covered with thatching. In the open space around the body of the king they bury one of his concubines, and also his cup-bearer, his cook, his groom, his lackey, his messenger, some of his horses . . . and some golden cups . . . After this they set to work and raise a vast mound above the grave. . . .

A year later further ceremonies were performed at the grave. More of the king's attendants were taken, strangled, and placed near the main burial. Fifty of his finest horses were killed, "their bowels taken out, and the cavity cleaned, filled up with chaff, and sewn up again." These dead animals were then impaled on stakes running lengthwise through their bodies, the ends of the stakes being mounted on "half the felly of a wheel placed archwise . . . Each horse is furnished with a bit and bridle, and then the fifty strangled youths are mounted on the fifty horses. . . . The fifty riders are thus ranged in a circle round the tomb and so left . . ."

Fantastic? Impossible, or at least improbable? Many people thought so, and Herodotus, some of whose stories are even taller than this, used to be called "The Father of Lies"—a jibe at his more conventional title "The Father of History." Some suggested that he had never seen the Scythians, but got his stories from the embroidered tales of travelers, which in some cases he may have done. For instance are we to take seriously this comment about Scythian behavior at a funeral of one of their kings:

. . . they make a booth by fixing in the ground three sticks and over them woollen felts, which they arrange to fit as close as possible; inside the booth a dish is placed . . . into which they put a number of red-hot stones . . . and creeping under the felt coverings, throw some hemp seed upon the red-hot stones; immediately it smokes, and gives out such vapours as no Grecian vapour bath can exceed; the Scyths, delighted, shout for joy.

From time to time grave mounds of these nomadic horsemen have been found, in places as far apart as Mongolia in eastern Asia to Hungary in eastern Europe. There are certain differences in the art and even of the racial types of the men and women found in these graves; Herodotus's Scythians seem to have been a fair-haired people not unlike the northern Europeans and their American kindred today, whereas those whose grazing lands were further east were of Mongoloid stock. But on this high, grassy roof of the world where the plains roll interminably to the horizon, there are few mountain barriers, and thus the inhabitants could wander freely, absorbing and imitating each others' customs and those of the settled folk with whom they came in contact. Thus the art of the Scyths of western Russia and eastern Europe is much influenced by that of Greece. Those in contact with China show a marked Chinese influence. But basically their way of life and mode of burial was the same.

Some of the finest graves were found at Chertomlyk in southern Russia. These were royal tombs, but had been robbed, probably not long after the kings were buried. In the richest burial mound there was an abundance of goldwork which the plunderers, fortunately, had to abandon when their entrance tunnel caved in. In the heart of the barrow (burial mound) was the central burial chamber and four smaller ones radiating from it. The walls of the chambers and the approach ramps leading to it had been boarded, and above the main chamber had been a gabled roof set on stout wooden columns. The walls had been hung with rush matting and on these and the ceiling were hooks, still in position, on which had hung clothes. These, of course, had perished, but on the floor lay scores of stamped golden plaques which had once decorated them.

There were niches in the walls, too, in which stood gold vases and other personal belongings, and in one of the side chambers stood six big wine jars (amphorae) in which the excavators found dregs of the wine. But all these wonders were overshadowed by the main burial, which was intact. There lay a skeleton of the king, his neck encircled by a bronze torque of fine workmanship, his left hand within reach of an ivory-handled knife and an ivory-handled riding whip ornamented with gold. There was a bronze *gorytus* or Scythian caldron, filled with bronze arrowheads, and numerous clothing ornaments of gold still lay about the tomb. In a nearby chamber lay two more bodies, each wearing a golden torque and bracelets and rings of gold. Here again were found an abundance of the gold ornaments with which their clothes had been trimmed.

A woman's body lay in another chamber, and on her head were still fragments of a purple veil with the fifty-seven gold plaques which had adorned it, and near her lay a bronze mirror.

Outside the burial chamber, as Herodotus had described, lay the bodies of ten fine horses; five had trappings embellished with gold, the others with silver. From this, one may imagine how splendid a sight a Scythian king must have presented at the head of his warriors, accompanied by the princes of the royal blood on their magnificent horses, their brightly colored garments glittering with gold and silver.

Like the riders of the American Far West, the Scythians were expert with the lasso but they seemed to have preferred to chase and shoot their prey from the saddle. The manes of their war horses were trimmed to permit them an unimpeded downward shot when necessary, and, like the famous Parthians of later times, they fired over their left side.

All this we have learned from archaeology, apart from the comments of Herodotus, and other Greek writers speaking from the western edge of the Asian continent, and Chinese historians speaking from the eastern edge. The latter refer to the Hsiung-nu, fierce horsemen from the Mongolian steppes whose plundering raids along the Chinese frontier eventually compelled the Emperor Shih Huang Ti to build the Great Wall. One Chinese observer, who may perhaps have had to face a Hsiung-nu charge, has left one phrase which glitters like a sword blade: *"They have no faces—only eyes . . ."*

These eastern barbarians, smashing like a storm tide against the bastions of Chinese civilization, were not Herodotus' Scythians, but their manner of fighting was much the same. And they show very clearly how the development of the human race, and the possibility or impossibility of civilization, has been governed by landscape and climate. The Indians of the North American plains were living very like the Scythians until less than a century ago. Yet their remote kindred of Central and South America had been able to create civilizations a thousand years ago, thanks to the invention of agriculture. Similarly the peoples of Egypt and Sumer, thanks to the fact that their ancestors had settled in fertile valleys, had developed the arts of civilization before 3000 B.C. Yet they were surrounded, and sometimes attacked, by peoples who, because of their harder geographic environment, were at a much lower level of development.

This does not mean that nomadic peoples like the Scythians, though they had no writing system or cities, were necessarily savages. The rich and vigorous art found in Scythian graves, even though confined to dress ornaments, harness trappings, and such objects as metal vessels which a nomadic people could carry on their marches, shows a wonderful feeling for design and that same lively delight in animal forms which one sees in the art of paleolithic man.

But the Scythians not only created works of art; they collected them on their travels. Most surviving examples are of durable materials like gold, silver, and bronze, but there are a few miraculous exceptions to this rule, and they were found by the Russian archaeologist Rudenko at Pazirik in Siberia. I say "miraculous" because the preservation of the famous Pazirik tombs *is* a miracle. The first clue to their existence was found in 1865, at Katanda, in the southern Altai district of Siberia. An explorer named Radlov became interested in the large number of barrows in the region; these were different from most Scythian burial mounds, being topped with huge boulders. On removing the boulders and digging down into one of the largest mounds, Radlov and his men were astonished to find a thick layer of *ice*. Yet it was then autumn in Siberia and there was no ice above ground at Katanda.

He then made a disastrous mistake. As it was late in the season and he was short of time, Radlov began pouring hot water into the barrow to melt the ice. Then, as the frozen layer dissolved the astonished archaeologist saw, opaquely through the thinning ice sheet, the bodies of the dead *still wearing some of their clothes* and surrounded by precious things. Alas, as soon as the water reached the bodies most of the fabrics disintegrated, though a few fragments were preserved, together with some furniture and other durable objects.

Although the discovery caused some excitement in Russia the rest of the world showed little interest, for this was the period when Schliemann had discovered the golden treasures of Troy and Mycenae, and the royal mummies had come to light in Egypt. Among the general public these marvelous finds overshadowed everything else. The Altai ice burial was a nine-day wonder and was soon forgotten. It was not until sixty years later that Rudenko set out on an anthropological expedition into Siberia. The year was 1924.

In the Pazirik valley he came upon forty mounds topped with heavy boulders, and was reminded of the one which Radlov had incautiously excavated. Five years later he returned with an assistant, Griasonov, recruited a staff of local workmen, and began the scientific excavation of one of the larger barrows. When the boulders were removed and the excavators dug down they were thrilled to find a layer of thick ice, as in the tomb which Radlov had found. But this time instead of melting the frozen layer, Rudenko and his assistants removed it piece by piece with infinite care and labor. Eventually they came upon an oblong burial chamber forty-five square yards in area, enclosed by double walls of logs, of which the inner wall had been smoothed on the inside and lined with felt held in place by copper or wooden nails.

Within the chamber lay coffins hollowed out of larch trunks, the rims being decorated with silhouettes of animals cut out of leather. The bodies had been embalmed, exactly as Herodotus described, and were laid on blankets of felt overlaid with rugs. Nearby, in another part of the mound, lay the bodies of horses with rich harness and trappings, lavishly decorated with gold and bronze plaques.

From 1947 to 1949 Rudenko worked at Pazirik and excavated several more mounds, some of which were even more marvelous than the first. For instance in Mound 2 and Mound 5 lay the well-preserved bodies of two chieftains, the preserved flesh of which had been tattooed with elaborate designs, again of animal forms, some realistic, the others fantastic. One of these men had been killed in battle, and the designs tattooed on his arms, chest, and back were "so lively and spirited in conception and execution that they must rank with the finest drawings of the Scythian school." Although the ancient thieves had entered the burial chambers, and in some cases hacked off heads and limbs to get at the jewelry, they had left the horse burials undisturbed. Miss Tamara Talbot-Rice, to whose excellent book *The Scythians* I am indebted for some of the material in this chapter, writes:

> As in the human graves, so in these all the walls were hung with felt which was just as elaborately worked as were the hangings in the human sections. Many of the horses had been in excellent condition at the time of their death. The best had been fed on grain . . . during the spring months and carried up to the summer encampment. All the riding horses were chestnut or bay geldings, and many were well-bred animals. . . . The condition of the feet of the finer ones suggests that they had been kept in stables for some time prior to their death.

In almost every detail Herodotus had been right, even though he had been describing the burial customs of Scythians occupying the western end of the Asian steppes, whereas the Pazirik tombs were much further east, indicating how widespread these customs were. For example he mentions a cart on which the dead chieftain was carried through his territory before burial. Such a cart was found in Mound 5, made of birch wood and mounted on four spoked wheels. It was so constructed that parts of it could be dismantled for carrying on the backs of pack animals when negotiating difficult country. Remember also Herodotus' description of the small felt "booth" with three poles into which the Scythians crept to inhale the vapor of burning hemp, whereat they "shouted for joy."

At Pazirik, in 1929, Rudenko found bundles of such poles, with their felt or leather sheets still attached to them, and nearby a caldron containing stones and hemp seeds. Each burial contained this essential piece of equipment; in the case of double burials there were two, one for the man and the other for his wife. It has been suggested that the fantastic character of Scythian art, in which animal forms develop into weird, mythical creatures, may be partly due to the influence of this drug which produced ecstasy and intoxication.

One question you will probably be waiting to ask, How did it happen that these tombs were preserved for some twenty-five hundred years under a layer of ice? We are still not quite certain, but what appears to have happened is this: When, not long after the burials, thieves entered the tombs and removed some of the more precious objects, water seeped through the disturbed boulders which thereafter acted as insulators; so that, during the summer months, though the ice melted from the surface of the ground, the water which had percolated into the inner chambers remained frozen.

Many more of these frozen graves still await exploration. One wonders what will be discovered next.

An
Expert at Work

FROM TIME TO TIME in this book I have emphasized how some of the ancient myths have been proved to have a basis of truth, and that modern archaeologists tend to take them much more seriously than scholars of a century ago. There are now three main "corridors" along which we can approach the remote past: the linguistic, through written records; the purely archaeological, through the material objects men left behind them; and the mythical.

In India an important group of myths is contained in the Rig Veda, a collection of Hindu hymns of very ancient origin. Just how old we cannot be certain, but these Vedic hymns, of which there are over a thousand, are addressed to the most powerful of the Hindu deities, praising their deeds and imploring them to accept their worshipers' offerings. The greatest of these Hindu gods was Indra, "the ruler of the bright firmament," equivalent in importance to Amen-Ra in Egypt and Zeus in Greek mythology. To Indra the Hindu warriors addressed themselves when they prayed for success in battle; in one of his aspects he is the god of war.

In certain of the Vedic hymns Indra is called *puramdara,* which means "fort-destroyer." And just as Amen-Ra assists the Pharaohs in battle, so Indra helps the leaders of the Aryan people who invaded and conquered India. To assist one of them Indra destroys "ninety forts," and these forts are evidently walled cities, since the word *pur* (rampart) occurs. Some of these are of stone— *asmamayi*—others of mud brick. He is also described as having destroyed one hundred "ancient castles" and in another passage he "rends forts as age consumes a garment."

So much for Hindu religious traditions, but was there any factual basis for them? Until thirty years ago no building had been found in the Indian subcontinent which could be dated earlier than about 500 B.C. Yet Indian civilization clearly went back much earlier than that. In 1922 Sir John Marshall, then Director of Archaeology in India, had stated: "Before the rise of the Maurya Empire [which began in 321 B.C.] a well-developed and flourishing civilization had existed in India for at least a thousand years; yet, of the structural monuments erected during those ages not one example survived save the Cyclopean walls of Rajagriha."

The first indication that Marshall was right in his assumption came almost at the same time that he made his statement. One year earlier, in 1921, an Indian archaeologist named Rai Bahadur Daya Ram Sahni had begun to dig into the foundations of Harappa, in the Punjab, attracted by some strange, undecipherable forms of picture writing that had been found, together with small seal stones inscribed with animal forms. The modern town of Harappa is built on a huge mound reminiscent of one of the "tells" (mounds) which, in Mesopotamia, indicate a long period of human occupation. The same proved true in this case. Under Harappa were found remains of an earlier city of unknown date, but whose inhabitants had lived during what archaeologists call the Chalcolithic period (between the ages of stone and iron). In Mesopotamia this period begins before 3500 B.C. Could this newly revealed city be equally old?

Next year another member of Marshall's staff of archaeologists, Mr. R. D. Banerji, began to excavate nearly four hundred miles from Harappa, at a place known as Mohenjo-Daro (probably

meaning "the hill of the dead"). Apart from a Buddhist stupa
(tower) on top of the highest of several great mounds, there were
few overlying buildings, so that archaeological teams were able
to remove thousands of tons of earth, stripping the mounds until
there lay, baking in the Indian sun, the skeleton of a great city,
the like of which had never been seen before. At the same time
other archaeologists, working at Harappa, were able to disclose
enough of the prehistoric city to show that it resembled Mohenjo-
Daro so closely that it was obvious both belonged to the same
civilization.

As to the methods by which this was achieved by archaeologists
trained in an older school of excavation, there has been some
criticism, not all of it fair or just. Little attempt was made to dig
downward and reveal the stratigraphy of selected areas, so that a
consecutive series of pictures could be assembled showing how
these cities originated, matured, and declined. Instead the ruins
were stripped bare at more or less one level. But as Sir Mortimer
Wheeler, when he became Director-General of Archaeology in
India, said of his predecessors:

> What the excavators, with their "Up Guards and at 'em"
> methods, *did* do, was something that in a sense transcended all
> this. They built barracks on this desert spot, imported whole
> regiments of hillmen with their families, and turned two thou-
> sand of them or more on to the dusty mounds. Day after day,
> building after building emerged from the soil, streets and lanes
> fell into place in a great townplan, walls and drainage on a scale
> altogether new to knowledge began to build a picture of an
> ordered policy that was in the fullest sense an evolved civiliza-
> tion.

This generous and deserved tribute was paid by the distinguished archaeologist who later interpreted this mysterious civilization, called the Indus Valley or sometimes the Harappan culture, *by archaeological methods alone.* I stress this because, as
stated before, the aim of this book has been not primarily to describe ancient civilizations and cultures, but the archaeological

methods by which they have been revealed. We have seen that in Ancient Egypt, Sumer, Assyria, the Hittite Empire, China, and Greece scholars have been assisted to some extent by written records. There is not a single written record of the Indus Valley civilization. It vanished from the face of the earth leaving not a trace of its existence.

The Indus people themselves had a pictographic writing-system but it cannot be read. The people who conquered and succeeded them left no record, except, perhaps, vague allusions in the Rig-Veda, which was once thought to be entirely mythical. When Marshall and his staff, followed by Mackay and then by Wheeler, set out to interpret these vast ruins and the lives of the people who had inhabited them, they had nothing to guide them save the buildings themselves and the things they contained. No royal tombs have been found; it is not even certain that the Indus Valley folk were ruled by kings. Such graves as have been found to date are paltry little sepulchers with scanty grave goods, which tell us little.

Neither is there any reference to this once-mighty civilization, remains of which have been found over a distance of more than a thousand miles, in the annals of Ancient Egypt or Mesopotamia. This demonstrates very strikingly how, in the ancient world, natural barriers such as deserts, mountains, and oceans cut people off from each other. Within a distance which a modern jet liner could cover in five or six hours (or less), three completely different civilizations—Egypt, Sumer, and the Indus Valley—grew up independently and apparently with little knowledge of each other. Admittedly there is Sumerian influence at work in early Egypt, and Mesopotamian cylinder seals and other small objects have been found in the Indus Valley, suggesting trading contacts at least. But that is all.

When Wheeler took up his post as Director-General of Archaeology in India in 1944 (after a distinguished war record), one of the first tasks he set himself and his staff was to unravel the secrets of this forgotten people, so far as they could be revealed. He had long been a stern critic of some of the earlier excavators who worked in the Middle East, whose sites, when they left them, were all too often "ghastly charnel-houses of murdered evidence." The words are Petrie's, but even that great master and teacher had his faults. Although he had rightly insisted on the importance of small objects, and had taught his students the method of sequence dating by observing subtle changes in the styles of pottery and other artifacts, he paid insufficient attention to making and "reading" accurate sections cut through a site from top to bottom, in order to establish the sequence of occupation (and sometimes nonoccupation) within the area he was digging. Generally he used the "mass-excavation" method, laying the whole place bare, and this system was still being used by some archaeologists as recently as twenty years ago.

Again, though Petrie was careful to make records, plans, and sections, the latter were sometimes skimpy and inadequate, and though he understood and used the principles of stratigraphy, he did not often give enough time and study to it, partly due to the speed at which he worked.

Before going to India at the age of forty-nine, Wheeler had spent most of his archaeological life working on Roman, Iron Age, and Bronze Age sites in Great Britain. There, ever since the days of General Pitt-Rivers, a school of archaeologists has grown up trained in the methods he invented: close attention to layers, careful, painstaking observation of the objects found in each layer and their relationship to each other, and infinite care in the recording of detail. By contrast a great many archaeologists who have made their careers in Egypt and the Middle East went out with only a basic training—in Petrie's case none at all. Then, working on their own in distant lands, often under extremely arduous conditions, they missed the critical discipline imposed by British archaeologists on each other. The latter met each other frequently, discussed and sometimes criticized their colleagues' work, and this constant interchange of ideas was of great benefit to their technique.

Before going on to describe Wheeler's work in the Indus Valley. I will quote some of his trenchant advice to students, advice worth remembering by any budding archaeologist.

However broadly we use the words, Man is in some sense the casket of a soul as well as five-shillings [seventy cents] worth of chemicals. And his recorder [the archaeologist] must therefore be a good deal more than a rather superior laboratory assistant.

The basis of scientific excavation is the accurately observed and recorded section . . . the successive accumulations of construction and debris on a buried occupation-site have much the same validity as the successive pages of a book, and to be understood, must be comprehended in their proper sequence, like the pages of a book.

But Wheeler also adds:

A chronologist is not an archaeologist. As an American writer has put it, "Chronology is admittedly an important factor in any archaeological research, and the earliest and surest method of establishing it is to be commended. But after a sequence of periods has been established, if then the very culture of those periods is unknown, we may justifiably ask "so what?"

At Mohenjo-Daro, Harappa, and other Indus sites, Wheeler applied, and taught his staff to apply, the same scientific methods of excavation which he had developed in Great Britain. First he had to establish the chronological sequence. In both cities, at carefully selected points, he began by making deep sections of the mound, from the top to as far down as he could get. In this he was limited by the fact that at the extremely low levels he had to cope with water.

Digging in the driest season of the year, we struck water at fifteen feet below the present surface, and, with mechanised pumps and careful engineering, we dived for a further ten feet into the streaming mud . . . Then, one night, when the pumps were labouring, a thousand jets of water burst from the sides of our cutting, and with a sullen roar it tumbled in. We had reached farther than any of our predecessors, but time and tide had beaten us.

He meant "beaten" only in the relative sense, of course. Wherever possible he cut his sections in squares, not by the old-fashioned "trenching" method. By sinking a square pit through the strata of the old city, the evcavator-observer, standing within the pit, had room to move about and study the section on four sides. Every successive change in the color or texture of the soil was then labeled and numbered, and the whole measured, photographed, and subsequently drawn. Then another square pit was dug adjacent to the first, and the sections within this also observed and "read." Between each pit or "square," a "balk" or wall of untouched earth was left along which the staff and workmen could move easily so that after a time a typical Wheeler excavation looks like a grid. Later the intervening balks could be removed, of course, but a great advantage of working in small units like this is that every piece of work can be carefully supervised by the head of excavations. The opposite was too often true of the methods used by Petrie and other nineteenth-century archaeologists. Unskilled workmen were left for too long unsupervised, although Petrie tried to overcome this difficulty with his sudden "surprise appearances" and his use of a long-range telescope.

I am not suggesting that Wheeler's method is the only correct one. It cannot be applied on all sites, as he himself admits, but it may stand as a typical example of good modern archaeological technique.

The excavation of a great mound or "tell" like that of Harappa or Mohenjo-Daro is difficult and complex. It is no good just skimming off layer after layer and automatically assuming that each represents a successive period of occupation. It may do so, or it may not. Nowadays when building a new skyscraper, for instance, the builders clear the site of any previous structure and sink their foundations on bedrock, or at least at earth level. Not so the men who occupied Mohenjo-Daro. Sometimes they built on the foundations of their predecessors' dwellings; sometimes they partially cleared them; at other times old buildings were left standing and continued to be occupied, whereas in another part of the city new buildings were being raised at a high level.

Again, take the rubbish dumps which accumulated for centuries

outside the city walls. These are of great importance to archaeologists because they frequently contain objects which the inhabitants of successive periods have discarded, but which may be of
great value for comparative dating. If the dump has been left untouched, then obviously objects found at the lowest level will be
the oldest, and those at the top the latest. But what happens if, at
some time or another, they have dug a pit in the dump? Then the
objects will have become mixed up and if the excavator is not
observant enough to spot this his stratigraphy will go haywire. But
it *is* possible, by noticing differences in the color and texture of
the earth to avoid making such mistakes. Hence the importance of
an accurate "section" or better still, many "sections" at different
points which can be compared.

Another valuable source of information is the city walls. To
the average onlooker at an ancient site a wall is just a wall but it
may tell the archaeologist much. Has it ever been rebuilt, and if
so when and why? Was the rebuilding normal repair due to age?
Or was it due to the threat of invasion? Is there any evidence
of an attack having been made on it, and if so when? I remember
seeing the well-preserved walls of a Roman city at Caerwent, in
Wales. To me it appeared to be just a normal third-century stone
wall with projecting towers or bastions. But I was told that it had
in fact been rebuilt several times, and that when clearing one of
the bastions the archaeologists found the skeletons of men slain
in battle, who had been dumped into the bastion and covered up.
Again, when Schliemann excavated Tiryns, a Mycenaean city near
Mycenae, he found the skeletons of its last defenders, or attackers,
lying among the debris outside.

It was Wheeler's keen eye for a site which enabled him to detect
what his predecessors had overlooked—that both Harappa and
Mohenjo-Daro had been fortified cities. Until 1946 it had been
assumed that both cities had developed without the need of strong
fortifications, which would have made them almost unique, save
for the palaces of Crete. But the archaeologist's training on British
sites had accustomed him to note differences of color and texture
in the earth, and at Harappa something about the shape and color
of the earth surrounding the central part of the mound made him

suspect that here there had once been powerful defenses. But defenses against whom? And of what date?

Excavating at this point he soon discovered mighty walls of mud brick which had once protected a citadel raised above the level of the rest of the city, and he found a similar citadel at Mohenjo-Daro. In both cases there was another feature, both peculiar and slightly sinister. At Harappa, below the citadel, which was 460 yards (over a quarter of a mile) long and 215 yards wide, with walls 45 feet thick, was a group of buildings which were identified as a double row of barracks, a double row of huge granaries, and remains of eighteen circular brick platforms, each with a central hole with fragments of straw and barley at the bottom.

In modern Kashmir grain is still pounded by this method. Coolies or laborers wielding great mortars grind the grain in similar pestles, and there can be no doubt that some three thousand years ago Harappan laborers were doing the same. But why were their threshing floors and granaries placed at this particular point, under the frowning walls of the citadel? At Mohenjo-Daro a similar arrangement was found, even better preserved. There the citadel was on an artificial mound forty feet high and protected by a massive wall of mud brick and timber set with towers. There too were the foundations of a great granary which had measured 150 by 75 feet. Some of the walls were still standing to a height of 20 feet and the outer walls of the working platform were sloped, except at one point where they were vertical. Here, it is believed, bales of grain were hauled up from below, probably from carts which had been driven in from the surrounding villages.

From archaeological evidence alone—since we have no understandable written records—this arrangement strongly suggests regimented labor working under powerful supervision. And if this was so, who were the supervisors? Examination of the citadel at Harappa revealed the remains of a huge bath or tank, made watertight with mortar and bitumen, and nearby were groups of buildings which, it has been suggested, may have housed a college of priests. The bath, other examples of which have been found at both cities, may be significant. Today ritual cleansing is an important part of the Hindu religion. But so far, neither at Mohenjo-Daro nor Harappa have any buildings been identified as temples or sanctuaries of a religious cult. Many little figurines have been found representing a woman, possibly a fertility goddess. Some of these figures have children at the breast; others have a pannier on each side, which, from the smoke stains found inside, may have been used for burning incense. But the Egyptians, Sumerians, Mycenaeans, Mayas, and Incas worshiped many gods. Whom did the Indus Valley people worship? So far we do not know.

There are so many things about them we would like to know, but a great deal has been established by the archaeologists. First they had no dwellings comparable to those of Egypt and Mesopotamia. The largest are comfortably spacious but not grandiose— the kind of houses one would expect prosperous merchants and officials to occupy. No royal palaces have been found, and no royal tombs. Most of the city area of Harappa and Mohenjo-Daro consists of row upon row of small dwellings fronting on to narrow streets, some of which are "dog-legged" to break the force of the prevailing wind. Everywhere there is evidence of planning and organization. Sewage was carried away from the houses in earthenware drains cased in brick, with manholes for regular inspection. There are many baths and latrines; the Harappans were ahead of both the Egyptians and Sumerians in the matter of sanitation.

Numerous small objects have been found in the houses which give us a clue to the kind of people the Harappans were. They had a system of weights and measures, examples of which have been found, from very small to large units. From these we know that they had a decimal system, as in modern Europe and the United States. They were a trading people, importing copper, silver, and lapis lazuli from Afghanistan, turquoise from Iran, and other products from ancient Sumer. Many Sumerian objects have been found, such as cylinder seals, and their art sometimes shows an affinity with that of Sumer; one even finds Sumerian religious motifs. But the Harappans were not Sumerians or offshoots of Sumer.

They grew wheat, barley, peas, and melons, and they domesticated cattle, of which many pictures appear in their art; animals
such as the buffalo, humped cattle, sheep, pigs, and goats. They
also had domestic dogs and cats. At one site the paw marks of a
dog and cat were found imprinted on a piece of clay. The dog, as
usual, had been in pursuit. It also appears that they grew cotton
and exported it, possibly to Sumer. The river was the main
source of communication, and they established settlements along
the southern coast of India. To pay for their imports of metals
and other items, they must have exported agricultural produce,
among which, judging from the huge granaries at their twin cities,
grain would predominate.

Like the Ancient Egyptians and the Sumerians, they were skillful hydraulic engineers, building great embankments to hold back
the waters of the flooding Indus, and channeling water to their
fields. Like Egypt and Sumer, the Indus Valley was a "riverine"
civilization but apparently not as old. The earliest levels found
so far have been dated to approximately 2500 B.C., but at this
time, two hundred years after the Egyptians had built the Great
Pyramid, the Harappans were still at a low level of culture and
had not emerged from the Chalcolithic period. At that same
period the Sumerians could look back over at least seven hundred
years of civilization and were living in great cities such as Ur,
Nippur, and Erech. Great efforts have been, and are being made,
to trace the origin of the Harappans. Hundreds of their village
settlements have been excavated all the way along the Indus River
from Harappa to Mohenjo-Daro and down to and along the coast.
The matter is still not settled, but objects found at the lowest
levels of these sites have some affinity with those found in the
mountains of eastern Persia and Baluchistan, though Professor
Stuart Piggott, an authority on Indian prehistory, says that since
no seals have been found in the Baluchistan villages whoever
brought what was to develop into Harappan civilization must have
come from Persia (Iran) where such seals have been found.

The current theory is that, just as the inhabitants of the west
Iranian highlands moved down into the Tigris-Euphrates valleys
and were among the founders of Sumerian civilization, so possibly,

about 2500 B.C. or earlier, the mountain peoples of western Iran
may have been tempted down from their inhospitable highlands
to the potentially rich valley of the Indus. The ancestors of the
Harappans already had the example of Sumer before them. They
must have known what could be achieved by harnessing and controlling the waters of a mighty flooding river.

It is not true of all ancient civilizations that, like Topsy, they
"just growed." It would seem that the founders of the Indus Valley
civilization consciously and deliberately copied that of Sumer.
There is evidence of this in the fact that among the buildings
examined by Wheeler was one which used the mud and timber
construction which is found in Sumer but which is quite un-
suitable to the climatic conditions of the Indus Valley; subsequently this method was dropped. It would also seem, judging
from the evidence available to date, that this extraordinary, not
very attractive civilization with its planned cities, planned drain-
age system, planned way of life—reminiscent of a modern authori-
tarian state—rose and fell in not more than about a thousand years,
less than one-third of the time during which the civilizations of
Egypt and Mesopotamia existed.

I said "not very attractive" whereas what I should perhaps
have said was "not very attractive to me," which is one reason why
I have unashamedly used the unfortunate Harappans as guinea
pigs for an exposition of modern archaeological technique. Their
art was not remarkable, their architecture, with its monotonous
rows of barracklike dwellings, extremely dull. They rarely depicted the human figure, and when examples have been found,
one's heart does not warm to them as it does to the Egyptians,
the Mycenaeans, or the classical Greeks. Yet they must have been
a valiant and resolute people, who could venture down from their
mountain homelands into a valley potentially rich in wealth but at
first full of danger of wild animals and diseases bred in that
marshy, unhealthy country. Who knows how many thousands
perished in the struggle to tame the valley before the Harappans
could make it produce wealth?

Remember that all these facts and theories are based on archaeological research alone. Does archaeology offer us any clue as

to how and why the Harappan civilization perished? It does, and the evidence is dramatic. When Wheeler and his assistants examined the upper levels of Mohenjo-Daro and Harappa they noticed that there had been a gradual deterioration. Just as, in modern times, former mansions become slums and are divided up into apartments, so in the Harappan cities the larger buildings had been, at a late date, cut up into smaller rooms by partitions, and the wider streets were encroached upon; the lanes were choked with humble dwellings.

Decay was evident, but why? Again it is necessary to apply imagination to fact. We know, nowadays, that if you strip a landscape of its trees and vegetation, the climate deteriorates, soil erosion sets in, and you end up with a dust bowl. This process is still going on today in various parts of the world, such as East Africa, though experts are doing their best to check it. Now the Harappans used a great deal of timber for firing the kilns in which they made their mud bricks—they had no building stone—and this must have come from the valley. It may be that this denuding of the landscape caused an increase of rainfall and uncontrollable flooding of the great river. There is evidence of embankments or levees being built higher and higher, and evidence that at times these were breached.

In time such conditions would disrupt the orderly planning of the Harappan state; crops would be ruined, irrigation systems would fail, and wealth decline. Such circumstances might—though this is pure speculation—also produce political unrest, perhaps revolution. The priest-engineer rulers, whoever they were, might well lose their grip on the people. Whatever the reason, there was deterioration and decay from within, but we do know that the final death blow was from without.

Again we owe the discovery and interpretation of this tragic disaster to Sir Mortimer Wheeler who, just as he had reconstructed the attack by the Twelfth Legion on Maiden Castle in England, now revealed the slaughter which had accompanied the sack of Mohenjo-Daro. Archaeologists often use the phrase "human debris" to denote objects made or used by man, but sometimes, as in this case, it can have a more poignant meaning. In some of the streets of Mohenjo-Daro skeletons lay in tumbled heaps, unburied and without funerary equipment. In others bodies of men, women, and children lay sprawled where they had fallen to the swords and spears of an unknown attacker.

Some of the Harappan buildings were "well houses" approached by flights of steps. In one such house lay the skeletons of two persons lying where they had died, on the steps, in a vain attempt to get to the street. Remains of a third and fourth victim lay close to the house. In another room the excavators found the bodies of thirteen women and a small child, some wearing bracelets, beads, and rings, but lying in the attitudes of violent death. Two of the skulls had sword cuts. In another part of the city the skeletons of nine people, in contorted attitudes, were found in a shallow pit together with two elephant trunks. Who were they? Perhaps a family of ivory workers who, in attempting to escape, had been cut down by the enemy. The bodies had been looted but the plunderers had no use for the tusks, which they left behind.

Who were the attackers, whose grim work was also found at Harappa and other Indus Valley sites? Archaeology cannot tell us, but perhaps the myths can. Who was Indra, the "fort-destroyer" who "rent forts as age consumes a garment"? Was he indeed a god, or a deified war leader? Before the discovery of Harappa and Mohenjo-Daro scholars probing for possible literal truths in the Vedic hymns thought that the "ramparts" and "castles" they mention were, at the most, primitive stockades erected by a barbarian people. Now there can be little doubt that the Indus Valley cities were meant; indeed one city mentioned in the Rig-Veda is *Hari-Yupuya,* which could have been Harappa.

The Indus Valley civilization, after a thousand years of existence, was destroyed by Aryan invaders who swept down into India in the fifteenth century B.C., bringing with them the language from which modern Sanskrit, the classical form of the principal modern Indian language, is derived. It is related to nearly all European tongues, including English, French, Italian, German, Dutch, Scandinavian, and the classical languages of Greece and Rome. It is important to understand the meaning of the term "Aryan" which we shall meet again in Greece and Asia

Minor. It does not mean "race" but refers only to a group of interrelated languages spoken by peoples who entered India, western Asia, and eastern Europe during the period roughly from 2000 to 1000 B.C. All these languages have a common root, but from which land they stemmed we cannot be certain; perhaps southern Russia.

The Aryan invaders of India became its rulers, but they seem to have adopted some of the customs of the people they conquered, for example ritual bathing (but not Harappan sanitary engineering) and certain art forms: the illustration of the little Harappan dancing girl is remarkably like classical Hindu art, though at least a thousand years earlier. More examples will doubtless be discovered, and many mysteries which at present shroud Harappan civilization cleared up by present and future generations of archaeologists.

Back
to the Heartland

Having completed our world journey, we return to the region from which we started, the Middle East, Egypt, and southeastern Europe where the world's oldest civilizations began, and where the pioneer archaeologists of the nineteenth and early twentieth centuries revealed them. Now that you have watched, in Pakistan, a first-class modern archaeologist at work, you will understand how much evidence was lost or overlooked by some of the early excavators of Egypt and Mesopotamia. However, let us do them honor; very few were mere treasure seekers and if they sometimes made mistakes which make their successors shudder, these were not necessarily due to carelessness or haste, but because, as pioneers, they lacked the technique which only accumulated experience can teach.

But from the turn of the century onward techniques of excavation improved; another generation of archaeologists appeared on the scene, some (but by no means all) better trained and equipped than those who had dug in the same areas during the exciting period during which the civilizations of Egypt, Mesopotamia, Syria, Asia Minor, and Greece were being revealed. And since we have been away from this heartland of civilization for quite a time, let us summarize very briefly what had been achieved up to World War I.

Petrie had surveyed many pyramids, dug numerous tombs, trained and inspired many students (one might almost say "disciples") and each year had alternated between digging in Egypt and lecturing at University College, London, where he held the Professorship of Egyptology. And each year he would publish reports on his season's work. He had produced order from the chaos left by Amélineau at the tombs of the First and Second Dynasty Pharaohs at Abydos, had identified these kings, and placed them in correct chronological sequence and thus pushed back the known history of Egypt by some four hundred years.

At the same time he had discovered the tombs of the predynastic inhabitants of the Nile Valley and established to his own and most people's satisfaction that these were the ancestors of the civilized pyramid-building Egyptians. He had taught Egyptologists to recognize the importance of small objects, and instilled into them his system of sequence dating. He continued to excavate in Egypt until after the end of World War I, but later transferred his attention to what was then Palestine, which he called "Egypt beyond the frontiers."

Meanwhile such scholars as Dr. George Reisner had systematically dug and cleared the mastaba tombs around the Giza pyramids, and, while so doing, came upon the tomb of Hetepheres, mother of Cheops, with all its rich funerary furniture. He had made a detailed study of the origins and development of the Egyptian tomb and worked as far south as Meroë in the Sudan where he found pyramid-tombs of Nubians who had become Egyptianized.

Other excavators had worked on the vexed question of Egyptian origins, and identified various predynastic cultures at Badari, Amrata, Merimda, and other places. But there was a strange, inexplicable gap between these primitives and the pyramid-building Pharaohs. One of the most important and significant excavations carried out during the past thirty years has been that of Professor Walter B. Emery, Petrie's successor as Professor of Egyptology at

University College, London. At North Sakkara, where the British Egyptologist Quibell had established, in 1912, the existence of archaic tombs, Emery has dug out a series of magnificent mastaba tombs belonging to kings and queens of the First and Second Dynasties (approximately between 3200 and 2800 B.C.). Among those whose names have definitely been identified are Hor-aha (who may have been Menes, unifier and first ruler of a united Egypt), Zer, Uadji, Udimu, Semerkhet, and Ka'a, all of the First Dynasty.

If you recall Petrie's work at Abydos, you will remember that what appeared to be tombs of these same Pharaohs were also identified there. The pyramid-building Pharaohs often had two funerary monuments (Snofru appears to have had *three* pyramids), one of which was a genuine tomb, containing the body, and the other a cenotaph. It is thought that this is a relic of the days when Egypt—before its unification by Menes in 3200 B.C.—was divided into two kingdoms, Upper and Lower Egypt. According to Egyptian belief, the *ka* or spirit of the dead man or woman could pass easily from one House of Eternity to another. We do not know whether the royal tombs were at Abydos, a holy place sacred to Osiris, or at Sakkara. Emery believes that the Sakkara mastabas, which are of great size and had evidently been richly furnished before they were robbed, were the royal tombs, and this view is gaining wide acceptance. However the matter is not yet settled.

What *is* interesting is the level of civilization, in respect of architecture, art, and craftsmanship, which these great mastabas reveal. In all these aspects Egyptian civilization was as rich then as it was when the Step Pyramid was built three to four hundred years later. Emery, who started his excavations at Sakkara in 1936, continued up to 1939 and resumed them from 1946 to 1956, has opened an absorbing new chapter in Ancient Egyptian history, which he unfolds in his recently published book *Archaic Egypt*.

It is difficult to overemphasize the importance of this revelation. The "missing link" between the hut-dwelling predynastic Egyptians and Joser's astonishing Step Pyramid—the first stone monument in the world—has now been made clear. The predecessors of that noble building were the royal mastabas of the First and

Second Dynasties, huge structures of mud brick, oblong in shape, with the paneled-façade elevations like the enclosure wall of the Step Pyramid, the interiors honeycombed with chambers surrounding a burial pit (sometimes stone lined) sunk into the rock beneath.

Emery has been able to trace a steady development of these tombs, as one would expect over so long a period (Emery says 550 years), but even the earliest known, that of Hor-aha, is extremely impressive. To take a few typical examples: the tomb of Hor-aha is over 150 feet long by 70 feet broad, about half the area of a football field. Within it are twenty-seven square chambers built to contain funerary equipment, and below, cut out of the rock, is a great rectangular pit divided into five chambers by cross walls. One of these chambers, which had all been roofed with heavy timber, may have contained the burial of the Pharaoh.

On the north side of the structure was a series of models, including one of the royal estate, and a brick-lined pit which had contained the "solar bark" in which the dead king expected to travel with Ra across the sky. The queens of the First Dynasty were certainly well provided for. The mastaba of Queen Meryet-Nit, possibly the third sovereign of the dynasty, measures about 130 feet by 50 feet, and when I was fortunate enough to visit it just after its excavation I was astonished to see, in a series of little pits surrounding the tomb, the skeletons of her sacrificed servants. Each had been buried with objects denoting his craft. Her vasemaker had his stone vessels and copper tools, her artist his paint pots, and her shipmaster his model boats. Those little, bleached skeletons, exposed to the Egyptian sun after some five thousand years, were a pathetic and moving sight.

However, it says much for the humanity of the Egyptians that they dropped this custom before 3000 B.C., later substituting little glazed-clay model servants called *shawabti* ("answerers") who, by a process of magic, could take the place of flesh-and-blood human beings. Other peoples, as we have seen, were still sacrificing their servants at a much more recent date.

In a general description of these tombs, of which no two are exactly alike, Professor Emery writes:

In the burial chamber there were chests and boxes containing garments, jewellery, games, etc., and ivory inlaid furniture, such as chairs, small tables, and beds. The other rooms adjacent to the burial also contained furniture, tools, and weapons, and in nearly every case one room was entirely reserved for the storage of food in the form of great joints of meat on pottery platters, bread kept in sealed pottery jars, and cheese in small tubular vessels. Other pottery dishes, bowls, and jars formed a sort of reserve dinner service. . . . In other rooms big wine jars were stacked in rows . . . In the magazines [small chambers] of the superstructure, more equipment was stored . . .

These magnificent sepulchers, in which the fragments of inlaid furniture, copper, and goldwork show how rich the interments must once have been, are seventeen hundred years older than the fabulous tomb of Tutankhamen, which is itself three thousand years old. Yet the kind of equipment—inlaid furniture, ivory game sets, lovely vessels of stone and metal, ornaments, jewelry, food offerings—anticipated that of the much later royal sepulcher, though Tutankhamen, living near the end of Egypt's Imperial Age, naturally took much more gold with him, together with chariots which were unknown in Early Dynastic times. But the basic conception of the things needed in the afterlife remained the same; nor was the craftsmanship of the objects found in the Early Dynastic tombs in any way inferior.

Tutankahmen's tomb, the objects from which have been described in the first chapter, was discovered in 1922 by Howard Carter, a British Egyptologist, financed and assisted by Lord Carnarvon. Its incredible survival, in an almost intact state, after three thousand years, was due to a happy combination of circumstances. First, the young Pharaoh, a relative of the hated "heretic king" Akhenaten, was unpopular, as were all members of Akhenaten's family, among the priests of Amen responsible for the burial. They interred him in quite a small tomb, one of the smallest in the Royal Valley. Secondly he reigned for only a few years and died young. Third, and most important, a much larger and later tomb was tunneled out of the hillside above Tutankhamen's modest sepulcher, and the stone chippings from the excavation

concealed the small flight of rock-cut steps leading to that of
the forgotten Pharaoh.

But we owe its discovery and preservation to the patience and
determination of Carter, who combed every square foot of the
valley, and had been urged by his patron to give up in the very
year before the great discovery was made. Carter persisted, and
in September 1922 struck the first of a flight of steps. These led to
a sealed door which, when removed, admitted the awestruck
discoverers to a series of chambers, each crammed with marvels,
and one of which contained the intact burial of the Pharaoh
in his coffin of solid gold. It is also due to Carter and his devoted
assistants, such as Winlock, Mace, and others, that these unique
treasures were removed with loving care, and preserved for
posterity. It is doubtful if such a rich discovery will ever be made
again in Egypt, although in 1940 Professor Montet, of Belgium,
found the intact burials of several Pharaohs of a much later dynasty
at Tanis, in the Delta area. Their silver coffins and gold face-masks
can be seen in the Cairo Museum.

From a strictly archaeological viewpoint Tutankhamen's tomb
told us little that we did not already know, whereas Emery's less
spectacular, though still impressive finds at Sakkara have broken
new ground, and set Egyptologists rethinking the whole problem
of the origins and early development of Egyptian civilization.

Other interesting discoveries made in Egypt in recent years
are the solar bark of Cheops, found intact with its hull, steering
oar, and cordage in a pit near the Great Pyramid, and, again
at Sakkara, Zakaria Goneim's excavation of an unfinished step
pyramid near that of Joser. Only a few of its steps had been
built before it was abandoned, but beneath it Goneim found a
deep descending gallery striking down through the rock and
leading to a rough-hewn burial chamber also unfinished. I was
fortunate to be at Sakkara when the climax of this excavation
was reached, the opening of the sealed alabaster sarcophagus. Alas,
it was completely empty and had never contained a burial.
Perhaps this was a dummy tomb, and the real one may still be
found elsewhere under the pyramid enclosure. The pyramid is
believed to have been begun by Sekhem-set ("Powerful of Body"),
successor to Joser.

Meanwhile, far to the south, in the Sudan, Professor Emery has excavated a number of splendid fortresses, some of the Twelfth Dynasty, which were garrisoned by those of the Pharaoh's troops responsible for guarding the vital trade routes between Egypt and the south. These mighty strongholds, some as big as medieval castles, with towers and arrow slits, will, alas, all be destroyed when the new High Dam is built and the rising waters flood most of ancient Nubia. Being of mud-brick they cannot be dismantled and removed.

Turning to Greece where we left Heinrich Schliemann enjoying his triumphs at Mycenae, the most revolutionary discovery was made at the turn of the century when Sir Arthur Evans unearthed, at Knossos in Crete, remains of a magnificent civilization which he called "Minoan," after the legendary King Minos.

Evans, unlike Schliemann, was a scholar from a family of scholars. It was his father, John Evans, who went to the Somme Valley with his colleague Prestwich, met Boucher des Pérthes, and confirmed that the worked flints he had found were the work of paleolithic man. Young Arthur grew up in an atmosphere of learning and scholarship. He traveled widely in eastern Europe, was for a time a war correspondent in the Balkans, and meanwhile made an intensive study of medieval, Greek, and Roman antiquities. He had intense curiosity about the remote past, and on being shown Schliemann's finds at Troy and Mycenae, pondered on whether a people capable of producing such art and creating such splendid buildings could also have been literate.

These Mycenaean treasures of inlaid bronze, gold, and silver, the vigorous yet sophisticated art which was neither Oriental or classical Greek, fascinated him. He could not accept Schliemann's naive belief that they belonged to the period of the Trojan War (twelfth century B.C.); to Evans they seemed older, although at the time he had no means of dating them. Even if they were as late as the twelfth century B.C., they belonged to a civilization which had existed at the same time as that of Egypt. Petrie had discovered vases in Egypt which he believed came from the Aegean area. And since the Ancient Egyptians had had a writing system as far back as 3000 B.C., why not the Mycenaeans?

Yet not a scrap of anything resembling a script had turned up on any Mycenaean site. Tombs, gravestones, objects were all mute. It was puzzling. Then, one day, when Evans and his friend Myres were browsing among the curio shops in the back streets of Athens, he picked up from a dealer's tray a tiny object of glazed clay, scarcely bigger than his thumbnail. Evans was very short-sighted, but when he held something very close to his eyes, he could see it almost microscopically; he had found this a great asset in examining ancient coins. This time he thought he recognized peculiar markings or "squiggles" on the object, which was a bead seal. He examined others on the dealer's tray and again found the markings. "Where did these come from?" he inquired. "From Crete, sir," came the reply.

Evans thought over this problem. He had already considered Crete as a possible place from which some form of hieroglyphic script might have been transmitted to Europe; the island was roughly equidistant from Egypt, Asia, and the European mainland. An Italian archaeologist, Frederico Halbherr, had already begun to excavate at Phaistos in Crete in the previous year.

Schliemann had also wanted to dig in Crete, and had even entered into negotiation with a Cretan landowner for the purchase of some land; but, counting up the olive trees on the property and finding the number somewhat smaller than he had been promised, Schliemann the businessman triumphed over Schliemann the archaeologist and the deal was called off.

Shortly afterward the great German died, in the year 1890. Four years later Evans landed at Crete for the first time, and immediately fell in love with the island. He was enchanted by the wild, mountainous landscape, the hospitable but fiercely independent islanders who reminded him of the Balkan peoples whose struggle for independence he had championed. On horseback, accompanied by Myres, he traveled the length and breadth of the country, noticing in many places evidences of buildings, ancient roads, which seemed to him of high antiquity. And in many villages he found numerous examples of the little seals which had first attracted his curiosity. The Cretans, he discovered, often found them in their fields, and as each seal had a little hole through the middle, the women wore them around their necks as charms when they were nursing their babies. The Cretans called them "milk stones" for this reason.

Several years later, having managed to purchase a piece of land at Knossos (the same land for which Schliemann had negotiated), Evans sailed again for Crete. He had determined to dig at Knossos, first because it is mentioned by Homer as the home of King Minos, and second because a little earlier a modern Cretan, appropriately of the same name—Minos—had dug into a large mound there and found a number of *pithoi* (clay jars as high as a man). March 1899 was a historic year for Evans and for archaeology. He arrived at Herakleion, the nearest port, in one of the worst thunderstorms in living memory. Lightning flashed from the towering peaks of Mount Ida, the legendary birthplace of Zeus. It seemed almost as if the King of Gods, lord of the thunderbolts, was marking this momentous day.

Accompanied by the archaeologist D. G. Hogarth, renowned for his work in Mesopotamia, and Duncan Mackenzie, a Scotsman known for his skill in recording the results of excavations, Evans went to Knossos, recruited workmen, and without delay began to sink shafts into the mound. Within a few days he had struck a row of great oblong stone chambers, some of which contained *pithoi,* and at the bottom of each chamber were stone-lined pits which looked as if they had once contained treasure; fragments of gold leaf were found in some of them.

Not long afterward he found what he had been seeking—large numbers of clay tablets inscribed with an unknown form of writing; not cuneiform, not hieroglyphic, not in any way resembling Greek characters. These tablets, he also discovered, had been baked, but not in a kiln. Originally they had been left to dry in the sun and would undoubtedly have perished but for one fact. At some unknown period the building had been destroyed by fire—there was ample evidence in the sooty stains on the oil jars and the surrounding masonry—and it was this which had baked the tablets.

But as week followed week, the excitement of the discovery of the tablets was overwhelmed by a much greater one. It soon appeared that the oblong chambers were merely the storage maga-

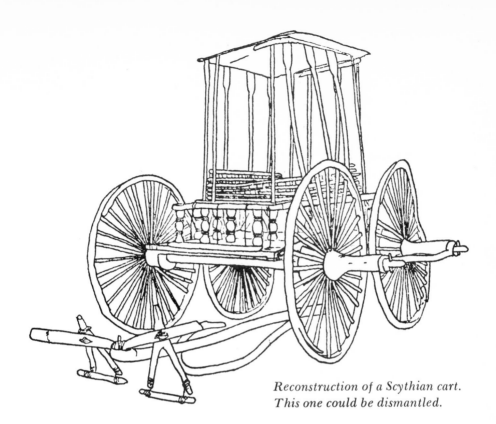

Reconstruction of a Scythian cart.
This one could be dismantled.

This silver beaker, decorated with embossed and chased figures of animals, was made
by Scythians who ranged the Danube region about the fourth century B.C.

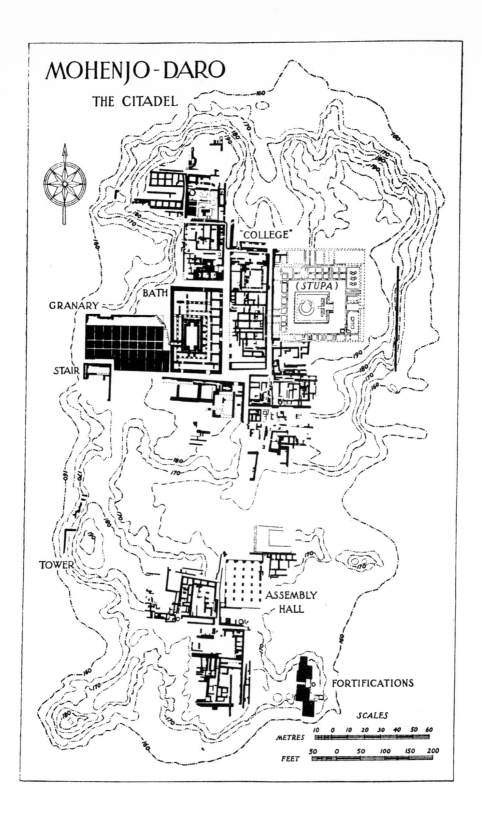

MOHENJO-DARO
THE CITADEL

"COLLEGE"

(STUPA)

BATH

GRANARY

STAIR

TOWER

ASSEMBLY
HALL

FORTIFICATIONS

SCALES
METRES   10 0 10 20 30 40 50 60
FEET   50 0   50   100   150   200

*Tutankhamen's coffin, of solid gold. Howard Carter's discovery
of this tomb was sensational news in 1922.*

Zakaria Goneim's excavation of an unfinished step pyramid at Sakkara. At left, workmen clear fill at the entrance approach. The stone vessels (below) were found in a side passage leading to a complex of storerooms. Part of a second blockage shows in the background.

Knossos. One of the storage magazines showing huge oil jars and the rectangular pits which contained precious objects. Below, the 3,000-year-old throne, with frescoes restored.

The Linear A and Linear B writing system of the Minoans
was finally deciphered by Michael Ventris

The "ghost" of a viking ship found at Sutton Hoo,
in Norfolk, England, during World War II

*Stonehenge. New findings by astronomers indicate that these stones
may have been used as an ancient observatory.*

*A scuba diver finds a pair of amphorae off the coast of Turkey. Submarine archaeology
is one of the most exciting developments in this field.*

zines of a great palace hidden under the mound—hillock is a better word. A labyrinthine complex of buildings was revealed, of which some architectural features resembled those of Mycenae. Objects found within the maze of rooms, mainly pottery at first, also seemed Mycenaean. But as he dug deeper and deeper, Evans realized that he had discovered something far older. In his own words, noted in his diary at the time: "The extraordinary phenomenom—*nothing Greek—nothing Roman* . . . even Geometrical [seventh century B.C.] pottery fails us—though as *tholoi* [tombs] found near the central road show, a flourishing Knossos existed lower down. . . . Nay its great period goes *at least well back to the pre-Mycenaean period."*

Evans had come to Crete in search of a writing system and had found it. But he had found something else, the remains of the first civilization in Europe, more than a thousand years older than Schliemann's Mycenaeans, more than two thousand years older than classical Greece. Its foundations stretched far back to the New Stone Age (before 3000 B.C.), and at the height of its power it was contemporary with, and equal to, the civilization of Ancient Egypt at the period of her imperial greatness.

Evans who, on his father's death, had inherited a large fortune, decided to devote the rest of his life to excavating and interpreting the Minoan civilization. For over thirty years he not only excavated Knossos, but partially restored it at his own expense so that future generations would see, not a tumbled heap of ruins such as Petrie would have left, but a Minoan palace, with its courts and staterooms, grand staircases and frescoed walls. That is what you will see if you go to Knossos today, and if you are at a loss for words to describe Evans' achievement, try those which are inscribed on the tomb of Sir Christopher Wren, architect of St. Paul's Cathedral, London: *"Lector, si monumentum requiris, circumspice"* (Reader, if you seek his monument, look around you).

The Miracle of
Crete

Evans, who is believed to have spent over three-quarters of a million dollars on excavating and restoring Knossos, built himself a villa near the site and called it the Villa Ariadne, after the legendary daughter of King Minos. He was not as readily susceptible to myths and legends as Schliemann had been, but the more he studied Knossos and other Minoan sites, the more clearly he heard echoes of the story of Theseus and the Minotaur.

You will remember the story. Minos, king of Crete, was a mighty ruler whose fleet controlled the eastern Mediterranean and who had conquered cities on the Greek mainland, including Athens. As tribute he demanded that each year seven noble Athenian youths and seven maidens be sent to Knossos as a sacrifice to the Minotaur. a monster who was half bull, half man, kept by Minos in a labyrinth under his palace. Many perished in this way until Theseus, son of the king of Athens, volunteered to go as one of the selected victims.

But when he reached Knossos, the beautiful daughter of King Minos, Ariadne, fell in love with the handsome Athenian and gave him a ball of thread. When he entered the dark labyrinth he paid out the thread behind him. Then he fought the Minotaur and "killed him with his fists," after which he found his way out again by following the thread. He married Ariadne, who had saved his life, and the two escaped from the island. Another legend describes how Daedalus, a mighty artificer, built the labyrinth for Minos, and also "Ariadne's dancing-floor," a name which Evans, who at heart was as romantic as Schliemann, gave to a paved area of the Knossian palace. Daedalus also made himself wings, and with his son Icarus fled from the island. But Icarus flew too near the sun, so that the wax which attached the wings to his body melted, and he was drowned.

Evans, though not himself a trained archaeologist, had the wisdom (and the money) to employ professionals throughout his thirty years of excavation. He also had a resident architect who helped him accurately to restore buildings which had been partially destroyed. But Evans, who was strong-willed, occasionally autocratic, and equipped with vast knowledge, patience, and a disciplined imagination, was the presiding genius of Knossos. Soon after beginning their excavations. he and his staff came upon fragments of brilliantly colored painted frescoes which had adorned the plastered walls of the stone-built palace. Some of these depicted dark, slim-waisted, muscular youths with black curling hair; others showed a charging bull; and in one extraordinary painting a young man is shown leaping over the back of the bull, with two other athletes, who were girls, standing on each side of the picture, one presumably to help the athlete make his leap, the other to catch him.

Had these some connection with the legend of Theseus and the Minotaur? Here was no "bull-monster" but a magnificent bull, which we know was often connected with religious worship, because of his strength and procreative power. There were the Apis bulls of Egypt, the Assyrian winged bulls which Layard found, and—going back twenty thousand years—the bulls painted in the Lascaux caves. As for sacrifice, these young men and girls were obviously taking part in a highly dangerous sport which was almost certainly more than a game but a ritual.

Among the frescoes which Evans found and restored were some showing men and fashionably dressed ladies (but the women were carefully drawn in the foreground while the men were mere "squiggles" in the background) seated or standing on some kind of grandstand, evidently watching some important event. In one of these pictures there is a sacred shrine, topped by the stylized horns of a bull. Evans also discovered a shrine within the palace, containing small figurines of a female figure dressed in full Minoan "court" costume: full, flounced skirt, tight waist, and bolero top revealing the breasts, and around her bare arms were wreathed snakes. He connected these statues with the worship of a Mother Goddess or Earth Mother since the snake is often associated with earth worship.

Again, at various places within the palace were stone-lined pits which at first he thought might be baths. But the Minoans were magnificent hydraulic engineers; they had an efficient sewage system, pipes for carrying away rain water, and when he discovered their baths he found they were rather like the Victorian "hip baths," usually set in chambers which had a drain hole in the floor to carry away the waste. In what he called the "Queen's Megaron" (house) there was a three-thousand-year-old toilet with remains of a seat and what appears to have been a "flush."

So these mysterious pits, which had no outlet for water, were obviously not baths. Evans wondered if they were "ritual pits" into which priests or priestesses of the Mother Goddess descended in order to make propitiatory offerings to the earth deity. Why this was necessary Evans discovered, in dramatic circumstances, much later. In interpreting Minoan religious beliefs he had nothing to guide him save the buildings, frescoes, and innumerable little engraved seals on which were often depicted religious scenes. Always the predominant figure in these scenes is a goddess; when men appear they are usually only priests, warriors, or worshipers. The long-sought-for tablets were a disappointment. Evans was unable to decipher them, nor were any of the linguists he consulted. All he could recognize was that they were lists or inventories of some sort, records of the palace stores; he observed pictograms of men, women, chariots, oil or wine jars, and other objects, and a numerical system. That was all.

He reached the conclusion that the Minoans had worshiped a mother-goddess, or perhaps several aspects of the same goddess, that this worship was connected with the "bull-leaping" sport, that the figures in the grandstand were watching it, and that the young athletes could have been, not precisely sacrificial victims, but people who had been selected and trained to take part in this highly dangerous ritual. On a stone *rhyton* (offering vessel) there is a relief showing an unfortunate athlete who has misjudged his leap and is being gored by the bull. Other scenes, on a pair of magnificent golden cups found at Vaphio, show young men and women catching wild bulls in rope nets; one scene depicts two animals, one of which is evidently a decoy cow, whose companion, a bull, stands bemused in admiration while a crafty Minoan is tethering one of its legs to a tree.

As for the Cretan labyrinth, the layout of the great palace itself is labyrinthine, so it is possible that the Dorians, ancestors of the classical Greeks, seeing Knossos in ruin, and having no such complex buildings themselves, may have wandered through its courts and narrow corridors, seen the "bull-leapers" on the frescoed walls, and conceived the legend of Theseus and the Minotaur. This is only a theory and an unsatisfactory one, in my opinion. Myths are not deliberately invented; they grow, develop, and change over thousands of years of human experience. Trying to understand them is like trying to read a medieval palimpsest in which there are pictures on top of pictures on top of more pictures. Behind every myth there is usually an older myth.

The whole complex and absorbing story has been told in a number of books, including two by the present author. Here there is space only to summarize what Evans and other archaeologists achieved in their interpretation of Minoan culture and how this was related to the Mycenaean civilization which Schliemann discovered. First, a few dates. The early period is misty, but it would seem that sometime between 4000 and 3000 B.C. people who were at a Neolithic (New Stone Age) level of development began to cross from the coast of western Asia to the then uninhabited islands of the Aegean. They were farmers and stock rearers and worshiped a fertility goddess, statuettes of whom have been found in many places. By about 3000 B.C. or perhaps earlier, some of these wanderers had begun to settle in Crete; as one would have expected, they chose one of the most fertile parts of the island, the Messara Plain on the east.

They lived in caves, and sometimes buried their dead in caves. Their rather crude pottery is varied in shape and design which suggests that they did not all come from the same place. Some may have come from Egypt, since archaeologists have found Egyptian stone vases of the type discovered in Early Dynastic tombs (3200– 2800 B.C.). It was this connection with Egypt, which lasted right down to the end of Minoan civilization, which enabled Evans and other archaeologists to work out its approximate chronology. This method was briefly mentioned in the first chapter.

If you find an Egyptian object of known date—say a small statuette bearing the cartouche of a Pharaoh—the layer in which you find it cannot be later than the date when the object was made. It may be earlier, but not much; the peoples of the ancient world, unlike us, were not interested in preserving old objects. Now, if you find the datable object among types of pottery which you have found in undisturbed strata in *other* parts of Crete, it is reasonably safe to assume that these layers too, with the objects they contain, are of the same approximate date as the object. Of course the statuette could possibly have been of earlier date than the layer in which it was found, though this is unlikely. But if later you find other Egyptian objects of the same date in other layers containing a similar type of pottery, then your dating, whether it is 2000, 1600, or 1200 B.C., is reasonably firm.

By establishing these firm dates, combined with a close study of the changes in pottery styles during the periods in between (Petrie's sequence dating), Evans was able to draw up a chronological table or time scale divided into main periods, with subdivisions within those periods. Let me give you an example which shows not only the approximate dates of successive phases in the development of Minoan civilization, but how these can be related, chronologically, to the cultures of other peoples living at the same time. Don't be put off by the technical terminology.

B.C.	EGYPT	CRETE	GREECE
2000	11th Dynasty	Early Minoan III	Early Helladic (las phase of)
1900 1800	12th Dynasty	Middle Minoan I	Middle Helladic
1700	13th to 17th Dynasties, Hyksos invasion	Middle Minoan II Middle Minoan III	Middle Helladic
1600 1500 1400	18th Dynasty	Late Minoan IA Late Minoan IB	Late Helladic I Late Helladic II Late Helladic IIIA (Mycenaean)
1300 1200	19th Dynasty	Late Minoan III	Late Helladic IIIB (Mycenaean)
1100 1000	20th Dynasty		Late Helladic IIIC (Mycenaean)

Though this may look alarming at first sight—although it only represents the latter half of the era we are considering—you may find it useful to consult this guide occasionally if you become muddled by names and dates of periods. As Sir Mortimer Wheeler says, a chronologist is not an archaeologist, but chronology provides the basis for sound archaeology.

The names Early Minoan, Middle Minoan, Middle Helladic, Late Helladic, are mere labels given by archaeologists, a technical jargon which one finds in most professions such as medicine and law, understandable by fellow specialists and not intended for the layman. So if one archaeologist writes in his report, "I found Late Helladic IIIB pottery" at a certain level, other archaeologists will immediately know the type of pottery he is referring to, and its date. "Minoan" is used when referring to Cretan pottery and other artifacts; "Helladic" for that of the Greek mainland. There is a third term, "Cycladic," used in connection with the Greek islands apart from Crete. Archaeologists working in Egypt, Mesopotamia, Persia, Mexico, all have their own technical classifications.

To return to the Minoans. Between about 3000 and 2500 B.C. —the period when the Egyptians were building their royal mastabas and pyramids—the descendants of the first Cretan settlers, reinforced, no doubt, by new arrivals, gradually occupied most of the island, although the main concentration was still on the Messara Plain. They gave up living in caves and learned to build houses with many rooms; these were of rough stone and mud, reinforced by timber framing. In Minoan times there was evidently an abundance of trees on the island. By 2500 B.C. or thereabouts, the craft of metalworking had reached Crete, presumably via new settlers; copper tools are found for the first time in graves.

Metalworking also appears, at about the same time, on the Greek mainland.

These Early Minoans cultivated the olive tree, grew vines and corn, and kept animals such as sheep, oxen, pigs, and fowl. With the growth and improvement of agriculture the population no doubt increased, as more food became available. But they had one blessed advantage enjoyed by few civilizations—complete freedom from armed invasion. Their isolation prevented that. When Homer writes of the Phaeacians who hospitably entertained Odysseus on his way back to Ithaca from Troy, he might well have been describing Crete. Nausicaä, the King's daughter, says to Odysseus: " . . . there is no man on earth, nor ever will be, who would dare set hostile feet on Phaeacian soil. The gods are too fond of us for that. Remote in this sea-beaten home of ours, we are the outposts of mankind . . ."

So the Minoans were free to multiply and develop. Copper tools were followed by the harder bronze, an alloy of copper and tin, and now it was possible to make more efficient cutting tools such as saws, axes, and chisels. Buildings of rough stone gave place to splendid constructions of precisely cut masonry, although timber balks, equally well cut, continued to reinforce the walls. Why did the Cretans do this, and not those other fine masons, the Egyptians and the Incas?

Here is another example of man's applied intelligence which has raised him above all other animals. Crete is in a zone of severe earthquakes. Long before 2000 B.C. the Minoans had found a partial solution to this problem. Whereas buildings entirely of stone would have been shaken down, the bracing of timber within the masonry gave them flexibility.

By 2000 B.C., the beginning of the Early Minoan III period, something extraordinary happened, comparable with the building of the first Egyptian pyramids. At three places—Knossos, Mallia, and Phaistos—the Minoans began to build great structures which we call for convenience "palaces," though they were much more than royal residences. Evans at Knossos, Halbherr at Phaistos, and French archaeologists at Mallia all discovered that beneath the buildings we see today, most of which date from about 1500 B.C., lie the foundations of earlier palaces. Digging still deeper they found remains of extensive settlements or small towns, which had been occupied, and repeatedly rebuilt, from Neolithic, through the Early Bronze Age, up to the building of the first palaces, all of which had been founded at about the same time—2000 B.C.

The layout and construction of these enormous buildings was like that of the later palaces—a main courtyard from which a maze of rooms opened; some obviously the apartments of the ruler and his family, others were administrative offices where clerks and storekeepers kept records on clay tablets. Near these were big storage magazines for oil, grain, wine, and other produce of the land, besides manufactured goods such as pottery and metalwork. These were exported and exchanged for raw materials which the Cretans needed for their industries. In the tomb of Rekhmire, a high Egyptian official at Thebes, there is a picture of men in non-Egyptian costume carrying, among other things, beautiful vessels of what were once thought to be Mycenaean weapons, and at least in one case the silver head of a bull. The Egyptian inscriptions describe these men as the "Keftiu" from "the Isles of the Great Sea." It was not until Evans revealed the Knossian frescoes of the slim-waisted young men in Cretan costume that archaeologists realized that the "Keftiu" were the Minoans.

The palaces in which these lovely things were stored were probably also where they were made—or at least some of them. Every Cretan palace has workshops; potters, smiths, craftsmen in faience, jewelry, and precious metals had their quarters within these labyrinthine buildings. The palaces also contained religious shrines, for example the one at Knossos where Evans found statues of the Snake Goddess, and the mysterious "ritual pits" which had puzzled him at first. A Minoan palace was, in fact, more like a combination of royal residence, cathedral, government office, factory, and warehouse—that is, if we try to seek modern parallels.

During the six hundred years following the building of the first palaces, Minoan civilization continued to develop and flourish. Feeding these centers of power were numerous towns and settlements throughout the island, linked by an excellent road system. There were ports, the sunken remains of which have been observed at several places, and a flourishing maritime trade with the Greek mainland, and with Egypt, Asia, and the Aegean islands. Minoan manufactures have been found throughout this area.

Some of the towns, such as Gournia, where two American scholars, Miss Harriet Boyd-Hawes and Mr. Richard B. Seager carried out important excavations, seem to have been occupied entirely by craftsmen and their families. Others were agricultural villages. There were also what we might regard as the country residences of the nobility, as at Nirou Khani. Other archaeologists —American, French, British, Italian, and Greek—came to Crete to probe the secrets of these and other sites.

Meanwhile Evans, at his beautiful villa overlooking Knossos, continued his excavations and restorations, and labored on his great book *The Palace of Minos,* in which he assembled all he had learned about the civilization to the study of which he had devoted his life. It is his masterpiece. If every Minoan city was destroyed tomorrow, provided one set of Evans' volumes survived, future generations would still know as much about the Minoan civilization as he did.

One of the problems which occupied his mind was the relationship between the Minoans and the Mycenaeans. Although the art of both cultures was similar in some ways, it differed in others, and it is now established beyond doubt that the Cretan civilization is far older. Since Evans had worked out his chronology of Crete it became possible to date Mycenaean buildings, tombs, and objects.

The shaft graves at Mycenae, which Schliemann thought had belonged to the twelfth century B.C., were in fact three hundred years older. The big tholos or beehive-shaped tombs at Mycenae were, however, later than the earliest of the shaft graves. But when the ancestors of the Mycenaeans entered Greece round about 1800 B.C. in Middle Helladic times, they were a rough warrior-caste with little pretensions to civilization, as we can tell from their early tombs. The Minoans, at this period, had already built their first palaces and enjoyed a civilization as developed as that of Egypt.

Noticing the similarities between Minoan and Mycenaean art, especially in their bronze and gold work, Evans believed at first that the Mycenaean cities were merely Cretan colonies. Other scholars, notably Professor Wace, an Englishman, and Professor Blegen, an American, took a different view, which has since been proved correct. Their theory was that the so-called Mycenaeans, who may well have been Homer's "bronze-clad Achaeans" were the first Greek-speaking peoples to enter Greece, related by language to the Aryans who invaded India. Before their coming Greece was inhabited by the same racial stock as the people who had migrated from Asia to Crete and other islands between 5000 and 4000 B.C. The Mycenaeans, or Achaeans (we do not know what they called themselves) brought their "blitz-weapon," the horse-drawn chariot, which was unknown in Greece and did not even reach Egypt until centuries later. On the gravestones which Schliemann found above the Mycenaean shaft graves, and in other places, we see these fierce warriors in their chariots. They overran Greece and in about 1600 B.C. began to build their strong-walled citadels from which they ruled the country.

They came in contact with the Minoans, and, just as the Scythians adopted the art of the civilized Greeks who had colonized the coast of Asia Minor in the eighth century B.C., so these former Greeks, a thousand years earlier, had learned civilization from the Minoans. Probably many of the objects found in the shaft graves, such as the gold-inlaid bronze swords and daggers, were made in Crete or by Cretan craftsmen working for the Mycenaeans.

Another problem which absorbed Evans was the reason why

the Knossian palace had been so frequently rebuilt. Minoan civilization appears to have reached its height between 1700 and 1400 B.C. and it would, of course, be natural that successive rulers, like the Pharaohs, would wish to improve on their predecessors' monuments. But rebuilding had taken place apparently at the same time in Phaistos and Mallia. Why? Evans had a theory that it might have been due to earthquakes. He had noticed, during his excavations, a part of the former palace which had been damaged by violence; there were broken walls and charred timbers. There had been an especially severe disaster in about 1700 B.C. and again round about 1400 B.C. Armed attack? Very unlikely, since at one place he found, in his own words: " . . . the corner of a small house . . . of the Third Middle Minoan period . . . this little house had been ruined by huge blocks hurled—some of them over twenty feet—by what could have been no less than a violent earthquake shock." Men could not have done such damage. Not far from this House of the Fallen Blocks the archaeologist came upon another, which had been damaged at the same time, and in the basement of this house were the heads of "two large oxen of the *urus* breed, the horn-cones of one of which were over a foot in girth at the base" set near tripod altars. When the damaged building had been filled in by the Minoans, to prevent its ever being occupied again, they had sacrificed a bull.

And then a curious and somewhat sinister thing happened. Just as Evans and his workmen were finishing clearing this House of Sacrifice, at 12:15 on April 20, 1922, "a short, sharp shock, sufficient to throw one of my men backwards, accompanied by a deep rumbling sound, was experienced on the site and throughout the region."

Four years passed, while Evans continued at his task. He looked up the records of earthquakes which had occurred in Crete within historical times, and noticed that the shocks appeared to follow a definite cycle. Six major earthquakes had struck Crete within a period of six and a half centuries. Doubtless there had been similar catastrophes in Minoan times—he had seen the evidence of them—but the Minoans would attribute them, not to what we call "natural forces" but to an earth deity. He had read the works of anthropologists who had studied the beliefs of primitive peoples living today, and discovered that among some tribes living within earthquake zones, there is a belief that when shocks occur they are caused by a great bull which is tossing the earth on its horns.

The classical Greeks also had worshiped a god, Poseidon, whose epithet in Homer is the Earth-Shaker. *"In Bulls,"* says the poet, *"does the Earth-Shaker delight."* One of the emblems of Poseidon (later named Neptune by the Romans) was the trident. In Minoan palaces the same symbol had been found, carved on stone pillars standing in small dark chambers like the "ritual pits." Was this the answer to the riddle? Was this why the Minoans placed such emphasis on an earth deity, and were these "ritual pits" and "pillar chambers" built for ceremonies of propitiation?

One sultry summer night in June 1924, Evans was resting in the Villa Ariadne, his mind, as he writes "full of past earthquakes and the foreboding of a new convulsion" when, at 9:45 P.M., the shocks began.

> They caught me reading on my bed in a basement room . . . and, trusting to the exceptional strength of the fabric [which was of reinforced concrete] I chose to see the earthquake through from within. [The house] creaked and groaned, and rocked from side to side, as if the whole must collapse. . . . A dull sound rose from the ground like the muffled roar of an angry bull; our single bell rang, while through the open window came the more distant jangling of the chimes of Candia Cathedral. . . . Meanwhile a mist of dust, lifted upwards by a sudden draught of air, rose sky-high, so as almost to eclipse the full moon, some house lights reflected on this dark bank giving the appearance of a conflagration wrapped round with smoke . . .

And he adds: "It is something to have heard with one's own ears the bellowing of the bull beneath the earth who, according to a primitive belief, tosses it on his horns."

Evans was seventy-five when he had that experience, twenty-five years after the day when Zeus had greeted his arrival in Crete with one of the worst thunderstorms in living memory. Few men have written so romantically about archaeology as Evans, yet few men have been more exact and scientific in their approach to it. But the gods are capricious. Many scholars have labored as long and as hard as Evans, Petrie, and Schliemann in seeking to unveil the ancient world. But only to a few does that world suddenly and dramatically reveal itself, as when Evans heard the roar of the Earth-Shaker and felt the same religious awe which the Minoans had experienced: as when Schliemann saw, glittering deep in the shaft graves, the golden ornaments of Mycenaean kings; as when Carter shone a torch through a hole in the sealed door of Tutankhamen's tomb and saw the gleam of a Pharaoh's treasure.

The collapse of Minoan civilization came in about 1400 B.C. when the palaces of Knossos, Phaistos, Mallia, and others were destroyed by fire and violence. There are several theories which seek to account for this. One is yet another violent earthquake, perhaps caused by the volcanic eruption which almost destroyed the island of Santorin, and which would also have caused enormous tidal waves. Another is that the Mycenaeans attacked and destroyed the palaces; it has been suggested that the legend of Theseus, who later became King of Athens, may be a memory of the war leader who led the Mycenaean host to Crete.

Certainly the Mycenaeans became the dominant power after the fall of Crete, and one of their kings, Idomeneus, was ruling from Knossos at the time of the Trojan War. Again, some scholars believe that there may have been an internal revolution against the rulers of Crete, perhaps supported by foreign aid. No one is certain. My own guess is an earthquake of unprecedented violence, from which the Minoans never recovered, and which the Mycenaeans exploited, taking over the island.

In Greece itself, since Schliemann's death, many more Mycenaean sites have been identified, including the Palace of Nestor at Pylos, discovered and excavated by the American Professor Blegen, who also re-excavated Troy and established, among many more important matters, the true level of Homeric Troy, which was much higher up than Schliemann had supposed. Mycenae and Tiryns have been re-excavated by Professor Wace and Dr. Papadimitriou; there the Greek archaeologists found yet another grave circle, containing older burials than those Schliemann found, and there also Wace discovered the first examples of inscribed clay tablets found on the mainland. This script, which Evans first discovered at Knossos, but which he failed to decipher, is called Linear B. A few years ago a young British architect, Michael Ventris, after seventeen years of study, and helped by the researches of American and other linguists, succeeded in reading it, at least in part. This feat was even more remarkable than that of Champollion and Young who deciphered the Egyptian hieroglyphs, because, unlike them, Ventris had no "bilingual clue" like the Rosetta Stone, which had identical inscriptions in a known and unknown language. Tragically, Ventris was killed in a motor accident at the very moment of his triumph. He was thirty-four.

The decipherment proved Wace and Blegen to have been right in their theory that the Mycenaeans were Greek-speaking; the language of the tablets turns out to be a very primitive form of Greek. But their contents are disappointing; mere lists and inventories, in the main; records of palace stores, allotments of grain, cattle, military and naval units, and other dry records. The best-preserved and most numerous of these were found by Professor Blegen, of Cincinnati University, at Pylos. Without the help provided by this new material, supplementing that found by Evans in Crete, it is doubtful if Ventris could have achieved his amazing decipherment.

The Pylos tablets, like those at Knossos and Mycenae, had been baked in the fire which destroyed all these palaces, although, if Evans' dating is correct (and this is under dispute) the sack of Knossos occurred in about 1400 B.C. whereas the Mycenaean strongholds were destroyed in the twelfth and eleventh centuries B.C., after the time of the Trojan War which Professor Blegen, from his researches at Troy, now puts at about 1250 B.C.

Some time between that date and about 1150 B.C., the great citadels of the Mycenaean rulers—Iolcos, Pylos, Gla, Thebes, Orchomenous, Tiryns, Mycenae, and others—fell one by one. In every one of these buildings archaeologists have observed charred timbers and calcined mud and stone—always at about the same date. The destroyers were with little doubt the Dorian invaders who began to pour down into Greece before the turn of the twelfth century B.C. It is from them that the Greeks of classical times were descended. After a Dark Age in which the worlds of Crete and Mycenae were forgotten, save in poems, myths, and folk tales, and when even the art of writing was lost, there arose in Greece the greatest civilization which Europe has ever known; but this, coming within historical times, is outside the province of this book.

The Future of

Archaeology

THE STORY I have tried to tell may appear complex, even bewildering at times. We have moved from continent to continent, from generation to generation, and watched the work of archaeologists in countries as far apart as Siberia and Spain, China and Peru. Nevertheless the reader will now see that throughout all these changes of country and period there is a continuing thread of development. Allowing for the differing pace of this development in various parts of the world, we see archaeology transforming itself from mere antiquity hunting and treasure seeking to something much broader and more exciting; the scientific study of the whole rich past of mankind, from the first appearance of our remote ancestor Homo sapiens, down through the long hunting and food-gathering periods, on to the arrival of the first farmers, then to the emergence, in Africa, Asia, Europe, and the New World, of man's earliest experiments in civilization. I have also emphasized—perhaps overemphasized—how information gathered by one scholar or group of scholars correlates with and stimulates the minds of other scholars working, perhaps, in a totally different field.

257

Nowadays it is fashionable to say that the days of the giants, the great individualists, are over; that progress in archaeology, as in science generally, will be made by many specialists each working in one small field of research. Certainly modern archaeology is becoming more and more scientific and it would be almost impossible for any one scholar to master all the varied and fascinating techniques now available to him. But he has them at his command, in the sense that he can, if he wishes, call in the help of specialists who, though not themselves archaeologists, can apply their own scientific knowledge to interpret what the archaeologist finds.

Among the most important of the new scientific allies is carbon-14 dating, or, as it is sometimes called, radiocarbon dating. This technique arose as a direct result of research into atomic physics. Cosmic rays from outer space penetrate our atmosphere and this leads to the formation of a radioisotope of carbon which has an atomic weight of 14 (normal carbon has an atomic weight of 12). This carbon 14 or radiocarbon, present in the atmosphere, is absorbed by plants. Animals, as well as humans, eat these plants and so also absorb this radiocarbon.

But the moment the animal or plant dies it ceases to absorb the radioactive isotope which then begins to break up *over a very long period of time, and at a constant rate.* For instance, after 5,700 years only half the amount of carbon 14 will remain in the piece of organic material which absorbed it. After 11,400 years one quarter will be left; after 22,800 years one eighth, and so on. Physicists have devised instruments which can detect the amount of carbon 14 remaining in an archaeological specimen, for example a piece of charcoal. Therefore it is now theoretically possible to establish an approximate date of a piece of organic material (one that has been alive). The system will not work with say, stone or clay or metal, but can be made to work with wood, charcoal, grain, and even burnt bones.

There are, however, considerable difficulties in applying the carbon-14 method; the laboratory equipment is elaborate and delicate, and any contamination of the specimen under examination will give a false reading. On the other hand when the method has been applied to archaeological specimens of known date, for example, Ancient Egyptian timbers from Joser's Step Pyramid, of 2800 B.C., or wood from Roman galleys known to have been built between 37 and 41 A.D., the results have been impressive, though not precise. For instance the reading for the Roman galley was 53 A.D. *plus or minus ninety-five years.* This may seem a very wide margin of error for an object known to date from between 37 and 41 A.D., but when applied to, say, objects found on paleolithic sites of some twenty thousand years ago, such margins of difference are less important.

Another scientific method now applied to archaeological sites is pollen analysis. Imagine you are driving through a rich rural landscape today, or looking out the window of your house at trees, bushes, grass, and flowers. Now imagine that ten thousand years have passed, and that the trees, grass, flowers have long since decayed and turned to soil. They lie some thirty feet below the level of the new landscape, and at that low level someone digs up the remains of your house.

If an archaeologist of the type of Petrie, or Koldewey, or Winckler had discovered the ruins of your house deep underground, he might still have told the world much about the life of the people in the second half of the twentieth century. But could he recreate the long-dead landscape which you had known and loved? Would he be able to discover what plants grew in your garden, what kinds of trees covered the hills, what kinds of animals, birds, insects were familiar to you? He would not—unless you had conveniently left some pictures for him to study, or unless he dug up animal bones which would give him a clue.

But the modern archaeologist, using the method of pollen analysis, *can* rediscover many of these facts, even when he is examining a water-logged site which has not known human occupation for some fifteen thousand years. The reason is interesting. Paleobotanists—people who study ancient plant remains—have discovered that pollen, the fertilizing powder discharged by flowers, has a very long life, especially if preserved in damp, peaty soil. Every summer there is a "rain" of pollen, distributed by the wind; not all of this seed germinates but some lies in the earth, and gradually becomes overlaid with successive bands of soil, each also containing pollen.

Thus, on a favorable site, as for example a peat bog in Ireland or Scandinavia, you could make a cross section through the soil and examine the successive layers of buried pollen under a microscope. The wonderful fact is that these tiny grains, barely visible to the naked eye, still retain characteristics which, under the lens, tell the paleobotanist from which tree, shrub, type of grass, or other plant form they came, even though those plants may have died more then ten thousand years ago.

So what the paleobotanist does is to take samples of pollen at short intervals through a deposit; then he examines these specimens in his laboratory and identifies, say, tree pollens in large quantities. If he goes deeper into the deposit he may find the type of pollen changing: different species of tree and plant, or perhaps a cessation of tree pollen and its substitution by that of grass or scrub. This might indicate a change of climate; but if the cessation of tree pollen is followed by the pollen of cereals such as man grew for food (accompanied by pollen of the inevitable weeds), this is a sure indication that man had been cutting down the trees and clearing the ground for his crops. Sometimes the experts even identify the thin layer of wood as showing where the forest had been cleared by burning, as some primitive peoples still do today.

Another, wider use of pollen analysis is in revealing the relatively slow but inevitable changes of climates as the northern icecaps advanced and retreated during periods covering many thousands of years. Professor Stuart Piggott, in his *Approach to Archaeology* writes:

If there is no human interference in a region, plant-cover (ranging from trees to the smallest forms) will reach what is called a botanical climax, which represents the maximum number of species which can exist within the limitations imposed by climate, soil, elevation and the competition of other plants for growing-space. The main controlling factor here is climate, and when successive deposits in peat-bogs or lake-beds were first examined by means of pollen analysis, it was soon seen that the trees in particular reflected a consistent series of changes in forest composition in Northern Europe.

These ranged from the arctic or sub-arctic conditions at the beginning of the final retreat of the ice-sheet, through improving conditions in which for instance the birch and then the pine could rise to the status of dominant forest trees, and so into conditions approximating to those of modern Temperate Europe north of the Alps, where the natural forest (if given a chance) would be one of the type which includes a mixture of oak, ash and elm.

To me there is something unusually marvelous about this conception, even in a world abounding in scientific marvels. Someone digs a deep trench through a peat bog somewhere in northern Europe; somebody else collects minute specimens of pollen, embedded in the peat, sorts them carefully into layers, and then puts the tiny grains under a microscope. Then, in the mind's eye, one sees unrolling the vast pageant of the earth's history; land at first clamped in the iron grip of the ice sheets, where nothing grows; then, as the glaciers retreat, trees and vegetation appear, birches, then pines, and at last oak, ash, and elm. *Multum in parvo* indeed!

Then there is the technique known as Varve dating. When retreating glaciers melted at the end of the Ice Age, they released sediment into lakes, the larger grains sinking rapidly, the smaller ones much more slowly. Each successive year, therefore, produced a different layer of sediment, grading from coarse at the bottom to fine at the top, the thickness of the layer indicating whether the summer had been warm or cool. The thicker the layer, the warmer the summer. Since the color in these layers often changes, the band as seen from the air appears striped. This is where we get the name "varve" in connection with this method of dating. It comes from the Swedish word *varvig,* meaning "banded." Counting the varves and correlating the data obtained from them with information from other sources makes it possible to estimate dates very accurately.

Aerial photography has also made an invaluable contribution to modern archaeological methods. Airmen in World War I were the first to notice and photograph marks on the ground which turned out to be the remains of early occupation. Banks, ditches, or barrows, invisible from the ground, may appear as shadow marks from the air. Ditches and pits may show as crop marks from a more luxuriant vegetation, and walls and roads will probably be indicated by poor, stunted vegetation. In plowed land ditches and pits may show up from the air as soil marks.

Two main methods are used by archaeologists in the exploration of ancient sites by aerial photography: vertical photographs and oblique photographs. When, for instance, a ditch that was dug across a chalk down is filled in, the resulting disturbance will show up on a vertical air photograph of crops growing hundreds of years later. Because the soil is more moist where the ditch was dug, the corn will grow more strongly there, and though quite indistinguishable from the ground, will show up as a darker band on a photograph. Conversely, crops planted over stony remains, such as roads and the foundations of houses, will grow less strongly and appear as a lighter patch on an air photograph. Oblique photographs taken when the sun is at right angles to the earth, will show up strips and boundaries by the shadows which these cast. In this way, not only has the likelihood of discovering ancient sites by chance been greatly increased, but the systematic survey of such sites has also been made very much easier.

Such techniques have so broadened the archaeologist's approach, and given him such sensitive awareness, that nowadays he is capable of making important discoveries on sites which would have yielded nothing of importance to scholars of earlier generations. To take one example among many, at a place called Star Carr— about five miles from Scarborough, on the coast of Yorkshire, England—there is one of the most important archaeological sites in northern Europe. Yet, from the standpoint of the old-time archaeologist, there is nothing to attract the eye; no pottery on or near the surface, indeed no surface indications at all, not even a few interesting-looking mounds or banks which might tempt the investigator. The land is mainly flat and water-logged, bordering on the gray North Sea.

Why, then, did anybody bother to dig there?

Partly because a geological survey suggested that the area might once have been part of the shore of an inland lake in Mesolithic (Middle Stone Age) times. Such sites had been discovered before at two places, Klosterbund in Jutland, and Vig in Zealand. Samples of pollen taken from the peaty soil at Star Carr confirmed that similar plant life had existed there as at the sites where excavation had disclosed remains of mesolithic human settlements.

A team of British archaeologists therefore decided to dig on this damp, water-logged, cold, and unattractive bit of land near the Yorkshire coast. All knew that even if they did succeed in locating a mesolithic site they would not find any remains of stone buildings, or metal tools, let alone rare objects of art. They also knew that they would have to work not in clean sand or under fresh turf, but in peat, mud, and slime. Try to imagine Layard, or Maspero, or Schliemann digging such a site and you realize how archaeology has changed.

The results of the excavation were a triumphant vindication of the archaeologists' theories. Deep under the layers of peat lay the remains of a settlement occupied by men and women of the Mesolithic Age, over ten thousand years ago. At that time Britain was joined to Europe, and where now the North Sea breaks in thunder along a bleak coast, there had once been a peaceful inland lake. On its swampy shores several mesolithic families had made their winter camp, occupying it intermittently. Their houses, probably of reed or skins, had rotted away, but remains of the birchwood platform on which the houses had rested still survived, preserved in the water-logged earth.

Below this brushwood "mattress," designed to prevent the lakeside dwellers and their dwellings from sinking into the swamp, lay the bones of the animals they had hunted and eaten; red deer, roe deer, elk, ox and pig, water birds and fish. But there were no evidences of domestic animals, nor of cultivated plants. These men of the Middle Stone Age in northern Europe were still hunters and food gatherers.

There was also an abundance of stone tools which had been shaped on the site; over seventeen thousand flint tools were found, of which less than 7 per cent were finished products. There were saws, awls, scrapers, burins, and points. These primitive hunter-fishermen also made barbed points from deer antlers, and they evidently had boats too, since one of the "treasures" found by the archaeologists was a wooden paddle, preserved in the peat for about one hundred centuries. What the boats were like we still do not know; they could have been dugout canoes of timber, or made of skins stretched over a wooden framework.

If the quotes around the word "treasures" seem unjustified, this book will have made at least one of its points, that true archaeology is no longer a mere treasure hunt. That wooden paddle, dug out of a bog in northern England a few years ago, was just as truly a treasure as the golden face mask of Tutankhamen. Its value lies not in its artistic worth but in the fact that it is the earliest navigational appliance which has yet come down to us. Whoever invented the paddle—thousands of years ago—was an early ancestor of the inventors of steamship propellers and airscrews. Similarly, the inventors of the sling, the bola, the bow and arrow, all weapons which can kill at a distance, are the technical ancestors of the long-range gun and the guided missile.

It is, therefore, hardly surprising that a thriving branch of archaeological research is concerned with just this question of origins, rather than in examining the remains of mature, sophisticated cultures such as those of Egypt and Minoan Crete which, by comparison, began only yesterday. Where, and how, and why, did what we call civilization begin? Was it in western Asia or further east? Did the science and art of agriculture truly spring from one source, as Professor Childe and others believed? Or were there comparable developments in other regions at about the same time?

Returning to more recent times—within the past five thousand years—there are many fascinating but as yet unanswered problems. Why did the earliest European civilizations arise in Crete and not in one of the other Aegean islands? How far back does Egyptian civilization go? And why did it decline and die? Who were the founders of the so-called Indus Valley civilization? What connection existed between the inhabitants of Harappa and Mohenjo-Daro and those of ancient Sumer and Akkad?

In the Americas one might ask why the oldest evidences of civilization appear in Peru, Chile, and adjacent countries near the

Pacific seaboard of South America. In Central America the Mayas were a great and formidable people who achieved architectural marvels almost equal to those of the Ancient Egyptians and Babylonians, though they were raised not in dry desert sand but in unhealthy tropical rain forests. What made them concentrate so much of their intellectual effort on the measurement of time? And why in the end did the Maya farmers desert these mighty cult centers which the sweat and blood of their ancestors had raised, and move away, leaving pyramids, temples, and ball courts to be swallowed by the jungle?

Another fascinating and possibly fruitful line of thought is the presence of ritual in the lives of ancient peoples. We have noted how animal worship, or at least great understanding and reverence for animals, is seen in the cave paintings at Altamira and at Lascaux. We recognize this again and again when men become civilized; in the Assyrian winged bulls guarding the palaces of Ashurnasirpal and Sennacherib, the animal-headed gods of Egypt, the rampant lions which guarded Mycenae's Lion Gate, the cult of the Cretan bull, and, over six thousand years earlier, the performance, by the mesolithic hunters of Star Carr, of dances in which men wore the specially lightened antlers of deer. Curiously, such dances, in which men wear deers' antlers, still take place each year at the village of Abbot's Bromley, in rural England.

To me, one of the principal fascinations of archaeological research is the intellectual discipline, plus controlled imagination, needed before one can hope to enter into the minds of our long-dead ancestors. We are living in a world of fantastic change, in which the marvel of yesterday is the commonplace of today. Who, nowadays, is especially excited by the news that yet another satellite has been put into orbit, or a rocket shot at the moon? By contrast our remote ancestors were not subject to constant, bewildering change and readjustment. For example there may well have been several thousand years between the discovery that fire could be created and controlled, and the discovery that cooked meat is more edible than uncooked meat.

Within historical times, the civilization of Ancient Egypt changed very little in its main essentials from 3000 B.C. to the advent of the Christian era many centuries later. And even today, despite the rapidity of modern travel and the much readier mixing of peoples, there are still human beings, in the Kalahari desert of South Africa, and in the hinterland of Australia, who are still living almost exactly like the Stone Age folk of twenty thousand or more years ago. The Australian aborigines and the African Bushmen still perform ritual spells in which they imitate the movements of animals they are going to hunt, still obey the commands of shamans or witch doctors dressed in animal skins, still fashion stone and wooden tools and weapons, and still make magical paintings which they hope will give them power over the animals depicted.

Occasionally something rich and strange is revealed by the excavator's spade and mattock, and this soon makes the headlines. One romantic example was the discovery in the early days of World War II, at Sutton Hoo in Norfolk, England, of the remains of a complete Viking ship, buried under a grass-covered mound. This in itself was not very remarkable since Scandinavian museums contain well-preserved specimens of Viking long-boats complete with seats and oars, the type of vessel which crossed from Iceland to North America about a thousand years ago. Not a scrap of timber remained of the Sutton Hoo ship, though the imprint of every plank and nail was revealed in the earth wherein the vessel had been buried. But within the "hollow womb" of this ghost ship, of which only the outlines remained in the Norfolk soil, lay a king's ransom: purse mountings of shining gold ornamented with semiprecious stones, a shield with an elaborate central boss, a helmet and visor, rich golden jewelry including a buckle five inches long, a splendid sword with golden pommel and jeweled crossguard, and rich dishes of silver of Byzantine design.

There were more practical things, too: an iron standard which may have been carried into battle, and a number of seven-foot spears. But nowhere could a body be found, and it is now believed that the dead monarch, whoever he was (perhaps King Aethelhere, killed in 655 A.D.) may have perished at sea so that his body could not be recovered for burial. The treasures of gold and silver can now be seen glittering in several cases in the British Museum,

London. Nor can there be any doubt that more treasures wait to be found.

One of the hazards of writing about archaeology is that no book can hope to be entirely up to date. At the present time the archaeological world is highly intrigued by Dr. Mellaart's discovery, at Chatal Huyuk, in Turkey, of a fortified city of great complexity, with houses grouped around courtyards, with temples containing painted frescoes and religious objects, all comparable to the walled cities which we normally associate with the Bronze Age. In western Asia this began in roughly 3000 B.C., but Chatal Huyuk is not Bronze Age—it goes right back to neolithic times, before 7000 B.C.

This, and another very ancient walled town, Jericho, so brilliantly excavated by Miss Kathleen Kenyon, who proved it to go back to 7000 B.C., is causing us to re-examine the whole problem of man's civilized beginnings; clearly city life which all its complexities began far, far earlier than we used to think. There is another recently found example, almost as old, at Jarmo in Iraq. And coming to relatively recent times, 1500 B.C., the Greek scholar Dr. Nikolaos Platon has just unearthed, at Kato Zakro in Crete, a major Minoan palace comparable to those of Knossos and Phaistos.

Even as this book is being written, great advances are being made in the newest of all the archaeological techniques, still in its infancy—submarine archaeology.

In much the same way as scientific excavation on land had its beginnings in digging for treasure, so in its early stages submarine archaeology was little more than diving for treasure, usually among the remains of shipwrecks lying at the bottom of the sea. Then among the divers there gradually began to appear men who were also archaeologists, though such men were rare. The most notable among them is the Frenchman Philippe Diolé. However, during the last two decades rapid strides in the development of underwater excavation have been made. New techniques of diving, raising objects, and removing sand and mud now make practical the excavation of sites lying at depths of 150 feet and more.

In the past, one of the main obstacles has been that archaeologists, with a few exceptions, have had to rely upon skilled divers with no particular knowledge of archaeology themselves to find and bring to the surface for examination objects of historical interest. Today, with the perfection of the art of skin diving and the introduction of the aqua lung, it is possible to train nonspecialists, in fact even people who can barely swim, to become fairly creditable divers in a comparatively short time. This means, of course, that more and more of the younger archaeologists are able to explore the possibilities of underwater excavation at firsthand and use their special skills and trained eyes to locate and examine objects found on the sea bed.

No reference to submarine archaeology would be complete without a tribute to Commander Jacques Cousteau and his wonderful work in the field of underwater exploration, particularly that of perfecting and introducing new diving techniques. His constant research has enabled men to live for days on end, in especially designed containers under the sea, going out daily from their underwater base to carry out their surveys, as indeed was done by members of one of his recent expeditions. In fact, Commander Cousteau has perfected and is now ready to begin experiments with a small, circular, one-man submarine, built for underwater observations. Although Commander Cousteau is not himself an archaeologist, professional archaeologists of the future in the submarine field will undoubtedly owe a great debt to men such as he for helping to open up a whole new field of research.

In the course of a single year hundreds of young people write to me and ask, "How can I become an archaeologist?" It is a difficult question to answer, as much depends on local conditions. For example, in Great Britain, certain universities run short-term training schools for amateur diggers, to familiarize them with the basics of excavation, classification of pottery, the measurement and assessment of stratified layers, and so on. Such pupils may later be called on to assist at other "digs." Others may try to get on the staff of a museum, with the hope of being sent on an expedition, when funds become available. Still others prefer to concentrate on studying and perhaps reinterpreting the excavation reports of an earlier generation of archaeologists; or they may prefer to become specialists in some particular field such as philology. And in a number of universities there are opportunities to study and take a degree in archaeology or one of its specialized branches.

Perhaps, as some of the pessimists say, archaeology is becoming so specialized that much of the glamour, excitement, and adventure which impelled such pioneers as Mariette, Schliemann, Layard, Petrie, Evans, and others has disappeared, to be replaced by dull, plodding routine. Personally (though this may only be an assertion of faith) I do not believe this. Increased specialization, and the use of new, scientific techniques, is inevitable. But however many new tools and weapons the archaeologist may have at his command—carbon-14 dating, pollen analysis, dendrochronology, aerial photography, submarine excavation such as that pioneered by Monsieur Cousteau, and a whole battery of scientific skills, what will ultimately matter in the long run will be that same quality of controlled, disciplined imagination possessed by the nineteenth-century excavators. For archaeology, despite the scientific tools now available to it, is still not a pure science. Art, imagination, human sympathy, speculation, joy, doubt, and at times even despair, still enter into it; and long may this remain so.

PHOTO ACKNOWLEDGMENTS

The author and The World Publishing Company herewith thank the following individuals and institutions whose co-operation has made possible the preparation of *Digs and Diggers*. All possible care has been taken to trace the ownership of every picture included and to make full acknowledgment for its use. If any errors have accidentally occurred, they will be corrected in subsequent editions provided notification is sent to the publisher.

p. 89 (bottom), pp. 90-91 (top), p. 95, p. 96, p. 161, p. 165, p. 166, p. 167, p. 168	Courtesy of the American Museum of Natural History
p. 50, p. 235	Courtesy of the Arab Information Center
p. 240 (Stonehenge)	British Crown Copyright
p. 239	The British Museum
p. 55 (bottom)	Courtesy of the Department of Antiquities, Cairo Museum
p. 56	Courtesy of the Department of Egyptology, University College, London
pp. 161-162	Courtesy of the French Government Tourist Office
p. 54, p. 55, p. 89 (top), p. 92, p. 234, p. 236	Courtesy of Leonard Cottrell
p. 237	Macmillan & Co., Ltd., London, for *The Palace of Minos,* by Sir Arthur Evans
p. 49 (Lahun treasure)	Courtesy of the Metropolitan Museum of Art
p. 93	Fletcher Fund, 1940
p. 94 (stela)	Gift of Mrs. Henry Marsden, 1890
p. 90 (bottom), p. 91 (bottom)	Gift of John D. Rockefeller, Jr., 1931
p. 49 (funerary model	Museum Excavations, 1919-1920: Rogers Fund, supplemented by contribution of Edward S. Harkness
p. 94 (relief)	Rogers Fund, 1943
p. 233 (beaker)	Rogers Fund, 1947
p. 51, pp. 52-53	from *Operations Carried on at the Pyramids of Gizeh in 1837,* by Richard Howard-Vyse
p. 164 (bottom)	Courtesy of Pan American-Grace Airways
p. 164 (top)	Courtesy of Panagra
p. 233 (cart)	Thames & Hudson, Ltd., and Frederick A. Praeger for *The Scythians,* by Tamara Talbot Rice
p. 238	Cambridge University Press, for *The Decipherment of Linear B,* by John Chadwick
p. 240 (scuba diver)	Wide World Photos, Inc.

GUIDE TO
FURTHER
READING
AND INDEX

Guide to Further Reading

THE BEGINNINGS

Cottrell, Leonard, *The Horizon Book of Lost Worlds*. New York, Doubleday and Company (American Heritage Publishing Company), 1962.

——, *Lost Cities*. New York, Grosset and Dunlap, 1963.

Crawford, O. G. S., *Archaeology in the Field*. New York, Frederick A. Praeger, 1953.

Dawn of Civilization, The, compiled by a number of distinguished archaeologists. New York, McGraw-Hill, 1961.

Deuel, Leo, ed., *The Treasures of Time*. Cleveland and New York, The World Publishing Company, 1961.

Diolé, P., *4000 Years Under the Sea*. London, Julian Messner, 1954.

Kenyon, Kathleen M., *Beginning in Archaeology*, rev. ed. New York, Frederick A. Praeger, 1961.

Piggott, Stuart, *Approach to Archaeology*. Cambridge, Massachusetts, Harvard University Press, 1959.

Shippens, Katherine B., *Portals to the Past*. New York, The Viking Press, 1963.

Wheeler, Mortimer, *Archaeology from the Earth*. Baltimore, Penguin Books, 1954.

Zeuner, F., *Dating the Past*. New York, Longmans, Green, 1958.

EGYPT AND THE EARLIEST CIVILIZATIONS

Baikie, James, *Egyptian Antiquities of the Nile Valley*. New York, The Macmillan Company, 1932.

Blegen, Carl W., and others, eds., *Troy*, vols. I-III. Princeton, Princeton University Press, 1951.

Breasted, James H., *Ancient Records of Egypt*. Chicago, University of Chicago Press, 1929.

———, *History of Egypt from the Earliest Times to the Persian Conquest*. New York, Charles Scribner's Sons, 1933.

Carter, Howard, and A. C. Mace, *The Tomb of Tutankhamen*, 3 vols. New York, Cooper Square, 1963.

Cottrell, Leonard, *The Anvil of Civilization*. New York, New American Library, 1957.

———, *Land of the Pharaohs*. Cleveland and New York, The World Publishing Company, 1960.

———, *Life Under the Pharaohs*. New York, Holt, Rinehart and Winston, 1960.

———, *The Lost Pharaohs*. New York, Grosset and Dunlap, 1963.

———, *The Mountains of Pharaoh*. New York, Holt, Rinehart and Winston, 1956.

———, *Realms of Gold*. Greenwich, New York Graphic Society, 1963. (Published in England under the title *The Lion Gate*.)

Edwards, I. E. S., *The Pyramids of Egypt*. Baltimore, Penguin Books, 1952.

Emery, W. B., *Archaic Egypt*. Baltimore, Penguin Books, 1961.

Erman, Adolf, *The Literature of the Ancient Egyptians*. New York, E. P. Dutton and Company, 1927.

Gurney, O. R., *The Hittites*. Baltimore, Penguin Books, 1954.

Goneim, Mohammed Z., *The Lost Pyramid*. New York, Rinehart and Company, 1956. (Published in England under the title *The Buried Pyramid*.)

Herodotus, *History*, trans. by G. Rawlinson. New York, E. P. Dutton and Company, 1910.

Homer, *The Illiad*, trans. by E. V. Rieu. Baltimore, Penguin Books, 1951.

———, *The Odyssey*, trans. by E. V. Rieu. Baltimore, Penguin Books, 1946.

Koldewey, Robert, *The Excavations at Babylon*, trans. by Agnes S. Johns. London, Macmillan and Company, 1914.

Kramer, Samuel N., *History Begins at Sumer*. New York, Doubleday and Company, 1959.

Layard, A. H., *Discoveries in the Ruins of Nineveh and Babylon*, 2 vols. London, 1853.

——, *Nineveh and Its Remains*. London, 1849.

Lloyd, Seton, *Early Anatolia*. Baltimore, Penguin Books, 1956.

——, *Foundations in the Dust*. Baltimore, Penguin Books, 1956.

Lucas, Alfred, *Ancient Egyptian Materials and Industries*, 2nd rev. ed. New York, Longmans, Green, 1934.

Lythgoe, A. M., *The Treasure of Lahun*. New York, Bulletin of the Metropolitan Museum of Art, December, 1919.

Peet, T. E., *The Great Tomb Robberies of the Twentieth Egyptian Dynasty*. Oxford, Clarendon Press, 1943.

Petrie, W. M. F., *Illahun, Kahun and Gurob*. London, 1890.

——, *Kahun, Gurob and Hawara*. London, 1890.

——, *The Pyramids and Temples of Gizeh*. New York, Charles Scribner's Sons, 1883.

——, *Royal Tombs of the First and Second Dynasties*. London, Egypt Exploration Fund, 1901–1902.

——, *Seventy Years in Archaeology*. London, 1932.

Schliemann, Henry, *Mycenae and Tiryns*. London, John Murray, 1878.

Waterfield, G., *Layard of Nineveh*. London, John Murray, 1963.

Woolley, Leonard, *Digging up the Past*. Baltimore, Penguin Books, 1950.

——, *Ur of the Chaldees*. Baltimore, Penguin Books, 1954.

MAN'S EARLIEST KNOWN ANCESTORS

Breuil, Abbé Henri, *Four Hundred Centuries of Cave Art*, trans. by Boyle. France, Montignac, 1952.

——, *The Cave of Altamira*, trans. by Boyle. Madrid, 1935.

Burkitt, Miles C., *The Old Stone Age*. New York, Atheneum, 1963.

——, *Our Early Ancestors*. Cambridge, England, Cambridge University Press, 1926.

Childe, V. Gordon, *New Light on the Most Ancient East*. New York, Frederick A. Praeger, 1953.

——, *What Happened in History*. Baltimore, Penguin Books, 1943.

Clark, Grahame, *World Prehistory*. Cambridge, England, Cambridge University Press, 1961.

Darwin, Charles, *The Origin of the Species*. New York, The Washington Square Press, 1963.

Grigson, G., *Painted Caves*. Chester Springs, Pennsylvania, Dufour, 1956.

Hawkes, Jacquetta, and Leonard Woolley, *Prehistory and the Beginnings of Civilization*. New York, Harper and Row, 1962.

Howells, W. W., *Mankind in the Making*. New York, Doubleday and Company, 1959.

THE NEW WORLD

Bingham, Hiram, *Inca Land*. New York, Duell, Sloan and Pearce, 1922.
——, *Lost City of the Incas*. New York, Atheneum, 1963.

Bushnell, G. H. S., *Peru,* rev. ed. New York, Frederick A. Praeger, 1963.

del Castillo, Bernal Diaz, *The Conquest of New Spain,* trans. by J. M. Cohen. Baltimore, Penguin Books, 1963.

MacGowan, Kenneth, and Joseph A. Hester, Jr., *Early Man in the New World,* rev. ed. New York, Doubleday and Company, 1962.

Morley, S. G., *The Ancient Maya,* 3rd ed. by George W. Brainerd. Stanford, Stanford University Press, 1956.

Peterson, F. A., *Ancient Mexico*. New York, G. P. Putnam's Sons, 1959.

Soustelle, Jacques, *Daily Life of the Aztecs*. New York, The Macmillan Company, 1962.

Thompson, J. E. S., *Mexico Before Cortez*. New York, Charles Scribner's Sons, 1953.
——, *The Rise and Fall of the Maya Civilization*. Norman, Oklahoma, University of Oklahoma Press, 1959.

Vaillant, G. C., *The Aztecs of Mexico*. Baltimore, Penguin Books, 1951.

von Hagen, Victor, *Highway of the Sun*. New York, Duell, Sloan and Pearce, 1955.

Wormington, H. M., *Ancient Man in North America*. Denver, Denver Museum of Natural History, 1957.

FROM THE PACIFIC TO THE MEDITERRANEAN

Atkinson, R. J. C., *Stonehenge*. New York, The Macmillan Company, 1956.

Basham, A. L., *The Wonder that Was India*. New York, Grove Press, 1959.

Chadwick, John, *The Decipherment of "Linear B."* New York, Vintage Books, 1958.

Childe, V. Gordon, *The Dawn of European Civilization,* 6th ed. New York, Alfred A. Knopf, 1958.

Cottrell, Leonard, *The Bull of Minos.* New York, Grosset and Dunlap, 1962.

——, *Land of the Two Rivers,* New York and Cleveland, The World Publishing Company, 1962.

Evans, Arthur, *The Palace of Minos at Knossos,* 7 vols. New York, Biblo and Tannen, 1964.

Evans, Joan, *Time and Chance* (biography of Sir Arthur Evans). New York, Longmans, Green, 1943.

Hilprecht, H. V., *Exploration in Bible Lands.* Philadelphia, J. J. Holman and Company, 1903.

Kitto, H. D. F., *The Greeks.* Baltimore, Penguin Books, 1951.

Marinatos, S., *Crete and Mycenae.* New York, Harry N. Abrams, 1960.

Marshall, Sir. J. H., *Revealing India's Past.* London, India Society, 1939.

Needham, J., *Science and Civilisations in China,* vol. 1. London and New York, Cambridge University Press, 1954.

Pendlebury, J. S., *The Archaeology of Crete.* New York, Biblo and Tannen, 1964.

Philips, C. W., and others, *The Excavations of the Sutton-Hoo Ship-burial.* London, Journal of Antiquaries, vol. XX, 1940.

Piggott, Stuart, *British Prehistory.* London and New York, Oxford University Press, 1949.

——, *Prehistoric India to 1000 B.C.* Baltimore, Penguin Books, 1950.

Talbot-Rice, Tamara, *The Scythians.* New York, Frederick A. Praeger, 1957.

Watson, William, *Archaeology in China.* New York, Taplinger Publishing Company, 1960.

Wheeler, Mortimer, *The Indus Civilization.* Baltimore, Penguin Books, 1953.

——, *Rome Beyond the Imperial Frontiers.* Baltimore, Penguin Books, 1955.

Index

ABOUT THE AUTHOR

LEONARD COTTRELL is well known internationally for his books on ancient peoples. His interest in archaeology began at the age of nine; that was the year of the discovery of Tutankhamen's tomb in Egypt by Howard Carter. From then on, the boy became increasingly absorbed in the subject, and this enthusiasm eventually led him to become a writer about it. Among his recent books published in the United States are *The Lost Pharaohs, The Bull of Minos, The Anvil of Civilization, Lost Cities, Realms of Gold,* all for adults, and *Land of the Pharaohs* and *Land of the Two Rivers,* both Major Cultures of the World books.

Mr. Cottrell is a native of Great Britain and divides his time "between the London world of TV, radio and the theater and the quiet rural life" of his country house on the fringe of England's Lake District. Mr. Cottrell also writes and directs sound and television programs for the BBC.